DATE DUE

DEMCO 38-296

Tom Stoppard in Conversation

THEATER: Theory/Text/Performance

Enoch Brater, Series Editor
University of Michigan

Tom Stoppard in Conversation

EDITED BY PAUL DELANEY

Ann Arbor

THE UNIVERSITY OF MICHIGAN PRESS

Copyright © by the University of Michigan 1994
All rights reserved
Published in the United States of America by
The University of Michigan Press
Manufactured in the United States of America
⊗ Printed on acid-free paper

1997   1996   1995   1994   4   3   2   1

A CIP catalogue record for this book is available from the British Library.

Library of Congress Cataloging-in-Publication Data

Stoppard, Tom.
    Tom Stoppard in conversation / edited by Paul Delaney.
        p.   cm.—(Poets on poetry)
    Includes bibliographical references and index.
    ISBN 0-472-09561-7 (alk. paper).—ISBN 0-472-06561-0 (pbk. :
alk. paper)
        1. Stoppard, Tom—Interviews. 2. Dramatists, English—20th
century—Interviews. I. Delaney, Paul, 1948-   . II. Title.
III. Series.
PR6069.T6Z47   1994
822'.914—dc20
    [B]   94-10262
                                                              CIP

For Elizabeth and Arthur—
funny, smart, and kind
and great companions at the theater

Contents

Preface

To begin at the beginning, Ned Divelbiss over the years has obtained much of the material reflected in the text and bibliography of this volume. A librarian of the old school, he can delve and glean with the best of them and has been unstintingly generous with his time. I am also happy to express my gratitude to George Blankenbaker, Academic Dean of Westmont College, for support in the form of a sabbatical and for additional assistance during the final preparation of the volume. The Cambridge University Library, the British Library, the British Library Newspaper Library, the BBC Written Archives Centre, the National Sound Archive, and the National Theatre Scripts Department allowed access to their collections and offered research assistance. Laurie Camp, Jennifer Root, and Marianne Walker helped transcribe recorded interviews and assisted in the preparation of the manuscript. Randy VanderMey offered my writing the same incisive attention he routinely lavishes on his students' work. Heather Speirs provided encouragement and advice both as a colleague and as department head. But the project would never have been completed without the support of Dianne. She made a cottage into a home, and taught the children, and trekked to the theatre, and watched as the students left and the snow descended and the daffodils bloomed and the ducklings grew up, and read every word, and discussed possibilities and helped clarify options. During that year when we were strangers at the gate, the people of St. Peter's Church in Bury St. Edmunds took us in and feted us right royally with fellowship and love. Steve Collington offered valued assistance as intermediary, liaison, and go-between. Elizabeth and Arthur provided laughter, hugs and joy. Again.

Acknowledgments

Grateful acknowledgment is made to the following authors, publishers, and journals for permission to reprint previously published materials.

Michael Billington, theatre critic of *The Guardian,* for "Stoppard's Secret Agent," *The Guardian,* 18 March 1988, p. 28. Copyright © 1988 Michael Billington. Reprinted by permission.

Calder Publications Ltd. for "Trad Tom Pops In," by David Gollob and David Roper, *Gambit,* 10, no. 37 (Summer 1981), pp. 5–17. Copyright © 1981 Calder Publications Ltd. Reprinted by permission.

Condé Nast Publications Inc. for "Tom Stoppard: Kind Heart and Prickly Mind" by Joan Juliet Buck, [American] *Vogue,* 174 (March 1984), pp. 454, 513–14. This article was originally published in *Vogue.* Copyright © 1984 Condé Nast Publications Inc. Reprinted by permission.

The *Daily Telegraph* for "Tom's Sound Affects," by Gillian Reynolds, *Daily Telegraph,* 20 April 1991, "Weekend" section, p. 24. Copyright © 1991 The Daily Telegraph. Reprinted by permission.

Giles Gordon for permission to reprint his interview with Tom Stoppard first published in *Transatlantic Review,* 29 (Summer 1968), pp. 17–25. Copyright © 1968 Giles Gordon. Reprinted by permission.

Ronald Hayman for "Double Acts: Tom Stoppard and Peter Wood," *Sunday Times Magazine,* 2 March 1980, pp. 29–31. Copyright © 1980 Ronald Hayman. Reprinted by permission.

Hugh Hebert for "A Playwright in Undiscovered Country," *The Guardian,* 7 July 1979, p. 10. Copyright © 1979 Hugh Hebert. Reprinted by permission.

Oleg Kerensky for his interview with Tom Stoppard, extracted from *The New British Drama: Fourteen Playwrights since Osborne and Pinter* (London: Hamish Hamilton; New York: Taplinger, 1977), pp. 168–71. Copyright © 1977 by Oleg Kerensky. Reprinted by permission.

Joseph McCulloch for "Dialogue with Tom Stoppard," from *Under Bow Bells: Dialogues with Joseph McCulloch* (London: Sheldon Press, 1974), pp. 163–70. Copyright © 1974 Joseph McCulloch. Reprinted by permission.

Chronology

1937	3 July, born in Zlín, Czechoslovakia.
1939	Family moves to Singapore.
1942	Evacuated to India with his mother and brother prior to the Japanese invasion. Father remains behind and is killed.
1942–46	Attends English-speaking school in Darjeeling.
1946	Mother marries Kenneth Stoppard, an Army major, and moves to England.
1948–54	Attends the Pocklington School, Yorkshire.
1954–58	Becomes a journalist on the *Western Daily Press* in Bristol.
1958–60	Journalist on the *Bristol Evening World*.
1960–62	Freelance journalism. Writes *The Gamblers* (a one-act play) and *A Walk on the Water* (later revised as *Enter a Free Man*).
1962–63	Theater critic at *Scene* magazine in London.
1963	*A Walk on the Water* televised.
1964	*The Dissolution of Dominic Boot* and *'M' is for Moon Among Other Things* (one-act plays) on radio. Three short stories published by Faber and Faber. Writes *Rosencrantz and Guildenstern,* a one-act verse burlesque, during five months in Berlin on a Ford Foundation grant.
1965	Marries Jose Ingle (divorced 1972). *The Gamblers* performed at Bristol University; *A Walk on the Water* televised.
1966	*If You're Glad I'll Be Frank* on radio; *A Separate Peace* televised. Translation of *Tango* staged by the RSC. *Rosencrantz and Guildenstern Are Dead* staged on the Edinburgh Festival Fringe. *Lord Malquist and Mr Moon,* a novel, published.
1967	*Rosencrantz and Guildenstern Are Dead* staged at the National Theatre (April) and on Broadway (October). *Teeth* and *Another Moon Called Earth* televised; *Albert's Bridge* on radio.

1968	*Enter a Free Man* and *The Real Inspector Hound* staged; *Neutral Ground* televised.
1970	*After Magritte* staged; *Where Are They Now?* on radio.
1971	*Dogg's Our Pet* staged by Inter-Action.
1972	*Jumpers* staged at the National Theatre. Marries Miriam Moore-Robinson (divorced 1992). First New York production of *The Real Inspector Hound* and *After Magritte*. *Artist Descending a Staircase* on radio.
1973	Translates *The House of Bernarda Alba;* directs *Born Yesterday*.
1974	First New York production of *Jumpers; Travesties* staged by the RSC.
1975	*The Boundary* (cowritten with Clive Exton) televised; adapts *Three Men in a Boat* for TV; coauthors screenplay of *The Romantic Englishwoman;* first New York production of *Travesties*.
1976	*Dirty Linen* staged; *Jumpers* returned to the National Theatre repertoire; *The (15 Minute) Dogg's Troupe Hamlet* performed outside the National Theatre by Inter-Action; *Dalliance* (an adaptation of a Schnitzler play) staged.
1977	*Every Good Boy Deserves Favour* receives one performance with the London Symphony Orchestra; *Professional Foul* televised.
1978	*Every Good Boy Deserves Favour* revived at the Mermaid Theatre with a chamber orchestra and given first American production in Washington, D.C.; *Night and Day* staged. Writes screenplay of *Despair*.
1979	*Dogg's Hamlet, Cahoot's Macbeth* staged. *Undiscovered Country* (an adaptation of a Schnitzler play) staged at the National Theatre; first New York productions of *Every Good Boy Deserves Favor* and *Night and Day*.
1980	Writes screenplay of *The Human Factor*.
1981	*On the Razzle* (an adaptation of a Nestroy play) performed at the National Theatre.
1982	*The Real Thing* staged. *The Dog It Was That Died* on radio.
1983	*The Love for Three Oranges* (translation of libretto for Prokofiev's opera) performed by the Glyndebourne Touring Opera.
1984	First New York production of *The Real Thing. Squaring the Circle* televised. *Rough Crossing* (an adaptation of a Molnár play) staged at the National Theatre.
1985	Cowrites screenplay for *Brazil.* Revises *Jumpers* for West End revival. Directs *The Real Inspector Hound*.

1987	Translates *Largo Desolato* by Václav Havel; writes screenplay for *Empire of the Sun.*
1988	*Hapgood* staged.
1989	Revises *Hapgood* for first American production in Los Angeles; first New York production of *Artist Descending a Staircase.*
1990	*Rosencrantz and Guildenstern are Dead,* in a film version written and directed by Stoppard, wins the Golden Lion at the Venice Film Festival. Writes screenplay for *The Russia House.*
1991	Film version of *Rosencrantz and Guildenstern are Dead* released. *In the Native State* on radio. Writes screenplay for *Billy Bathgate.*
1992	*The Real Inspector Hound* revived on Broadway. Writes screenplay for *Shakespeare in Love* (film production canceled in October).
1993	*Arcadia* staged at the National Theatre (April); *Travesties* revived by the Royal Shakespeare Company (September). *A Separate Peace* broadcast on BBC (March); *Arcadia* on radio (December). Writes new narration for Lehár's *The Merry Widow* performed by the Glyndebourne Opera in Festival Hall (July). Writes screenplay for *Hopeful Monsters,* a novel by Nicholas Moseley.
1994	First New York production of *Hapgood*; revises *In the Native State* for the stage. *Arcadia* and *Travesties* both transfer to West End theaters.

A Note on the Text

Any omission of material written by an interviewer (of background biographical information which would, cumulatively, prove redundant) is indicated by a line of spaced dots. Other ellipses and material in editorial brackets appear here as they did in the interview as originally published. Typographical errors and misspellings have been silently corrected; and in a few instances Tom Stoppard or his interviewers have provided emendations of punctuation or phrasing. Titles of plays, newspapers, and other publications here appear in italics; similarly, boldface type has been replaced by italics and speaker names are given in small capitals. In nearly all other instances the spelling and punctuation of the original form of each interview has been maintained.

Introduction

Fresh out of school and without having spent a day at university, seventeen-year-old Tom Stoppard landed a job as cub reporter on Bristol's *Western Daily Press.* At the time, his ambition "was to be lying on the floor of an African airport while machine-gun bullets zoomed over my typewriter."[1] However, he soon discovered that he "wasn't much use as a reporter" because he felt he "didn't have the right to ask people questions": "I always thought they'd throw the teapot at me or call the police. For me, it was like knocking at the door, wearing your reporter's peaked cap, and saying: 'Hello, I'm from journalism. I've come to inspect you. Take off your clothes and lie down.'"[2] Indulging his gift for dialogue, Stoppard preferred to create possible answers of his own instead of actually confronting another person with questions. Although he hated people-in-the-street interviews worst of all, "it was OK when they didn't use a photograph" because "I just sat in the canteen and made up quotes from people who always lived in one of Bristol's longest streets."[3]

Perhaps as a result, when the very first reporters came to question the unknown twenty-nine-year-old who had just become the youngest playwright to have a play produced at the National Theatre, Stoppard could already assure them that "I'm very well prepared for interviews" because "I'm always interviewing myself."[4] Honing responses to questions, polishing his replies until they attained an exquisite patina, Stoppard achieved a reputation for as much verbal brilliance in person as in his stage plays. Clive James described Stoppard as "a dream inter-

---

1. Anonymous, "Footnote to the Bard," *The Observer,* 9 April 1967, p. 23.
2. Jon Bradshaw, "Tom Stoppard, Nonstop: Word Games with a Hit Playwright," *New York,* 10 January 1977, pp. 47–48.
3. Hunter Davies, "Stoppard Goes," *Sunday Times,* 23 April 1967, p. 13.
4. Peter Lewis, "How Tom Went to Work on an Absent Mind and Picked up £20,000," *Daily Mail,* 24 May 1967, p. 6.

viewee, talking in eerily quotable sentences whose English has the faintly extraterritorial perfection of a Conrad or a Nabokov."[5]

Like Henry, the playwright protagonist of *The Real Thing*, Stoppard values "well chosen words nicely put together."[6] But while priding himself on uttering precise words in a precise order, he can become almost apologetic for his own verbal felicity. "I feel I should preface this with an epigram, which is: 'Nothing is more studied than a repeated spontaneity,' "[7] Stoppard warned one interviewer before responding to questions with such ostensible spontaneities as "Well, I write fiction because it's a way of making statements I can disown. And I write plays because dialogue is the most respectable way of contradicting myself." To the duly impressed interviewer's "Not bad. May I quote you on that?," Stoppard replied—with what degree of irony it is impossible to say—"There's no point in being quoted if one isn't going to be quotable."[8]

After encounters with the quotable Stoppard, some interviewers emerged in near-babbling incoherence. "Conversation with him is like wearing an oxygen mask while touring an amusement park," gasped Tom Topor of the *New York Post*, "the air is so exhilarating and the stops so enticing that the destination doesn't matter."[9] But perhaps, as Kerner observes in *Hapgood*, "you get what you interrogate for."[10] Joan Juliet Buck speculates that because of his "reputation as the foremost intellectual playwright" the "atmosphere around Stoppard was so rarefied that male interviewers approached him in the manner of dueling dons, goaded by his wordplay into somewhat incoherent one-up wordsmanship, a little like people who can't resist stretching when there's a ballet dancer in the same room."[11] After reports of conversations with Tom Stoppard being "full of verbal acrobatics and intellectual cartwheels,"[12] or "an intellectual and a semantic trampoline,"[13]

5. Clive James, "Count Zero Splits the Infinite," *Encounter*, 45 (November 1975), p. 70.

6. Tom Stoppard, *The Real Thing*, 2d rev. ed. (London and Boston: Faber and Faber, 1984), p. 51.

7. Bradshaw, "Tom Stoppard, Nonstop," p. 48.

8. Bradshaw, "Tom Stoppard, Nonstop," p. 51.

9. Tom Topor, "Lunch with a Playwright," *New York Post*, 10 April 1974, p. 64.

10. Tom Stoppard, *Hapgood* (London and Boston: Faber and Faber, 1988), p. 12.

11. Joan Juliet Buck, "Tom Stoppard: Kind Heart and Prickly Mind," [American] *Vogue*, 174 (March 1984), p. 454.

12. Mel Gussow, "*Jumpers* Author Is Verbal Gymnast," *New York Times*, 23 April 1974, p. 36.

13. Bill Hagen, "Today's Truth, by Tom Stoppard," *San Diego Tribune*, 6 November 1981, sec. C, p. 1.

those who sought to engage Stoppard in thoughtful dialogue rather than verbal gymnastics have been surprised by his quiet patience and warmth. Fearing that Stoppard's scintillating mind might make for rather disconcerting company, Joseph McCulloch prepared for dialogue "like an average tennis-player about to encounter a Wimbledon star." But such fears proved "quite groundless with Tom Stoppard": "Nobody could be less showy in manner or less intoxicated with his own personality. He is the best of company, easy to talk with, constantly interested in what others have to say, totally unaffected and natural in conversation."[14]

Throughout his career, the number of interviewers who have found him dazzlingly cerebral is counterbalanced by those who have found him to be "urbane and courteous ... patient and attentive to a journalist's questions."[15] Composer Stephen Sondheim contrasts Stoppard's "relaxed ... spontaneity" with the "manicured articulateness in his plays."[16] When told that he "doesn't talk like his characters," Stoppard professes to be disappointed: "Well, I'd rather more work gets put into their speeches than mine. One puns and cross references to raise a laugh among your cronies. One does that to impress. But in an interview that would be a very silly way to proceed. Trying to get the thing epigrammatic rather than merely grammatic."[17] Of course, Stoppard's pithy contrast of things grammatic and epigrammatic itself contains the makings of an epigram. And Stoppard's reputation for both patience and verbal pyrotechnics reflects the simultaneous seriousness and frivolity of his temperament.

"I must tell you," Stoppard told Jon Bradshaw in 1977, "There's something you should know right away. I'll say *anything* to an interviewer."[18] "I often give a frivolous answer to a serious question, which is a kind of a lie," Stoppard explained. "I don't lie about my age or the number of bathrooms in my house, but if you ask me whether I write comedy because I am too insecure to make a serious statement, well, that's a complex question and rather than getting into it, it's

14. Joseph McCulloch, "Dialogue with Tom Stoppard" [20 March 1973], in *Under Bow Bells: Dialogues with Joseph McCulloch* (London: Sheldon Press, 1974), p. 162.

15. Richard Stayton, "The Mysterious Tom Stoppard," *Los Angeles Herald Examiner*, 14 April 1989, "Weekend" section, p. 6.

16. Mel Gussow, "The Real Tom Stoppard," *New York Times Magazine*, 1 January 1984, p. 23.

17. Buck, "Tom Stoppard: Kind Heart and Prickly Mind," p. 513.

18. Bradshaw, "Tom Stoppard, Nonstop," p. 47.

much easier to say yes. One doesn't tell lies. I now have a repertoire of plausible answers which evade the whole truth."[19]

Given such a repertoire, it is not surprising that Stoppard would—if pressed—qualify many of the epigrammatic gems he has imparted with regularity over the years. When he could scarcely have been regarded as "politically correct," amid the politically committed world of British theater in the 1960s, Stoppard spoke of having "the courage of my lack of convictions." Asking in 1979 about that line, Hugh Hebert came away with the explanation that Stoppard had "over-reacted with a bon mot."[20] Stoppard went into greater detail two years later, conceding to *Gambit* interviewers that "when the climate was such that theatre seemed to exist for the specific purpose of commenting on our own society directly,... I took on a sort of 'travelling pose' which exaggerated my insecurity about not being able to fit into this scheme."[21] But in 1984, when his words were thrown up at him yet again, he dismissed the "lack of convictions" quote as "a flip remark from a former existence."[22] In fact, Stoppard has retracted several of his glittering bons mots. Even though he used to say "with complete sincerity" that "ideas are the end-product of the play, not the other way round," he admitted to *Gambit* in 1981 that the remark has "the overstatement of most epigrams" and, in any event, "stopped being applicable round about the time I started writing *Jumpers*."[23] Stoppard also told the *Baltimore Sun* that his reference to writing plays "because dialogue is the most respectable way of contradicting myself," was "a fairly flip comment" which "used to be more true than it is now."[24]

More surprising is Stoppard's response to a completely open-ended question from Dan Sullivan, who in 1986 wanted to know "What would Tom Stoppard, successful middle-aged playwright, say to Tom Stoppard, bright young playwright on the way up?" Sullivan could scarcely have been prepared for the one piece of advice Stoppard would give: "I would say, don't give interviews." "Once you give one,

19. Bradshaw, "Tom Stoppard, Nonstop," p. 48.
20. Hugh Hebert, "A Playwright in Undiscovered Country," *The Guardian*, 7 July 1979, p. 10.
21. David Gollob and David Roper, "Trad Tom Pops In," *Gambit*, 10, no. 37 (Summer 1981), p. 11.
22. Ros Asquith, "City Limits Interview: Tom Stoppard," *City Limits*, 19 October 1984, p. 79.
23. Gollob and Roper, "Trad Tom Pops In," p. 10.
24. J. Wynn Rousuck, "In *The Real Thing*, Stoppard's Trying for Realism—For Once," *Baltimore Sun*, 28 April 1985; repr. in *Performing Arts* microfiche, vol. 11 (May 1985), card 110:D7–D8.

you're trapped," Stoppard explained. "You have to keep living up to the last one. You present a version of yourself that you think will gratify the interviewer, and the next day you read about this person who puts himself forward in ways that you don't." "It's embarrassing," Stoppard added, "And strangely enough, the more accurate the interview is, the more you're embarrassed."[25]

To be sure, Stoppard has always felt uncomfortable about self-revelation. Two decades earlier, the youthful playwright who declared "I simply don't like very much revealing myself"[26] could also lament that "I have a feeling that almost everybody today is more trying to match himself up with an external image he has of himself, almost as if he'd seen himself on a screen."[27] After twenty years of media exposure, Stoppard's concerns about the limitations of that screen were, if anything, greater than ever. Talking of the contrast between himself and "the imaginary Stoppard" as conceived by journalists, Stoppard told one journalist, "I know exactly who I am now. I am this sort of wordsmith, unpolitical, dandified wit, you know, who writes plays which are very wordy but quite entertaining. It's all true and false. I don't mind, really. But on the other hand, I'm beginning to understand people who just simply never do any interviews of any kind."[28] "Each interviewer breathes from the previous interviews," Stoppard continued, "so the error is being reinforced each time. In the end it's just been cemented into this person."[29] Stoppard insists that such statuary may conceal as much as it reveals. "People wish to perceive me as someone who works out ideas in a cool, dispassionate way but I don't think that's my personality at all," Stoppard protested to Michael Billington just after the premiere of *Hapgood;* "I am a very emotional person."[30]

However, interviews with Stoppard are not, finally, primarily valuable for what they reveal of Stoppard the man but for what they may reveal of Stoppard's plays. While acknowledging the complexity of the

25. Dan Sullivan, "Stoppard: Getting the Right Bounce," *Los Angeles Times,* 2 June 1986, sec. 6, p. 6.

26. Giles Gordon, "Tom Stoppard," *Transatlantic Review,* no. 29 (Summer 1968), p. 19.

27. Dan Sullivan, "Young British Playwright Here for Rehearsal of *Rosencrantz,*" *New York Times,* 29 August 1967, p. 27.

28. Sean Mitchell, "Just Who, Really, Is Tom Stoppard?" *Los Angeles Herald Examiner,* 18 December 1986; repr. in *Performing Arts* microfiche, vol. 13 (November 1986—February 1987), card 110:A5–A6.

29. Mitchell, "Just Who, Really, Is Tom Stoppard?"

30. Michael Billington, "Stoppard's Secret Agent," *The Guardian,* 18 March 1988, p. 28.

plays, Clive James maintains that "no author has ever done a better job of explaining himself."[31] Whatever Stoppard's patience or reluctance in talking about himself, he can be exceptionally forthcoming regarding his plays. "Tom is just great," said Jeremy Irons after working with Stoppard in rehearsals for the Broadway production of *The Real Thing*, "He's not like Pinter, who believes that you don't have to explain because the work is it, it's all in the writing. Tom explains."[32] Irons's experience has been shared by actors who have worked with Stoppard throughout his career. In preparing for the 1967 National Theatre premiere of *Rosencrantz and Guildenstern Are Dead*, says John Stride—who played Rosencrantz—the cast "turned more and more from the director to Tom Stoppard." "We [ask]ed him about certain passages where the meaning was still elusive to the actors," Stride adds, "and he explained those."[33] When Stoppard "came in about half-way through rehearsals" for *After Magritte*, Prunella Scales found him "enormously helpful."[34]

The explanations Stoppard offers range from the global to the minute. Diana Rigg, who created the role of Dotty in *Jumpers*, reports that when she responded to the play with bafflement, "Tom came over to see me and spent two hours making a path in the carpet telling me what it was all about."[35] If Stoppard sometimes will expound on what a play is "all about," at other times he will explain individual words—and the space between words. The actor delivering Archie's "jabberwock" speech in the *Jumpers* Coda, Remak Ramsey, recalls that Stoppard "wanted 'Darwin different' said together with no breath so that you got a repeat of 'indifferent' at the beginning of the speech."[36] If "the notes he gives you" are "not specific enough," Ramsey adds, "he will sit and discuss them with you until there's no question what he means."[37] Michael Hordern, who had the triumph of his career as George in *Jumpers*, concurs that

> some authors you don't awfully welcome at rehearsal, but Tom you do. He's a marvellous word-carpenter and he knows to the

31. James, "Count Zero Splits the Infinite," p. 70.

32. Leslie Bennetts, "Friendship Characterizes Stoppard Play Rehearsals," *New York Times*, 22 November 1983, sec. C, p. 13.

33. Cheryl Faraone, "An Analysis of Tom Stoppard's Plays and Their Productions (1964–1975)" (Ph.D. diss., Florida State University, 1980), p. 34.

34. Faraone, "An Analysis," p. 207.

35. Margaret Tierney, "Marriage Lines," *Plays and Players*, March 1972, p. 26.

36. Remak Ramsey to Faraone, p. 76.

37. Faraone, "An Analysis," p. 208.

full-stop why he's written a certain thing. Most plays that have a contemporary author sitting in the stalls are rewritten a very great deal, but he's always got an answer. But he'll never put himself forward at rehearsal. If we come to any sort of impasse, he'll always go through the director. "Do you mind if I . . . ? Would you like me to explain this?"[38]

At times, of course, we do not so much hear the playwright who "knows to the full-stop why he's written a certain thing" as we hear the private individual explaining personal views. While Stoppard has repeatedly acknowledged that his plays emerge as part of "an ongoing debate with myself," that he writes plays because "dialogue is the most respectable way of contradicting myself," that he engages in a kind of intellectual leapfrog, from time to time he also declares that some characters in his plays do speak for the author. Stoppard tells us, for example, that in *Night and Day* "the person in the play who says that information, in itself, is light—about anything—does speak for me";[39] that in the argument between Joyce and Tzara in *Travesties* "I find Joyce infinitely the most important";[40] and that Henry in *The Real Thing* expresses "some of the notions I have about writing."[41]

Still, the preeminent value of interviews with the most articulate playwright since Shaw is how much light they cast on the way the plays themselves work. Here again Stoppard is, from time to time, surprisingly forthright. Of *Jumpers*, the play Kenneth Tynan described as "a farce whose main purpose is to affirm the existence of God,"[42] Stoppard says, "I wanted to write a theist play, to combat the arrogant view that anyone who believes in God is some kind of cripple, using God as a crutch."[43] Encountering a critic's observation that he "gave equal weight to Joyce, Lenin, and Tzara" in *Travesties,* Stoppard demurs that "when they have that argument about art at the end of the first act,

38. Ronald Hayman, "Michael Hordern—Playing the Intellectual," *The Times,* 22 January 1972, p. 9; repr. in Ronald Hayman, *Playback* 2: Essays and Interviews (London: Davis-Pointer, 1973), p. 81.

39. Hebert, "A Playwright in Undiscovered Country," p. 10.

40. Ross Wetzsteon, "Tom Stoppard Eats Steak Tartare with Chocolate Sauce," *Village Voice,* 10 November 1975, p. 121.

41. "The Event and the Text," a lecture in conjunction with the Third International Conference on the Fantastic, Boca Raton, Florida, 13 March 1982.

42. Kenneth Tynan, "Withdrawing with Style from the Chaos," *New Yorker,* 19 December 1977, p. 85; repr. in Kenneth Tynan, *Show People: Profiles in Entertainment* (New York: Simon and Schuster, 1979), p. 93.

43. Oleg Kerensky, *The New British Drama: Fourteen Playwrights since Osborne and Pinter* (London: Hamish Hamilton, 1977), p. 170.

notice that Joyce has the last word. I wanted him to murder Tzara, and he does."[44] And Stoppard concurs with those who believe that "fundamentally everything is okay" in the relationship between Henry and Annie in *The Real Thing* because what keeps them together is "Love. They're right for each other. They love each other."[45]

While information about anything—including information about what playwrights see in the plays they have wrought—may be light, we need to approach Stoppard's "interview talk" about his plays with care. Stoppard's comments on his plays in no sense constitute the last word on the subject. Having just described *The Real Thing* "schematically" as a play in which a man "leaves a woman who is pretty much his equal at the stuff which doesn't matter" and marries a woman who is "wiser than he is," Stoppard immediately offers the caveat "But, there's no superior truth in my description of the play."[46] Such disclaimers suggest that Stoppard would agree with the principle—a sound one—that authors' observations about their work need to be tested against the works rather than treated as somehow more authoritative than the works themselves. Stoppard's discomfort in talking about the way his plays work stems in part from reluctance to attribute intention and forethought to every facet of a play. He is well aware that some aspects of a play may owe as much to serendipitous discovery as to conscious authorial shaping.

Prior to writing *Night and Day*, Stoppard "spent a long time wondering how to write a play about journalism" and pondered such possibilities as "a day in the life of the *Western Daily Press*." Then, Stoppard says, "driving down the M-4, suddenly I thought, 'Oh. It's got to be abroad. Got it.' "[47] But to account for why *Night and Day* had to be set abroad would involve an attempt to "explain" a sudden burst of insight that came with the inexplicable force of an epiphany. More modestly, Stoppard observes that "*Night and Day* came out the way it did because it came out the way it did."[48] The contemporary Irish poet Seamus Heaney, while talking incisively and illuminatingly about his poetry, expresses a similar reluctance to speak too assertively about authorial intention:

---

44. Wetzsteon, "Tom Stoppard Eats Steak Tartare," p. 121.
45. Buck, "Tom Stoppard: Kind Heart and Prickly Mind," p. 514.
46. Buck, "Tom Stoppard: Kind Heart and Prickly Mind," p. 514.
47. Interview with Melvyn Bragg, "The South Bank Show," London Weekend Television, 26 November 1978 (recorded 22 November 1978).
48. Interview with Melvyn Bragg, "The South Bank Show."

It is dangerous for a writer to become too self-conscious about his own processes: to name them too definitively may have the effect of confining them to what is named. A poem always has elements of accident about it, which can be made the subject of inquest afterwards, but there is always a risk in conducting your own inquest: you might begin to believe the coroner in yourself rather than put your trust in the man in you who is capable of the accident.[49]

Similarly, Stoppard declares that "the main trouble" with issuing confident assertions about what he was calculating in a given moment "is that none of these thoughts is a consideration while writing a play. It's all kind of fake, and the interview makes you fake by allowing retrospective ideas to masquerade as some form of intention."[50]

The problem Stoppard here addresses is not just the accuracy or inaccuracy of the reporter but the inherent dynamics of the interview situation itself: "You see, the unstated supposition to any interviewing situation is that I know the answers to the questions you're asking."[51] And, as Kerner in *Hapgood* says of particle physics, "the act of observing determines the reality."[52] "The interview situation changes you," Stoppard explains, "You're trying to oblige somebody by making more sense of things than you normally feel. So you end up as somebody who has much clearer positions, much more definitive positions on all kinds of topics because you somehow didn't realize you could sit there and say, 'Actually, I have no idea.' "[53] Being interviewed for a *New York* magazine profile, Stoppard cautioned that "somewhere in the middle of the piece, there ought to be a warning, like on cigarette packets. A warning which states: This profile is in the middle truth range. Don't inhale."[54]

The warning not to inhale, the warning to be wary of statements "in the middle truth range," might apply to all of Stoppard's interviews. The author's words should not be taken as a complete or infallible guide; the author's words need to be tested against the plays themselves; the author's words will never plumb the fullest depths—or expose the full range of playfulness—of the play itself. And yet. An

---

49. Seamus Heaney, *Preoccupations: Selected Prose, 1968–1978* (New York: Farrar, Straus, Giroux), p. 52.

50. Buck, "Tom Stoppard: Kind Heart and Prickly Mind," p. 514.

51. Bradshaw, "Tom Stoppard, Nonstop," p. 48.

52. Stoppard, *Hapgood,* p. 12.

53. Mitchell, "Just Who, Really, Is Tom Stoppard?"

54. Bradshaw, "Tom Stoppard, Nonstop," p. 47.

author discussing what he has authored does speak with *some* measure of authority. While none of Stoppard's comments will contain the last word on his plays, the refusal to take into account what we can gather of an author and of his perceived intention, the "denial of intentional context," as George Steiner reminds us, is "as absurd" as approaching such statements with "blind trust."[55]

Steiner draws a telling analogy between the critical process and the geometry of tangents. Any attempt to delineate the work of art "will always entail approximation" as we seek to use straight lines to approach the elusive round. As "we advance step by step towards a delineation of the given space," Steiner says, "our perceptions are more and more justly incident to the circumference of possible intent and meaning" but "the congruence is never complete."[56] Some attempts at drawing tangents simply miss the mark, but any circle still has an infinite number of tangents. Critics draw relatively crude rectangles or increasingly complex polygons that the curving lines of art inevitably elude. Something always gets left out because none of us— including the author—ever succeeds in squaring the circle. Nevertheless, while interpretative debate will necessarily continue, "where it is seriously engaged in, the process of differing is one which cumulatively circumscribes and clarifies the disputed ground."[57]

While we should trust the tale and not the teller, while we should expect interpretative disagreement to continue, while the words of an author—even when articulate and candid—do not enjoy a privileged claim to truth, nevertheless the insights offered by an author just may prove more illuminating than much critical reflection. Tom Stoppard in conversation takes us some way at least into the complex question of authorial intention in his plays. A Stoppard play will always be something more—and less—than what is reflected in a Stoppard interview. What I would claim is that in conversation "Stoppard the critic" is usually a pretty fair geometrician when he graphs some boundaries of Stoppard the curvilinear artist.

Stoppard's most extended chartings of his plays have been with the editors of *Theatre Quarterly, Gambit,* and the *Paris Review.* Those wide-ranging discussions are included here. But equally revealing in their way are explanations Stoppard has offered to members of the press. In an interview that appeared in the American edition of *Vogue,*

55. George Steiner, *Real Presences: Is There Anything* in *What We Say?* (London and Boston: Faber and Faber, 1989), pp. 174–75.

56. Steiner, *Real Presences,* p. 175.

57. Steiner, *Real Presences,* p. 214.

Stoppard offered one of the clearest statements of how he sees the relationship of Henry and Annie in *The Real Thing*. Stoppard's strongest denials that *Travesties* is absurdist occur in remarks he made to Bay Area journalists when the play opened in San Francisco. Appearing originally in such publications as the *San Francisco Examiner* and the *Palo Alto Times,* these interviews are here made available to a wider circle of readers. Also included are transcripts of Stoppard talking about his work in one of his highly conversational, "free-associative 'lectures'" and responding to interviewers on BBC Radio. Throughout, I have sought to include those interviews which contained the most substantive conversations regarding the full range of Stoppard's plays while offering as little repetition as possible. Some cogent interviews have been omitted simply because they covered ground already mapped elsewhere. I have sought both the piquant insight and comprehensiveness of coverage, but when I had to choose one or the other, I have opted for what seemed more incisive.

The chronologically arranged conversations with Tom Stoppard begin at the beginning, with a glance at the dazzled but dumbfounded young playwright the morning after the National Theatre premiere of *Rosencrantz and Guildenstern Are Dead,* and conclude with the 55-year-old Stoppard returning to the National Theatre at the peak of his form with *Arcadia,* the 1993 work that may be his finest play to date. In between, Stoppard tells why in preparing to write *Artist Descending a Staircase* he "spent half a day in the B.B.C. Library listening to Goon Show records of fried eggs hitting fans," why he finds it "very hard to turn down offers to write an underwater ballet for dolphins or a play for a motorcyclist on the wall of death," why *Jumpers* begins "as a strange pig's breakfast of visual images," why in *Travesties* "Joyce has the last word" in his argument with Tzara about art, and why he left out over half of *Rosencrantz and Guildenstern Are Dead* to transform his most famous play—a quarter of a century after its stage debut—into an award-winning film. The insights Stoppard offers into his intentions for his plays and the process by which his plays have been altered during rehearsals should be of interest to anyone who has been puzzled, intrigued, or fascinated by a Stoppard play and has harbored a desire to engage Tom Stoppard in conversation.

Success Is the Only Unusual Thing about Mr. Stoppard

John Dodd

With *Rosencrantz and Guildenstern Are Dead* Tom Stoppard became the youngest playwright ever to have a play put on at the National Theatre. The play actually had its premiere in August 1966 on the Edinburgh Fringe performed by a group of Oxford undergraduates who were baffled by their script's repetitions until the twenty-nine-year-old playwright breezed in, laughed off the repetitions as a massive typing error, and put things to rights. Years later Stoppard said he had been nonchalant in Edinburgh because his novel, *Lord Malquist and Mr Moon,* came out the same week and he was sure the novel would make his reputation and the play would be of little consequence either way. But then came the life-changing review by Ronald Bryden, which prompted a telegram from Kenneth Tynan at the National, and young Stoppard was on his way to international acclaim. If he could approach the Edinburgh opening of *Rosencrantz* with unaffected breeziness, he was anything but nonchalant when his play faced its professional premiere by the august National Theatre Company. Just four years earlier he had been a journalist reviewing plays, but on 11 April 1967 it was his play that was being reviewed. Two decades later he confided that he missed most of the opening performance, including the final curtain: "Early in the first act a man sitting in front of me turned to his companion and said, 'I do wish they'd get *on* with it.' That finished it for me. I went to the pub and never came

From *The Sun,* 13 April 1967.

back." When the response by audience and reviewers finally dawned, the young playwright was more than a little staggered by the adulation being heaped on a play he had once thought of little consequence. A reporter for *The Sun*, a London tabloid lacking any intellectual pretensions, caught up with the unknown twenty-nine-year-old the morning after the night before.

Tom Stoppard was drinking glucose and water yesterday, partly for the benefit of his stomach, partly for his hangover, and partly to help him recover from the most wildly successful night of his life.

The morning newspaper critics had, a few hours before, confirmed that Mr. Stoppard is a very good playwright indeed. His first stage play, *Rosencrantz and Guildenstern Are Dead*, performed by the National Theatre Company at the Old Vic, produced theatre-poster adjectives from almost all of them.

Mr. Stoppard read the notices one by one after dashing up and down Fleet Street from one machine-room to the next following a first-night party.

The morning after, however, he was even a little apologetic about the whole thing.

He sat on a table at the National Theatre offices nursing his glass of glucose, trying very hard to think of anything unusual about his personal life.

No, he had never starved, never lived in a garret, never contracted TB. The only thing he could think of, he said, was that he occasionally smashed typewriters.

"I have broken two, so far. I hit them when I cannot think of the word or phrase I want. I suppose it is a substitute for hitting my wife. But apart from that, I am afraid there is not much to write about me."

Mr. Stoppard makes no pretensions about being a social comment playwright, he is not particularly angry about anything, and not especially ashamed about being middle class.

By birth he is Czech, but came to Britain soon after the war. He went to prep school, public school and then into journalism.

"I really wanted to be a great journalist, but I wasn't much use as a reporter. I felt I didn't have the right to ask people questions. So I went on to theatre criticism."

He came to London from Bristol and began writing. He has so far had three television plays performed and written a novel. To date, the novel has world sales of 688 copies.

"The novel came and went," says Mr. Stoppard. "The play came and stayed." Quite obviously, Mr. Stoppard having arrived amongst us at 29, is going to stay as well.

His greatest enjoyment is from writing. He is the proverbial man who is so in love with his work that he can only sit and contemplate it.

"I find it difficult to put down the first word," he says, "in case during the succeeding 24 hours I think of a better one.

"With my novel, I was incapable of writing it because it was so important to me. I eventually began it two days before it was due to be handed in. Perhaps pressure of work is my salvation."

He seems a pleasant, amiable, young man, a far cry from the explosive playwrights of the 1950s. He is still not terribly sure of his ground.

"As I went to bed last night, I had an awful thought that this was some monstrous hoax the world was perpetrating on me."

He is now to write a play for BBC 2. "I don't have a title yet, and the plot is so vague I don't want to talk about it. I will have to do a lot of thinking about it."

Tom Stoppard

Giles Gordon

Almost from its first appearance *Rosencrantz and Guildenstern Are Dead* was hailed as Beckettian or Pirandellian, as absurdist or existentialist. Years later Stoppard would claim that he did not know what the word *existential* meant until it was applied to *Rosencrantz*. But speaking to Giles Gordon in March 1968, five months after *Rosencrantz* had become the first National Theatre production to transfer to Broadway, Stoppard began to respond to those who claimed to hear divers echoes in his Shakespearean antechamber. Gordon now says he regrets a somewhat belligerent tone that was struck in his interchange with Stoppard. But despite an occasional testiness, the conversation allowed Stoppard his first extended opportunity to discuss in print the work that remains his most-discussed play. Pressing Stoppard regarding his distrust of self-revelation, Gordon provoked Stoppard's acknowledgment that in retrospect his play "just seems a classic case of self-revelation."

"Heads. Heads. Heads. Heads. . . . " The coin is spun by Rosencrantz (or is it Guildenstern?) and each time, many times, it lands the same way up. Irving Wardle has written of the play which brought immediate acclaim to Tom Stoppard, "It is probably the first play in theatrical history with a pair of attendant lords in the lead. Stoppard does nothing to fill out their blank outlines. Their blankness is the whole point. They exist only to be occasionally involved in great events. When they are not wanted they are left together in a bare anteroom of the palace, spinning coins and playing word games to pass the time until the next

From *Transatlantic Review*, no. 29 (Summer 1968).

call comes.... But he manages to provide his two heroes with an existential development. They discover the letter authorising their execution, and choose to continue the voyage and deliver it, so as to emerge from the shadows of nonentity for a single moment."

Tom Stoppard was the first dramatist to be interviewed by me for the *Transatlantic Review* who seemed reluctant to have me visit his home. There would be little peace with the baby being put to bed, he indicated. The fact that he is a very private person comes out in the interview, which took place in my rather dark office in Covent Garden during a lunchtime in March. The place and time may account for the somewhat muted effect. Mr. Stoppard certainly seemed more head than tail.

The National Theatre programme for *Rosencrantz and Guildenstern Are Dead* provides the following biographical information, in addition to what emerged in the interview. Tom Stoppard was born in 1937. He is married with one child. He lives in London. He began his career as a journalist in Bristol, subsequently freelancing in London. In 1964 he went to Berlin for five months on a Ford Foundation grant and wrote a one-act verse burlesque, *Rosencrantz and Guildenstern*. On his return from Berlin he started work on *Rosencrantz and Guildenstern Are Dead,* which owes little to the one-acter except momentum.

GORDON: I was lucky enough to see *Rosencrantz and Guildenstern Are Dead* when it was done at the Edinburgh Festival of 1966, before it was performed in London at the National Theatre at the Old Vic in 1967. In Edinburgh it was mounted by the Oxford Theatre Group in an austere and slightly musty church hall in the Royal Mile, yet it seemed to me that it was a better play there, for two reasons. First, because it was shorter, the right length for its material; second, because it was more pointed. Seeing the highly professional production in London, I felt that the argument was drawn out unnecessarily. You'd made a joke, a witty remark, but the effect was often spoiled because the dialogue pertaining to it would carry on for a few lines beyond the denouement, after the laughter.

STOPPARD: You're the victim of an illusion. The National Theatre script was in fact a little longer than the Edinburgh one but this was mainly because I wrote an entirely new scene for London. At the same time I cut quite a few things out of the script which was performed in London. I remember a meeting with Sir Laurence Olivier and Kenneth Tynan which went on until five o'clock in the morning and quite a few things went that night. Mind you, I put a lot of them back later.

It is also true that we didn't even attempt to do the very last scene at Edinburgh; it was simply unstageable in those circumstances, the circumstances being a stage the size of a ping pong table and a dozen actors instead of 35. The *production* in London certainly went on a great deal longer because there was a great deal more of it. Anyway, there is no question of there having been any extra lines beyond the point where we reached a denouement in Edinburgh. Perhaps the Edinburgh audiences laughed at penultimate rather than ultimate moments, for some gnomic Scottish reason. Not that I heard them do it myself. I was only there for the first two or three days of the production and the play was received, well, politely rather than with hilarity. On the day I left—it was a Sunday—Ronald Bryden wrote in the *Observer* that the play was very funny and I understand that after that people tended to laugh at it rather more.

GORDON: What struck me more about the play than anything else was that of any play written by a British playwright since 1956 and *Look Back in Anger* it was the least personal. One had the impression that nothing was revealed about you as its author. It was objective rather than subjective. It wasn't, in fact, autobiographical.

STOPPARD: That's quite true. It wasn't deliberate in the sense that I take pains—or took pains in that play—not to reveal myself, or that I take pains in my writing not to reveal myself. Or should I immediately contradict that remark, because in point of fact I am sensitive about self-revelation. I distrust it. I've written very little which could be said to be even remotely autobiographical and I've been subsequently somewhat embarrassed by what I have written. On the other hand, I suppose that that play, as well as almost everything else, probably has revealed quite a lot about me without it necessarily revealing it in autobiographical terms.

GORDON: Why do you distrust self revelation? Do you think it tends to result in less good plays than might otherwise be the case?

STOPPARD: No it doesn't, at least not from other people. I think probably the real answer would lie concealed somewhere in my history. I simply don't like very much revealing myself. I am a very private sort of person. But there again one has to distinguish between self-revelation and autobiography. A further point is that of course autobiographical work would tend to be on a realistic level since one's life is lived on a realistic level, and it happens that I am not any longer very interested in writing realistic drama. Now, do I not write realistic drama because I don't like to reveal myself autobiographically, or do I not reveal myself autobiographically because I don't like writing realistic drama? I would say the former. I have after all written a realistic play. I started by writing a realistic play and really there is nothing of me in it, that is to say nothing of my life in it, just perhaps the odd stray remark that I have picked up and wrapped up and saved up and thrown up. I did one or two small things, a few unpublished short stories and a couple of published ones which sprang more obviously from my own life, but I don't much like them as short stories now. And I think probably that if I had written my slab of fiction about a young fellow born in Czechoslovakia, brought up in India, went to school in England, joined a newspaper, started writing his first novel, I would probably hate that too.

GORDON: Why do you choose *Hamlet?* Why Rosencrantz and Guildenstern?

STOPPARD: They chose themselves to a certain extent. I mean that the play *Hamlet* and the characters Rosencrantz and Guildenstern are the only play and the only characters on which you could write my kind of play. They are so much more than merely bit players in another famous play. *Hamlet* I suppose is the most famous play in any language, it is part of a sort of common mythology. I am continually being asked politely whether I will write about the messenger in *Oedipus Rex,* which misses the point.

GORDON: But in a way it is difficult to see the point. It is all very well for you to say that, but it was brilliant insight on your part to see that you could—or someone could—write a play about Rosencrantz and Guildenstern.

STOPPARD: But as I said they are more than just bit players in another play. There are certain things which they bring on with them, particularly the fact that they end up dead without really, as far as any textual evidence goes, knowing why. Hamlet's assumption that they were privy to Claudius's plot is entirely gratuitous. As far as their involvement in Shakespeare's text is concerned they are told very little about what is going on and much of what they are told isn't true. So I see them much more clearly as a couple of bewildered innocents rather than a couple of henchmen, which is the usual way they are depicted in productions of *Hamlet.*

GORDON: And this presumably is why you wanted to write about Rosencrantz and Guildenstern.

STOPPARD: Yes, it presumably is. I can't actually remember.

GORDON: This is why to the playgoer, at least to myself, the play is the first post-McLuhan (if that means anything), post-Beckettian drama because the two protagonists are bewildered innocents rather than henchmen, and their anonymity is magnified to such an extent that they become positive people. Do you feel that either Rosencrantz or Guildenstern corresponds to you at all? What you were saying earlier about your distrust of self-revelation seems to fit here.

STOPPARD: They both add up to me in many ways in the sense that they're carrying out a dialogue which I carry out with myself. One of them is fairly intellectual, fairly incisive; the other one is thicker, nicer in a curious way, more sympathetic. There's a leader and the led. Retrospectively, with all benefit of other people's comments and enthusiasms and so on, it just seems a classic case of self-revelation even though it isn't about this fellow who wrote his first novel.... But of course the saving thing is that I'm the only person who really knows to what extent and at what points the play reveals me. There's a great deal, of course, which has nothing to do with me, which satisfactorily obscures the photograph.

GORDON: Nobody can write anything which doesn't reveal a certain amount about himself.

STOPPARD: That's perfectly true. It's merely the difference between reflecting one's experience and reflecting one's personality.

GORDON: Was *Rosencrantz* the first play you'd written?

STOPPARD: No, by no means. The first play I wrote was a stage play called *A Walk on the Water,* which has now opened in London under the title of *Enter a Free Man.* I wrote it in 1960. I subsequently wrote a one-acter which has only been done by students, and I've written several radio plays—*The Dissolution of Dominic Boot, M is for Moon among other Things, If You're Glad I'll Be Frank,* and *Albert's Bridge*—and television plays, and another one act play which is going to be done later. *Rosencrantz* was about the twelfth play I'd written.

GORDON: Do you want to go on writing plays?

STOPPARD: I do really. I don't like the process of getting a play on, and when one is actually in rehearsals or on tour with a play, a career as a writer of novels becomes very attractive indeed. On the other hand, I've written one novel, *Lord Malquist and Mr Moon,* published in 1966, and it didn't compare in any way with writing a play—in terms of involvement, in terms of excitement, in terms of satisfaction. It's a much colder occupation, much less dangerous. When one writes a play one is really exposing oneself to every rotten tomato on the horizon. I think there's a certain satisfaction in the danger of committing the conceit of writing a play and having it performed at the expense of some effort by quite a large number of people, and then having it judged in one go. It's like having one's novel read by all the critics in a room.

GORDON: Do you enjoy the actual work involved in putting your plays on the stage?

STOPPARD: Yes, I find much of it very stimulating. This is only the second time I've had a play staged and in each case I've been very closely involved in the sense that I turn up at all the rehearsals and I suggest things and I give notes and whatever. At the time, I don't enjoy it very much. There are certain occasions when one goes home in the evening and one knows that because of one's presence there that day something in that play will be very much better when it's done. Of course the director does a great deal more than I do. I hang about. What one is there for is to prevent oneself from being misrepresented, because the first and real truth about having a play put on is that with the most intelligent and sympathetic director possible and the most accomplished and intelligent actors available you will only actually get about 70 percent of what you meant, because a script turns out to be a great deal more obscure in its intentions than one could possibly imagine oneself. It's taken me a long time to shake the illusion that everything I write is self-evident, that it's self-evident in the way it is intended to be performed, spoken, moved and so on. Not at all!

I write with a very dominant sense of rhythm in the dialogue, and to me the orchestration of that dialogue has a kind of inevitability. The words on the page appear to me to be able to be said in only one particular way to achieve an optimum effect. Of course one finds that not only is this way something that one sees privately and which is not at all self-evident but also that there are other ways which often work better which one hadn't even thought of.

GORDON: Did you do a lot of rewriting of *Rosencrantz*? The words and nuances seem very precise.

STOPPARD: I rewrote a great deal before I reached a final draft, but having got to a final draft I did comparatively little, though I did change the ending. We worked a lot on the ending with the National Theatre actors in the last two or three weeks of rehearsal. And, furthermore, between Edinburgh and London I wrote the scene to which I referred earlier. It was suggested by Sir Laurence, who pointed out that I had omitted a key scene in *Hamlet*. This is the scene where Rosencrantz and Guildenstern accost Hamlet after he has hidden Polonius's body. It arose because Olivier pointed out that when Claudius came on and instructed them to find Hamlet, who happened to have killed Polonius, it was the one time in the play when they were given an actual specific duty to fulfil, and it was a pity that it had been lost in the sort of cinematic cut we had then. So I wrote that scene. It's there, and I'm glad it's there.

GORDON: The only scene which reveals them in action.

STOPPARD: Though it's not very active for all that.

GORDON: Who do you feel you've been influenced by as a writer, or don't you feel it's important?

STOPPARD: It's not important to me, but I suppose it's interesting. Influences such as appear in *Rosencrantz,* and any play of anybody else's, are I suppose admirations that have been unsuccessfully repressed or obscured. I don't mean consciously! But, of the influences that have been invoked on my behalf, and they have been Beckett, Kafka, Pirandello of course, I suppose Beckett is the easiest one to make, yet the most deceptive. Most people who say Beckett mean *Waiting for Godot.* They haven't read his novels, for example. I can see a lot of Beckettian things in all my work, but they're not actually to do with the image of two lost souls waiting for something to happen, which is why most people connect *Rosencrantz* with *Waiting for Godot,* because they had this scene in common.

GORDON: Beckett's novels are mainly about one lost soul waiting for nothing to happen.

STOPPARD: I wasn't thinking so much of what they are about so much as the way in which Beckett expresses himself, and the bent of his humour. I find Beckett deliciously funny in the way that he qualifies everything as he goes along, reduces, refines and dismantles. When I read it I love it and when I write I just guess it comes out as other things come out. As for Pirandello, I know very little about him, I'm afraid. I've seen very little and I really wasn't aware of that as an influence. It would be very difficult to write a play which was totally unlike Beckett, Pirandello and Kafka, who's your father, you know?

GORDON: What about your play *Enter a Free Man?*

STOPPARD: I have worked on it a bit over the last year. In fact I wrote a new scene for it about three weeks ago while it was on tour, but it is basically the play I wrote in 1960. I mean it is still a play about the same people in the same situation. There is some new stuff in it and I have thrown out certain things. There was some imagery which went bad on me as things do, I suppose about a third of it has been written in at various times over the last few years. It was done in Germany in 1964 and I put some new stuff in then, and actually I took some of it out again. So it is a play which has been around my consciousness and my conscience for longer than I like to think. Anyway, as you know, it opened a week ago and it was patted on the head until it was dead. I think it ought to have been done, if only once, because plays are written to be performed. On the other hand, I was scared about it, because plays go off like fruit. They're organic things, they're not mineral. They change their composition in relation to the time they exist, or are seen to exist, and in relation to oneself; they start to decompose the moment the word is on the page. A lot has happened since I wrote the play—to me and to the times.

If I'd written a page of dialogue last night—and I wish I had—this morning there'd be a couple of lines which I wouldn't be quite sure about, and this time next week there'd be a line I'd absolutely loathe, and in a month's time probably only half the page would still exist, and the other half would have been thrown away. Certainly there are things in *Rosencrantz* which for me have gone off, and the soft bits go first, as in fruit. Well, *Enter a Free Man* is now pushing eight, which is quite a long time if one is a young writer. I think that if one writes a play at the age of 45 then it doesn't very much matter if it's not done until one is 52, but if one writes a play at 23 by the time one is 30 one has changed a great deal, and I no longer think of it as the kind of play I would write now or would ever write again. But following it around on tour I've been somewhat heartened by the fact that the kind of audience response which I was hoping to get out of the play when I was doing it is actually coming back at me now, which in a sense surprises me.

GORDON: Do you pay close attention to the work of your contemporaries?

STOPPARD: I read an enormous amount, at least I used to read an enormous amount. Now I read less, but of the countless books I've read and plays I've sat through there are very very few where I feel that I've been given an experience which differs from all the other experiences one gets from books and plays. There are very few books which seem to me to actually get away from what everybody else is doing. I think that a book like *At Swim-Two-Birds* is going to influence writers for a century. It's influenced writers already. It's certainly influenced B. S. Johnson. How far back can one go? *Tristram Shandy, Ulysses, At Swim-Two-Birds?* Of plays, of course *Look Back in Anger* had an enormous effect on everybody but it doesn't seem as important now as some others. There are plays which had much less effect at the time which I actually prefer, mainly because of one's own idiosyncrasies. I think *Next Time I'll Sing to You* is one of the best plays written since the war, simply because it's written like music. It's a most beautiful and brilliant use of language.

GORDON: I have the impression, from *Rosencrantz* and from what you've been saying, that you're more interested in form than content.

STOPPARD: No, I'm not actually hooked on form. I'm not even hooked on content if one means message. I'm hooked on style.

GORDON: I wonder if we don't mean the same thing by style and form. Style to me is modish, more superimposed than form, which is structural, integral. To me, *Rosencrantz* is formal, and has style; *Look Back in Anger* has neither, though it has a lot of other things.

STOPPARD: I think it has both. It is as formal as a quadrille, if you can have a quadrille with two girls and a man—you could draw that play on graph paper, with lines for Jimmy, Alison and whatsername—Helen?—crossing and recrossing in a formal construction. And although at first glance it has a sort of freebooting, free-associating flow of a compulsive talker with a certain wit and coherence, it is in fact constructed with an intense and ever-present recognition of the fact that it has got to be done in front of an audience and work in a particular way, and this concern for structure pops through to the surface at key points. The way that, for example, you end an act on a point where Jimmy and Helen, whom he has despised for the previous twenty minutes, come to a clinch—she hits him and he kisses her—act! It's exactly the same thing as ending a serial in a woman's magazine at a point where the reader is intrigued to buy it next week. As for style—the play seems merely emotional, but you can't really talk like that in real life without feeling self-conscious. And the reason you feel self-conscious is that you are aware that you are doing it with style, with just as much style as an Oscar Wilde character contriving to speak exclusively in epigrams.

Our Changing Theatre, No. 3: Changes in Writing

John Russell Taylor

In 1970–71 BBC Radio aired "Our Changing Theatre," a series of six monthly programs "surveying different aspects of the many changes now taking place in the British Theatre." In the third program Tom Stoppard and Howard Brenton spoke to John Russell Taylor (in separate interviews) about "Changes in Writing." The highly politicized Brenton began the second half of the program by announcing that "the theatre is breaking up, which is something that I welcome." Quite to the contrary, Stoppard—even in 1970—was talking about what is changeless in the theater and was praising form and structure in art. Affirming that he responds wholeheartedly to "a free mind working within a disciplined form," Stoppard dismissed plays that are intentionally incomprehensible as "pointless, self-indulgent and ultimately patronizing." Stoppard's affirmation of the need for structure and clarity in art provides the background for the discussion of his own play dealing with "barely explicable" events, *After Magritte,* which had opened earlier in the year.

TAYLOR: In our changing theatre the changes in the writer's situation have been more remarkable, more immediately notable than those of anyone else, and have perhaps led on to changes elsewhere.

STOPPARD: I think you ought to have one programme where you interview a West End audience to complete the picture because what has happened as far as I can see is that while the plays have changed,

Broadcast on BBC Radio Four, 23 November 1970 (recorded 12 October 1970).

the fact that the audiences are still there suggests that they have changed too. On the other hand, an audience tends to like the same sort of things all the time really because they don't change their humanness.

TAYLOR: How far do you think that this reacts on your own work. Are you conscious of being in any way an innovator, of pushing the limits of what audiences expect, or do you feel that you're just a dramatist writing as you do because it comes out of you...?

STOPPARD: Absolutely the latter. I think that essentially one writes what one writes because that is what comes out.

One is the victim and beneficiary of one's environment, history, subconscious, say, and—for me personally—80 percent of my time is spent in looking for something to write *about.* To put it crudely, it's a bit like waiting to be struck by lightning, because in order to invest the amount of energy and time necessary to write a play, one really has to be bowled over by a thought and I stumble about trying to leave myself receptive to this kind of violation almost, but when it actually happens, it's a moment of sublime bliss. It's as though at the far end of this gilded hall, the double doors have opened and a butler bearing a silver tray turns up and slowly approaches with the idea or even the manuscript, in a curious sense, in front of him, which he just puts in front of me while the trumpets sound. At that point, one has this surge of relief, that there is perhaps one more play left in one, and the last thing one worries about are these circumstantial and social aspects of what one is doing and what the effect is in the universe of the theatre. It really doesn't enter into it at all.

TAYLOR: Well, I'm relieved to hear you say so, because I find that it does in fact enter into it to an extraordinary degree for many of the dramatists that I speak to. They are very conscious of having some sort of mission, some sort of image of the theatre as they think it ought to be which they want to impose, or some sort of image of themselves, sometimes even, though it's not very fashionable at the moment, some political or religious message that they want to put over, that they are, in this way, very conscious of what they're doing, very conscious of their intentions in a most general extra-dramatic sense.

STOPPARD: Well I am as square and traditional, let's say as reactionary, a person as you could hope to meet because I operate on the premise that a theatre's job is to prevent people from leaving their seats before the entertainment is over. My absolute primary aim is that what I write should be engrossing. One writer will reveal society's contradictions while another will reveal society's essential uniformity, and it's no good saying that one is speaking the truth and one is not speaking the truth.

TAYLOR: Most of your drama is extremely verbal. I wonder how far this may have something to do with your having begun your writing career writing radio plays.

STOPPARD: I like radio and I write verbally, as you say, but not as a result of that. Long before I did any radio, I spent years writing for newspapers. I really dig words more than I can speak them. There are no words to say how much I love them. (Isn't that nice?) I sometimes wonder whether it's anything to do with the fact that I was actually brought up to speak two languages at least, in that I was born Czecho-slovakian. And Nabokov... there's a chap who wrote in Russian until he was in his twenties, and consequently he was able to sort of dash down into the English language as though it were the sea, and conse-quently he spends all his time splashing about in it and singing. I'm sure that being mature enough intellectually to respond to all the subtleties of the English language would make one a very verbal writer, as he is. In my case, I don't know whether that would have more than a marginal effect because I was going to English-speaking schools from a very early age. On the other hand, I haven't got any more plausible reason, if there has to be a reason at all, why my attitude to the English language is one of awe and admiration.

TAYLOR: It strikes me that you would be in a very difficult position as a dramatist if the theatrical revolution, so devoutly hoped for by many of your colleagues, actually took place. Because your plays have to be acted in the traditional manner and have to have very precise and disciplined productions.

STOPPARD: Yes, that's true. I really don't see any danger of that kind of play disappearing at all. It's survived for 3,000 years and I don't know that the Theatre Upstairs is going to do much about it.

TAYLOR: You are not worried about who is coming downstairs?

STOPPARD: No, I'm not. What's interesting is that people go to the theatre in large numbers and they are going to different kinds of theatre. I don't feel remotely hostile to the kind of theatre which bores me. This is not always the case with people I know. The first and only time I met Peter Barnes—I met him as I was on my way to see Arthur Miller's *The Price* and he said I really shouldn't waste my time. Not essentially because it wasn't a good play but because it was a type of play which ought not to be encouraged *at all.* I thought he was a nice fellow, but I thought it was a pretty daft attitude to take. I ought to add that I went to *The Price* and I was looking forward to it, being an old admirer of Miller anyway, and I was bored. I wouldn't have been particularly alarmed, I wouldn't have been all of that despairing had Mr. Barnes advanced down the aisle and smashed the whole thing to bits before my very eyes, you know. It would seem to me a slightly extreme and superfluous gesture, but I wouldn't have gone to the stake for Arthur Miller's *The Price.*

Certain people like Beckett and Pinter have re-defined the minima of theatrical experience. And if, like me, you appreciate economy—in other words, getting the most effect with the least—then one gets a little tired with fairly small effects being gigantically arrived at.

We have got more subtle, more receptive, more perceptive perhaps. But the thing which I respond to whole-heartedly is a free mind working within a disciplined form. What I *can't* take is an anarchic mind—not an anarchic spirit, which I admire, but a mind which has no formality to it when it comes to structuring and communicating its thoughts. And a great deal of modern art, I mean pictorial art, I look at it and what I don't get is what went *in.* And—I've probably got all my football teams wrong here—but I have a private test known as the Goodison Park test. The test consists of putting this work of art into the middle of a football pitch at half-time, and if the whole crowd screams "Easy, easy" then forget it. In other words, I don't care how far out a writer is, I like to get the feeling that enormous care, enormous feeling for structure and formality, to get its optima out of it, has gone into that work of art. This is what for me separates geniuses like Pinter and Beckett from fakes like . . . mumble, mumble.

TAYLOR: What you are saying helps to explain your own plays which are frequently obsessively detailed and finished. I mean a play like *After Magritte* is finished and tied up to an almost insane extent.

STOPPARD: I'm delighted to be given an opportunity to talk about that since I was to have indulged myself by doing so anyway. But taking as read the fact that when I actually see a Pinter play it makes me feel like I was made in Hong Kong, there were certain things which I was trying to do in *After Magritte* which I think I did do. A succession of barely explicable, small domestic events occur and furthermore the conversation is largely about some equally inexplicable events witnessed in the past. And it is all to do with using what *you* call the well-made play bit—because I think the theatre ought to be a series of ambushes and you can't sort of ambush anybody by just sort of laying about it in all directions.

TAYLOR: I think it's true to say that you are not really a difficult playwright because you are determined not to be. But at the same time there is a lot in your plays, the sub-structure of the plays, if you like, which most of the audiences are not going to get. The plays are bright enough on the surface to keep them entertained without really understanding what is going on underneath.

STOPPARD: Well, it isn't as simple as that because you *imply* that I put an underneath *in*. What, in fact, happens is that one casts about, as I say, waiting to be struck by lightning, and what one is struck by is the top, the top of the idea. One reacts to the possibilities—in my case usually comic possibilities—of a concrete situation. What one depends on is that those things which appeal to one will have a bottom to them and—I hope I make myself clear—it is important to me to find a subject which I can exploit dramatically and theatrically in terms of comedy or anything else. The reason why *that* idea appealed to me rather than another one is that it does have this under-structure to it. And that's the only way round that it *can* happen—because if you start worrying about sub-structure and instilling deliberate ideas about society into one's work, this sub-structure will be there but it will be sufficiently ambiguous so as to defy analysis, because the important thing about a successful work of art is not that it should communicate X to everybody but that it should run through the absolute alphabet for each 26 people. I get approached by chaps telling me that my plays are, in one case, about Vietnam and in another case about, oh God knows what. And I invariably concede that that may very well be the case.

TAYLOR: Up to now you have been perhaps lucky in that the ideas which have come to you have been ones which can work on a number of levels, but how would you feel if you suddenly found yourself writing a play that was bound to be regarded as experimental and incomprehensible?

STOPPARD: I hope to God I'd have the sense to throw it away. When I'm writing a play it is my constant concern that it should be wholly and continuously entertaining. The point is that you are in control of what you do with it and what I try to do with it is to write a play which means that people have to sit in a room and watch it and pay for the privilege. And bearing all that in mind, it is pointless, self-indulgent and ultimately patronizing to make it incomprehensible.

TAYLOR: Obviously from what you say and indeed from your work in general you are very much an unclassifiable among modern dramatists. But perhaps the whole question of classification is artificial. How do you feel about your position?

STOPPARD: Oh, I would endorse that heartily. I think that the classification thing is essentially a convenience. I think that consistency itself is a much over-valued trait because people's responses don't conform to the categories which they're invited to respond to. I personally can be thrilled to bits with, let us say, *The Importance of Being Earnest* and bored solid by a three-act comedy. I can equally be engrossed and bowled over by something seen on the fringe of the fringe in Edinburgh or Soho and sit in a sort of torpor of apathy and boredom and irritation in what would be called a temple of the avant-garde.

The whole thing is just lunatic really because it implies that kind and quality have an equation going between them which I would refuse absolutely. It would be as though somebody invoked Eliot's *Book of Practical Cats* to prove that *The Waste Land* was essentially the work of a frivolous author. It's lunatic. I personally would like to feel that about every five years I could put absolutely everything into a big play and make it as deep as I know how and in between knock off in five weeks a pass and the following month a play for school's radio, designed for an audience of 13-year-olds and so on. I mean the whole feeling of being pressured into being, you know, a post-Osborne or a pre-Osborne type of writer or a . . . upstairs of the Royal Court or downstairs of the Globe, I've really got no time for that at all.

Stoppard Refutes Himself, Endlessly

Mel Gussow

In late 1967 Stoppard spent three and a half months in New York for the rehearsals and Broadway opening of *Rosencrantz and Guildenstern Are Dead* (whereupon he was hailed by Clive Barnes as "among the finest English-speaking writers of our stage"). When he returned in 1972 for the American premiere of *The Real Inspector Hound* and *After Magritte* off-Broadway, *Jumpers* had been running for almost three months in London and Stoppard was already at work on *Travesties*. Meeting an interviewer from the *New York Times*, Stoppard spent less time talking about the pieces just opening in New York than about the theist affirmations of his more recent play, *Jumpers*. Stoppard concludes by offering the original ground plan (later revised) for the structure of *Travesties*.

In Tom Stoppard's new comedy, *The Real Inspector Hound*, two drama critics become inextricably involved in the action while watching a murderous parody of an Agatha Christie mystery. One of the critics is a second-stringer who, among other obsessions, is contemplating assassinating the first-stringer.

During a brief visit to New York for the opening at Theater Four, the author insisted that the play was not specifically about critics. "In a way it's about wish fulfillment," he said, "about the danger of getting what you want."

However he readily admitted that he had drawn inspiration for

---

From the *New York Times*, 26 April 1972.

the work from his own years as a second-string drama critic on a newspaper in Bristol, England.

"I was an awful critic," the lanky, modishly attired Englishman recalled. "I operated on the assumption that there was an absolute scale of values against which art could be measured. I didn't trust my own subjective responses. And I never had the moral character to pan a friend. I'll rephrase that. I had the moral character never to pan a friend."

As a playwright Mr. Stoppard is keenly interested in matters of morality. "I write plays because writing dialogue is the only respectable way of contradicting yourself," he said. "I'm the kind of person who embarks on an endless leapfrog down the great moral issues. I put a position, rebut it, refute it, refute the rebuttal, and rebut the refutation. Forever. Endlessly."

At the same time he believes there is an absolute "ceiling view of a situation." Who is looking down from the ceiling? Mr. Stoppard leans toward God.

"They found traces of amino acid in volcanic rock—the beginnings of life," he said. "Now a straight line of evolution from amino acid in volcanic rock all the way through to Shakespeare's sonnets—that strikes me as possible, but a very long shot. Why back such an outsider? However preposterous the idea of God is, it seems to have an edge in plausibility."

And that, he said, is what his newest play, *Jumpers,* is about. Now in repertory at the National Theatre, it is "a sort of Gargantuan extravaganza with a million and a half words.

"The cast includes a number of acrobats and gymnasts and also a man called Jumper who is the villain, a pragmatist. There is also a moral philosopher who believes in metaphysical absolutes."

Mr. Stoppard sympathizes emotionally with the latter character, "but intellectually I can shoot him full of holes. As much as anything this is an anti-Skinner play. [B. F.] Skinner is a highly provocative, fascinating, intelligent, brilliant, wrongheaded oaf. If people write well and epigrammatically and clearly, their ideas gain in authority."

As for Mr. Stoppard, he can see two sides to almost every issue—for example, Ireland. "Two things seem to me to be indisputable about Ireland. One is that the Catholics have an absolutely genuine grievance and the other is that the Catholics are incredibly irresponsible, dangerous maniacs who have to be put on board floating hulks in Belfast Harbor as soon as possible."

The point is that each side "invokes the ceiling view." Who is right? "If I had read all the papers and had gone to Belfast," said Mr. Stoppard, "I still wouldn't know the answer."

But one continually has to make choices. "We live in an age where the leper is the don't-know," he said. "It gets to be like binary roulette. You go by gut instinct. I don't respect people who are rigorously consistent. That denotes a kind of atrophy of spirit. I like people who repudiate everything they've written every five years. Probably up until the age of 50 that's a healthy thing to do."

About his own plays, he said, "There's stuff I've written I can't bear to watch. They get rotten like fruit, and the softest get rotten first. They're not like ashtrays. You make an ashtray and come back next year and it's the same ashtray.

"Beckett and Pinter have a lot more chance of writing ashtrays because they've thrown out all the potential soft stuff."

Compared to Beckett, Mr. Stoppard thinks he writes "absolutely traditional straight plays," such as *The Real Inspector Hound* and its curtain-raiser, *After Magritte.*

In the latter, his intention—in the manner of the painter René Magritte—"is to exhibit an absolutely bizarre set of components within an academic context." Mr. Stoppard's context is Agatha Christie, and there are witnesses.

Rival witnesses to an incongruous event is a favorite device of his. In Mr. Stoppard's *Rosencrantz and Guildenstern Are Dead,* the bizarre happening is *Hamlet,* as viewed by "two people driving past Elsinore."

The idea for *Rosencrantz* was suggested by a friend. Another friend gave him an idea for his next play by telling him, "In 1916 in Zurich living within a stone's throw of each other and using the same cafe were the Dadaist, Tristan Tzara, and Lenin, and I think Freud, maybe. Look into it."

He plans to begin the play this summer. "I think it might be nice to do a two-act thing, with one act a Dadaist play on Communist ideology and the other an ideological functional drama about Dadaists."

The playwright, who has never directed before, is considering staging that play himself. "I enjoy working with actors enormously," he said, "and I'm very dogmatic about how I think things ought to be done. When you write plays, you don't write à la carte. One writes set menus. Take it or leave it."

Arts Commentary

Richard Mayne

Four days before his radio play *Artist Descending a Staircase* was broadcast, Stoppard was a guest on the BBC Radio Three "Arts Commentary," where he revealed that his aim in *Artist Descending a Staircase* was to write a work that *had* to be broadcast, a radio play that was unstageable. In 1988 Stoppard finally allowed the King's Head Company to mount a fringe production of his "unstageable" radio play in their north London pub. That production transferred to the West End and a Broadway production followed in 1989. Still, Stoppard's comments on the BBC just before the play's first airing, including his unwavering identification with Donner's rejection of avant-garde "rubbish," perhaps constitute his most forthright statement on the issues raised by *Artist Descending a Staircase*.

MAYNE: Can I ask you a very simple question, is this play a comedy or a tragedy?

STOPPARD: That's not a simple question at all, that's about as complicated a question as I've ever been asked. It's an extremely comic tragedy, and I think that everything I write is supposed to work, at least on one level, in a comic way and, as probably most writers hope, I hope that nothing I write is only funny. I think that I have a definite preoccupation with what I think of as being an obligation to make things funny. It's not an obligation imposed upon me, it's an internal one. It may be the expression of a certain insecurity. I've asked myself the question quite a lot in the past. I think that comedy is something which I understand much more than tragedy and, furthermore, I can recognise a comic moment which works as opposed to one which

Broadcast on BBC Radio Three, 10 November 1972.

33

doesn't. Were I to write a genuine tragedy, I'm not sure that I'd ever really know for certain whether the thing was working or not. The silence of deep boredom is the same sound as the silence of a deep appreciation of a tragic muse.

MAYNE: Do you think so? I'm not so sure, I think from . . .

STOPPARD: Well to the author's ear, you know, they don't sound too different. It might be a bit worrying.

MAYNE: Well, there's a kind of close-knit quality about the silence. In some of the silences in this play, one is aware that the thing is still very much held in a grip by the author, by you, and one of the things I liked about it very much, and I like about all your plays, is the way in which the audience to some extent is led up the garden, continually, there are little surprises and traps; you think you're walking on firm earth and then suddenly Whoop you don't know quite where you are.

STOPPARD: I like to proceed by a series of ambushes, not necessarily anything as dramatic as an ambush but perhaps the word *quirk* might be useful here, a series of quirks, a series of small unimportant surprises and this is, I think, an expression again of what I was talking about, the need to just surprise—it might be a small joke or a large murder.

MAYNE: Yes. Or an accident or a suicide?

STOPPARD: Indeed, indeed, indeed.

MAYNE: You never know. Listening to the play, of course, you realize that it's very much a radio play. It's very hard I should imagine to do this kind of thing either in television or on the stage because it so much depends on the co-existence of recorded and actual sound, of the quick flash-back to a period you're not quite sure of, the effects that might be effects but might be reality but yet might be effects after all. Are you fascinated by radio more than any other medium?

STOPPARD: I wouldn't say that but having been asked to write a radio play, I did set out consciously to try and write one which had to *be* a radio play. On the other hand I have gone into two or three other plays with the same attitude. One was set on, sort of, Forth Bridge.

MAYNE: *Albert's Bridge?*

STOPPARD: Yes, and another one was about the telephone speaking-clock lady, and . . .

MAYNE: *If You're Glad I'll Be Frank.*

STOPPARD: Indeed. Both of them have been staged and this time I thought I really ought to try to do something which was unstageable and I don't know that I've succeeded. There is a part of it where the

First World War appears to be starting around people as they're walking through woods [*laughter*] and I quite expect to be invited to some university theatre in the future where the First World War will indeed be seen to start around these people. When I actually set out doing it, I had intended to take this to an extreme as follows: I wanted to write a play with a minimum of dialogue and, as it were, stitch one together using the grammar of sound effect, not merely, you know, bangs and crashes but let us say the grammar of mood music. We're all conditioned to read all kinds of messages from quite simple sounds, and I wanted to do a play which consisted *only* of these sort of sounds, perhaps the odd line here and there when I was in trouble. I spent half a day in the B.B.C. Library listening to Goon Show records of fried eggs hitting fans, and cucumbers being brought down on the heads of fat men, and tried to sort of juggle them about but the whole thing was quite a fiasco. I never got beyond even a skeleton of an idea of what I could do with it and I ended up writing something much more conventional than I'd intended. But I've got the other one saved up.

MAYNE: Good. I was once asked to do a very brief programme for a children's radio on 'Laughter' and the idea was to try and have a programme made up entirely of different sorts of laughter with again the minimum of dialogue. I think it's very difficult to do this. Will you be able to do it, do you think?

STOPPARD: Yes, that's a lovely idea. Not of the sort of length which *Artist Descending a Staircase* lasts. I think that one might be able to do something which lasts twenty minutes.

MAYNE: Talking about the theme of the thing again, it seemed to me that one of the themes . . . was 'time' which has always seemed to me to run right through your work. I'd like to quote a little bit from *If You're Glad I'll Be Frank* when the lady who is playing "TIM," that is giving the time signals on the telephone, says "and they count for nothing measured against the moment in which a glacier forms and melts. Which does not stop them from trying to compete; they synchronize their watches, count the beats, to get the most out of the little they've got, clocking in, and out, and speeding up, keeping up with their time-tables, and adjusting their tables to keep up with their speed." This seems to me to be a very profound statement and a rather, well, it's the sort of area of your work that made me ask you the first question, you know, is it tragedy? Because there's something tragic about these three people who were once so marvellous—they were sort of dashing. They seemed to this girl so dashing, all of them, and they were going to overthrow everything and start afresh, just like the Vorticist Wyndham Lewis's *Blast!*, all that, and now here they are, three old mice, really, living at the top of those stairs, and falling down it in one case, and it's all so pathetic and time is passing, the girl is dead and so on. Is this really what you're saying in the play, that all these things die finally?

STOPPARD: There's a cart before a horse here. Going back to your example, the great wheeze was to write about a time-clock girl, just that instant idea was where the appeal originated and what you've read is part of what followed from that impulse. The play is not the result of an apparent obsession with time. The obsession is the result of the play, and I didn't go into it thinking that time is an interesting subject so much as being attracted to the idea of this person being a real girl in the basement of the Post Office somewhere forever intoning the hours. In the case of the radio play it's a much more mundane sort of world I live in, you know. I said OK I'd do it by the end of June and I had this thought about this tape gag where we play a tape at the beginning and 75 minutes later we'd peg it off by showing that the whole thing had been, as it were, misinterpreted. So there was the need for 74 minutes of padding or brilliant improvisation, if you like, or very carefully structured and meticulously built-up plot. A bit of all that. And bit by bit you sort of assemble things which you drag out without really inspecting them for their resonance or what they speak of one's own predilections. In other words the question perhaps assumes a much more self-conscious process than I'm aware of when I write. The problems are, in a way, practical problems to do with finishing up with a play as opposed to a few ideas.

MAYNE: It's quite clear that the play is a contraption that works. But I think that inside the contraption, whether you intended to put it in there or not, there are these living animals which are your preoccupation.

STOPPARD: I very much hope so, yes. I think that in that particular play there's what you referred to as the sort of Munnings'-like diatribe ... That's a kind of old score which I've been meaning to reward myself with for years, but of course the whole point of writing plays is that you can't contradict yourself in public without becoming less than respectable.

MAYNE: Well, that's one of the things I like about it, that because of these different levels, different voices, different times, different attitudes, all the time there's a sort of very complicated dialectic or dialogue going on between all the people you are and all the ideas you have.

STOPPARD: I think that really the great release and attraction and perhaps secret point of being a playwright is that we are all different people, and one is writing dialogue for oneself, different facets of oneself, and that's certainly true of much of the work I've written.

MAYNE: In a way, I suppose, Beauchamp is you, because here he is playing with these tapes and producing what Donner describes as rubbish. "Yes," he says "Magnificent rubbish from the humus heap of life." But he says, "No, rubbish."

STOPPARD: No, I'm ... Donner is me. I'm a very square, conservative and traditional sort of mind. I absolutely think that Beauchamp's tapes *are* rubbish, and I think that what Donner says about them is *absolutely* true. I think that when Donner says that much of modern art is the mechanical expression of a very simple idea which might have occurred to an intelligent man in his bath and be forgotten in the business of drying between his toes, that is me. I did give Martello a line or two to counterbalance that, and I think that Martello's argument is not unreasonable. Dot, dot, dot, ad infinitum.

MAYNE: Yes. That's marvellous. . . . Thank you very much, Tom Stoppard. *Artist Descending a Staircase,* in John Tydeman's production by the way, is being broadcast next Tuesday evening at 10.10 on Radio Three.

Dialogue with Tom Stoppard

Joseph McCulloch

In June 1964 the Reverend Joseph McCulloch instituted a series of Tuesday lunch-break dialogues at the Church of St. Mary-le-Bow, in the heart of the City of London, for the purpose of "keeping open the dialogue between the Church and the world." When Stoppard was the guest on 20 March 1973, *Jumpers* had returned to the National Theatre repertoire after a six-month hiatus and Stoppard had written a play about Galileo that he hoped to present at the London Planetarium. Speaking from facing pulpits at Bow Church, the comic showman and the churchman seemed at times to have traded places, with the parson insisting that all is comic and the playwright declining to give "brief, flippant" answers because some issues were "too serious." However, questioned about *Jumpers,* Stoppard offers perhaps his clearest affirmation that there is more to a person "than meets the microscope" and that evolution may account for a man's "tripes and pipes and liquids" but not "his ability to discuss it." Although his play about Galileo was never performed live as Stoppard hoped, his work on that project provides the background to his remarks here about the dance between science and theology, remarks that prefigure in uncanny ways some facets of *Arcadia* (1993).

McCULLOCH: I daresay many of you have already been to *Jumpers*. It was, without a doubt, more than anything for a very long time, what I mean by comedy, and I'm not saying that merely to say the right thing.

From *Under Bow Bells: Dialogues with Joseph McCulloch* (London: Sheldon Press, 1974). Interview took place on 20 March 1973.

I do mean it. It was very, very funny and yet had an underlying serious theme. When I say that many wives, including my own, have seen much of their husbands in your self-absorbed don, you will know how near the knuckle you got!

I am going to take a text from *Jumpers,* if you don't mind, from the last speech of the Professor of—was it Moral Theology, or something?

STOPPARD: Moral Philosophy.

McCULLOCH: Moral *Philosophy,* which is worse—slightly. He says: 'A remarkable number of apparently intelligent people are baffled by the fact that a different group of apparently intelligent people profess to a knowledge of God, when common sense tells *them,* the first group of apparently intelligent people, that knowledge is only a possibility in matters that can be demonstrated to be true or false, such as that the Bristol train leaves from Paddington.' Now, this seems to me the crunch of the modern world. Do you think this is true?

STOPPARD: I will tell you what was at the back of my mind in that speech. It is a fact that I know dozens of rational humanists who have a very hard-headed attitude to any mysticality in the theological tradition, and are very articulate and sceptical and scathing about it—*and read their horoscopes.* One does find that people accept horoscopes, not with any sort of firm conviction or absolute belief, but the very fact that horoscopes exist *at all* in a world which is said to be—at least in Western Europe—over sixty per cent non-church-going at best, suggests that everybody has a repository of a 'mystical' awareness that there is a lot more to them than meets the microscope. It's a difficult thing to express in terms which are not, if you like, 'spiritual' or 'mystical', but I think that almost everybody would admit to having this sense that some things actually are better than others in a way which is not, in fact, rational.

That, roughly, is the central concern of the play—*Jumpers*—if one can put it like that. But I am glad you called it funny, because I don't think it is very effective if it doesn't work as a comedy.

McCULLOCH: Horace Walpole once said that the world is a comedy to those that think, and a tragedy to those that feel. Don't you think that it should have been, 'this world is a comedy to those that think they think'? What perhaps is worse, is that they think they think they *know!*

STOPPARD: One knows what Walpole meant, and it is probably a little unfair to analyse too much because, of course, like a painter, he wishes to actually *convey* an idea. The outer edge may not be clearly defined, but as long as the message is central, that is enough.

McCULLOCH: I am intrigued by your statement that it is unfair to analyse too much. Why?

STOPPARD: A better word would have been 'irrelevant'. I think that as long as one understands what a man means by a statement, what he really *means,* then his failure to put it into a precise capsule which has absolutely no ambiguity about it, in a sense, doesn't matter. If you and I both know what we mean by *x,* then it doesn't actually matter if we express it ambiguously. That is all I meant.

McCULLOCH: I would go further. I would say that, provided you and I think we like each other, or *feel* we like each other, then our words will not matter very much.

STOPPARD: Oh, oh. I am not sure that I would think that I think that I know that I like you if we hadn't been able to communicate. It is not that you look so nice, is it?

McCULLOCH: You would have to have oculist attention if you thought that! What I am trying to say is, that I have a profound suspicion, which seemed to me to ring out in *Jumpers,* and in other things you have written, that people who are clever, love to hear themselves being clever, but are not, in fact, saying anything very much.

STOPPARD: You have a sort of anti-academic scepticism?

McCULLOCH: I'm afraid so, yes. Ever since Oxford, I have been profoundly suspicious of academics.

STOPPARD: There is a lot to be said for an academic life. Goodness! the pulpit doesn't half make one pontifical.

I think that my definition of an academic person is not merely somebody who *lives* in a university, but whose major, professional pre-occupation is a critical one towards other people's creative work, for example. There is a level of academic criticism which I think is its own justification, in that it gives an entirely innocent and entertaining occupation to a great number of people. I agree with you that much of it doesn't really have a useful application to that with which it presumes to be preoccupied. Some of it obviously does. Some academics are wholly admirable people—at any rate, they are people with admirable brains.

I think that the only thing which really puts me into an anti-academic frame of mind sometimes, is the sheer scale of the enterprise. I mean if there were a number of people here and there, innocently stimulated by analysing literature or doing some sort of demographic study of entirely hypothetical societies, I would find this absolutely fine—why not? But there are now millions of people studying a few hundred other people and their works, and the gearing is slightly ludicrous. They are living their whole lives in this sort of capsule, which I think feeds the brain and doesn't really feed the neighbors, if you see what I mean. The thought of those incredible American campuses, which are like cities full of people doing theses on Virginia Woolf, is quite monstrous. I don't know, when you use the word 'academic', whether you are using it in the sense that I am, as a writer. Perhaps you are thinking of other fields?

McCULLOCH: No, I was thinking of the peculiar, introverted system in which I found myself at Oxford, where this curious idea that you could concentrate on a little piece of knowledge and assume that you *knew* something at the end of it, was extremely dangerous and misleading. I would go further and say that the great value of your play was that it revealed to most people who had not thought of it before, that man is never so comic as when he thinks about God.

STOPPARD: That's left me rather short of words. Is that a demonstrable proposition, or the opposite? It's an impression you have, is it—that it brings out the comic side of people?

McCULLOCH: Yes. I mean, the moment that anybody starts to talk about whether God is, or is not, which your delightful professor did—Michael Hordern played him brilliantly, I thought—you show quite clearly how absurd we all are. If God *is,* then obviously our only possible justification could be that we exist in his mind. If God *is not,* then our bombinations about God, in a vacuum, don't matter at all.

STOPPARD: Well, I don't suppose that there is anybody in the church now, who has never been confronted with that notion, at one time or another. But because—and this is the real problem, I think—one knows in advance that time, which will reveal all truths, is infinite, one actually begins with a hopeless quest, doesn't one?

McCULLOCH: Is time infinite, by the way? Surely time *must* be finite.

STOPPARD: On what grounds would you say that?

McCULLOCH: Because time is obviously measurable, therefore it cannot be infinite.

STOPPARD: It is one of those things with which I cannot bring myself to agree—such as that parallel lines meet at infinity.

McCULLOCH: I hope *we* are not parallel lines! What I am trying to say is, that the moment a man begins to talk about God, instead of refraining his soul and just trying to love and worship God, he has become an absurdity.

STOPPARD: Quite honestly, I would not have said that it brings out the comic side of people. I think it brings out, in a funny way, a sort of *embarrassed* side about them, because it is not really an area which gets much exposure. I think that there is a central confusion. You and I, even now, are talking about God in a way which has nothing to do with religion as such, nothing even to do with worship. I think that the kind of questions which ordinary people ask themselves, are the questions which actually give rise to academic philosophy: academic philosophy doesn't give rise to these questions. So when you make the sort of statement that you have just made about people thinking about God, surely they are doing so in ways which are bringing up questions of logical possibility, rather than a sort of mystical instinctive conviction about a Supreme Being.

McCULLOCH: It is precisely what you meant in the last part of *Jumpers*. Surely it is the limiting of knowledge to one particular method of objective observation which makes man ridiculous at present. The scientist is the most ridiculous of men the moment he strays outside the question of 'How does this thing work?' But what it is for and indeed the whole problem of ends, is right outside the scientist's purview. This has led the twentieth century astray more than anything else. Pulpits *are* places where you pontificate—you have said precisely that.

STOPPARD: I rather think that science and theology will always find a way to dance together to the music, because the whole of science can be said, by a theologian, to be operating within a larger framework. In other words, the higher we penetrate into space and the deeper we penetrate into the atom, all it shows to a theologian is that God has been gravely underestimated. In Galileo's time the view that the earth was at the centre of the universe, and everything else went around it once a day, meant that the whole thing could not be that big, however fast it was all going; it had to be a reasonable size; and in the still centre of this mechanism was the apple of God's eye. The awful thing about a *rotating* earth was that suddenly the whole machine became infinitely huge. There was no reason for it to stop anywhere at all, and, to quote Brecht, 'In such a universe, even the Pope might lose the eye of God'. It is the thought that suddenly one was no longer this privileged little unique world in the middle of these marble globes, but that one was simply on a lump of rock, barely distinguishable from millions of others, flung out into unimaginable space like a dice flung out of a cup—it was this, surely, which upset the theologians of the time. And I think the lesson which derived from that confrontation was the thought that God *had* been underestimated and that all this changed nothing. It simply, as it were, glorified God.

McCULLOCH: I think that God *is now* beginning to be underestimated, not *has been*. In the Middle Ages they had an *Organum,* the idea of the whole in which all branches of knowledge had their proper place. Today we have got analysts of various kinds, all breaking down knowledge into tiny little bits, and having no context into which to fit each. The idea that space, size, and so on should be important is a *modern* idea. I mean, no decent medieval theologian was worried about the *size* of things. This is much more a modern idea.

STOPPARD: Is it?

McCULLOCH: Oh, surely. What does it matter how big space is, or how small the micro-organism is? Does it matter? It only goes to show how totally compendious the mind of God is.

STOPPARD: I think it is one of those things which doesn't matter now because the thing is demonstrably huge. I'm not sure that in the early seventeenth century it was of such little concern.

McCULLOCH: Perhaps I can make clearer my main point by asking another question. Your play portrays a philosopher who does marvellous mental acrobatics. But isn't the far more marvellous thing the fact that he should exist at all? Isn't that the real question he raises in himself?

STOPPARD: I can accept everything about him in purely mechanistic terms except one thing. I can accept the evolution of the tripes and pipes and liquids which are in him. I can accept the evolution of the button on his cuff and the cathode-ray tube he watches, and everything about him—except his ability to discuss it, because there, to me, is a break in—what would you call it—philosophical logic, perhaps? There is a gap between an object becoming as complex, as prolific, as intelligent and as extraordinary as it can be, of itself, and actually *knowing* all these things about itself. This seems to me, in the imagery in which it occurs to me, to create a gap where you need to make a jump.

McCULLOCH: Is there not something peculiarly missing in your Professor Moore that makes him comic? Is there not something that makes me or anybody else, comic? Wherever I trip up and am not humble, when I am not confronting the universe and saying, 'God, how magnificent', I reduce myself to absurdity. 'Whoso exalteth himself shall be abased.' Jesus was always pointing to the comic aspect of our tragic situation, where we become so above ourselves that we no longer can become what we really are.

STOPPARD: Yes, but this is talking of comedy on a much more elevated plane than I practise it. I actually do two things: I write comedy but I also write jokes.

McCULLOCH: So did Jesus—at least, he spoke them. But he wasn't box-office then!

STOPPARD: I don't think that I really go along with you on the importance you give to the comic aspect of things. Because to me it is not the important thing. It is the cart in front of the horse, in a way.

McCULLOCH: What's the horse? The tragedy?

STOPPARD: No, that is really the point. I don't actually see it in those terms. I ought to say briefly, so you can just know it and forget it, that one has to bear in mind, in writing for the theatre, that one is also actually involved with a lot of practical problems which are nothing to do with philosophy, comedy, art, drama or anything else. They are entirely to do with actually writing the next line and doing something which will keep people in a room reasonably preoccupied and interested—the practical things.

I must say that until *Jumpers,* I had never set out to write a play about an idea. In every other case, I've written plays about specific people in a specific situation, and ideas tended to be the end-product of the play, rather than *vice versa.* Something between the two happened in *Jumpers.* What I am saying is, that the notion of seeing cosmic comedy in those terms, as something which one can, as it were, have in the back of one's mind while one is writing, doesn't really happen. I know what you mean and I can see why you see it in the text, but in a way, it is not part of the play for me; it is not part of the *writing.*

McCULLOCH: One final question, perhaps an unfair one. Viewing the modern mind, and seeing that it is totally analytical—always trying to take the motor car to pieces while it is on the way—would you, if you were really sick, which you are not, but if one *was* sick, that is to say, bewildered in one's mind, would you rather have two years with a psychoanalyst, or five minutes with a priest—a good priest, by the way?

STOPPARD: I would much rather have five minutes with a priest, but not necessarily for the reasons you would wish me to give. You may not accept that my reason might be simply that I don't have two years for anybody. To answer this question fairly, I share some of your scepticism about mind-medicine.

McCULLOCH: But if you had the chance of going to someone you believed—although he was just a person like yourself—was speaking in the name of one who said, 'Go and sin no more; neither do I condemn thee', wouldn't that be a more wholesome thing than having yourself taken to pieces and your mind concentrated upon your own ego, as must happen a great deal in psychiatry?

STOPPARD: I think it *is* an unfair question, because you must be more empirical than that. I don't want to be evasive but I don't really *want* to answer that question, because it is too serious a question to answer in a very brief, flippant way.

I think two things: first of all, about professions which deal with human welfare and particularly mental welfare—it is unknown territory in which a lot of people appear, perhaps, to be obsessives, who are actually feeding something into themselves. On the other hand, all progress which is broadly beneficial, of course has within it odd people whom one doesn't trust—which doesn't really matter. I think, generally speaking, that one person in ten probably needs it.

What you are really asking me, is what are the important things. Here is somebody else's answer. After a philosophic lecture, in which, I think, a lot of things which we have said were incorporated, somebody said to the speaker, 'I think that everything you say is true, but is it important?' and this philosopher replied, 'I'm not at all sure that importance is important—but Truth is'.

Tom Stoppard

Janet Watts

As the original Ophelia in the Edinburgh Fringe production of *Rosencrantz and Guildenstern Are Dead,* Janet Watts enjoyed a certain rapport with Stoppard when she interviewed him for *The Guardian.* Seven years earlier the London journalist and the internationally famous playwright had met as two nonentities involved in mounting an unknown play about two Shakespearean nonentities. After raves for *Rosencrantz* both in London and New York, Stoppard had another success with *Jumpers,* which was proving to be one of the most popular plays in the National Theatre's repertoire. But Stoppard's plays had come under attack for being "apolitical," uninvolved with "the social problems of life in Britain today." To the playwright's chagrin, *The Guardian* editors ran the interview beneath these words emblazoned in fourteen point bold: "When Auden said his poetry didn't save one Jew from the gas chamber he'd said it all. I've never felt that art is important. That's my secret guilt. I think it's the secret guilt of most artists." A year later in his interview for *Theatre Quarterly,* Stoppard would qualify his remarks by saying that he was talking about the short-term rather than the long-term efficacy of art.

Tom Stoppard arrived in Edinburgh in August, 1966: the unknown young author of the unfinished play being gloomily rehearsed in the Cranston Street church hall by some Oxford undergraduates for the Festival fringe. *Rosencrantz and Guildenstern Are Dead* had fallen to the Oxford Theatre Group from the Oxford Playhouse, where it had

From *The Guardian,* 21 March 1973.

rested after the National Theatre, having sat on it for a year, had let it go.

The play's first stage production looked doomed to failure. The director and his leading lady had quarrelled and dropped out, the stage manager had taken over the direction, and the actors (I was one of them) were mutinous about that and bewildered by the play, which seemed clogged with repetitions and had no proper ending.

Stoppard breezed in for a two-day visit: elegant, eloquent, engagingly good-humoured about the shambles he found. He revised the last two acts, laughed the repetitions off as a massive typing error, and set the direction to rights.

"I was very light-hearted about the whole thing," Tom Stoppard recalls now, "because I had a novel published in the same week that the play opened, and there was no doubt in my mind whatsoever that the novel would make my reputation, and the play would be of little consequence either way." That Sunday, scanning the papers for his dream book reviews, he came on the *Observer*'s rave of *Rosencrantz* instead. "So I was slightly taken aback."

Amid the play's subsequent world-wide acclaim, Stoppard retained his fondness for the novel, *Lord Malquist and Mr Moon*, which went down particularly well in Venezuela. (Almost as many copies sold there as in England, "which I thought was something.")

He admits now that it must have been from "some psychological quirk, because it had never been embraced by anybody. . . . Only since Faber have said they'll bring it out again have I begun to suspect that it wasn't all that good." But it "stayed together in my mind for a long time": unlike the plays which tend to "go off" for him, "like fruit." He goes on revising a play even after its production, "trying to scoop out the soft bits and make it cohere again."

Yet in spite of his agonies over the rotting process, Stoppard enjoys his own work. "I laugh at my own jokes loudly and quite unashamedly," he admits; and I remember him once in Edinburgh, when an actor queried a speech, explaining lyrically, "That's poetry, man." It was, too.

What's he doing now? Dividing his time, mainly, between family life in a spacious house in the Green Belt beyond Slough and the Greenwich Theatre, where his adaptation of Lorca's *The House of Bernarda Alba* opens tomorrow, and Garson Kanin's *Born Yesterday* under his direction opens next month.

"I would like ultimately before being carried out feet first to have done a bit of absolutely everything," he explains. "Really without any evidence for any talent in those other directions, I find it very hard to turn down offers to write an underwater ballet for dolphins or a play for a motorcyclist on the wall of death. I would never have planned to do what I'm doing now. . . . I get a phone call so I say Okay, I'll have a crack at adapting Lorca; and another phone call and I say the whole thing is terrifying, but I suppose I would like to direct *Born Yesterday.* . . . " Meeting Trevor Nunn, an old friend, socially the other day, Stoppard ended up promising to write him a play. "It seemed a good way of getting a play done, if I had a moral obligation to deliver one." He wants to take his children but not the play on holiday with him this summer, so that was how he fixed his deadline. (Tom Stoppard learned about those as a reporter and film critic on two Bristol newspapers.)

Other offers are all too easy to refuse: the chance to be playwright-in-residence at the University of Nevada, Las Vegas, for example. "Can you *imagine?*" A speaking laugh. "I'm a very domestic person. The idea of doing glam things just fills me with deep depression. I absolutely prefer being at home. I'm much more prolific now with my second marriage. . . . I hate being away from my wife and children for more than about two days. I'm quite insecure if I leave my immediate sort of blanket where I can just write and see my own family." The great drawback for him in getting *Jumpers* put on in America is that he'll have to go there to "make sure it's all going to be okay." But he will go? "Of course."

Sitting in on rehearsals is a vital part of the Stoppard operation. "It just cuts a lot of corners. It's always worth trying what the author had in mind, even if you decide not to do it, and if he's not there you can waste a day trying to decide what he's on about."

There's a deeper participation, too: Stoppard almost directs his plays as he writes. Take a bit of the rubric of *Jumpers:*

" . . . (*She weeps on George's uncomprehending heart. He strokes her hair . . . he really doesn't know what to do. So he plays with her hair for what seems a long time, lifting up her hair, running it through his fingers, looking at it, separating strands of hair. His mind grapples with hair, and then drifts and stops.*)"

"When I write, I have the production unrolling in my skull," says Stoppard. His plays often begin from an image, and move towards other images. *After Magritte* looks a bit like a painting by his favourite artist for most of its action: it began from a friend's funny story about the morning he was quietly shaving when he saw (from the bathroom window) his pet peacock leap over the garden hedge and make off down the road. Peacocks being rare birds, he dropped his razor, pursued it as he was (pyjamaed, barefoot, and foamy-faced), caught it and returned with the peacock tucked firmly under his arm. "I tend to write plays about people who drive by in a car just at that moment. They see this man in pyjamas, bare feet, and shaving foam, carrying a peacock, for about a third of a second. They never see him again. They never quite understand what it is they've seen. They probably wouldn't even agree on what it was." ("I lead an extremely happy and contented dull life where I never see anything as interesting as that," he adds; "but people tell me about them.")

Stoppard (a true ex-journalist) has a gift for quotable remarks. "I write fiction because it's a way of making statements I can disown, and I write plays because dialogue is the most respectable way of contradicting myself," he once said on television. He looks wry when reminded of it: "It seems pointless to be quoted if one isn't going to be quotable . . . it's better to be quotable than honest," he says (doing it again). His plays' dialogue is often "simply stuff which I've ping-ponged between me and myself," he says this time. He plays a deft game. "A truth is always a compound of two half-truths, and you never reach it, because there is always something more to say," he said on the television programme, which was a document of positive uncertainty. After a sequence of Stoppard stone-walling a barrage of interview questions, the words were typed deliberately on to the screen, "Tom Stoppard doesn't know."

Yet he never loses control. "I would think it a personal failure to write a play which is not consistent in every way . . . They've got to make absolutely logical sense to me. Otherwise you're drifting over the edge into a kind of artistic anarchy. My plays might have quite unusual things going on within them, but they stick to traditional playwriting rules. They are much the same sort of play as Terence Rattigan wrote, in the sense that there's a kind of play I don't write and Rattigan doesn't either—a play where one says all these outmoded forms of drama are such a bore, and I'm going to free the whole thing from these fetters . . . and the result is an absolute boring mess . . . " So, as he admits, he's a bit of a reactionary in some ways. Not much time for abstract art. He has a handsome collection of eighteenth and nineteenth century watercolours on his sitting-room walls.

His purpose in play-writing is purely theatrical, which can disconcert earnest students who want to theorise about his work. "I don't write plays for *discussion*—plays with secrets in them which are only to be discovered after patient research. I think of a play as an event in the theatre: to look for a kind of cryptogram in a play is to approach it in a way not really to do with theatre." He doesn't *mind* the academic theses—"I'm always pleased by the fact that the play gave pleasure," and so far nobody has written a thesis out of dislike—"It's just not what I write for, that sort of approach."

And the new play? Even the highly-articulate Stoppard finds it hard to explain where that begins. A clue: he's reading Marx and the Dadaists, and it's concerned with the proposition "that committed art is really a kind of bogus enterprise."

There's a line in *Artist Descending a Staircase* that says that in any community of 1,000 people there'll be 900 doing the work, 90 doing well, nine doing good, "and one lucky bastard writing about the other 999." Stoppard laughs. "I've always felt that the artist is the lucky man. I get deeply embarrassed by the statements and postures of 'committed' theatre. There is no such thing as 'pure' art—art is a commentary on something else in life—it might be adultery in the suburbs, or the Vietnamese war. I think that art ought to involve itself in contemporary social and political history as much as anything else, but I find it deeply embarrassing when large claims are made for such an involvement: when, because art takes notice of something important, it's claimed that the art is important. It's not. We are talking about marginalia—the top tiny fraction of the whole edifice. When Auden said his poetry didn't save one Jew from the gas chamber, he'd said it all. Basically I think that the most committed theatre in the land—I suppose that might be the Royal Court—has got about as much to do with events in the political arena as the Queen's Theatre in Shaftesbury Avenue. I've never felt this—that art is important. That's been my secret guilt. I think it's the secret guilt of most artists."

Ambushes for the Audience:
Towards a High Comedy of Ideas

Roger Hudson, Catherine Itzin, and Simon Trussler

Stoppard's interview with the editors of *Theatre Quarterly* is not only the longest interview he has ever given but in several respects the most substantial. He not only responds to biographical questions but volunteers a detailed explanation of the genesis of *Rosencrantz and Guildenstern Are Dead*, distinguishes between his "serious" and farcical plays, and offers extensive commentary on *Jumpers* and *Travesties* as well as lesser works. He also finally faces head-on the charges of being apolitical and therefore somehow frivolous for not being a more socially committed playwright. The editors—Roger Hudson, Catherine Itzin, and Simon Trussler—confront Stoppard on such issues from their first questions about whether his family were "'poor whites,' or reasonably well-off," whether they had enjoyed "a step-up to the sahib class," whether Stoppard had had "a 'privileged' education." In response to persistent questioning as to why his work is not more political, Stoppard offers an animated defense of his political beliefs, his moral beliefs, and his reasons for valuing art. The interview took place in January 1974 when *Jumpers* was in rehearsal for its American premiere and RSC rehearsals for *Travesties* were just about to begin.

You left Czechoslovakia with your family when you were still a baby, just before the war?

That's right. My father was employed by a very large shoe com-

From *Theatre Quarterly* 4, no. 14 (May 1974).

pany, Bata, as company doctor—they transferred many of their employees to different parts of the world, and we went to Singapore.

And it was there that your father was killed after the Japanese invasion, when you were—what, four?

Yes—it was women and children first, and he remained behind, while my mother and my brother and I were evacuated to India.

How much do you remember of all this?

I've very little recollection of Singapore, but vivid memories of India, for which I have a huge nostalgia. But I've never been back. I imagine I'd be fairly disillusioned and despairing if I did, with the population increase, for one thing.

Were you 'poor whites,' or reasonably well-off?

Neither, really. My mother was manageress of the Bata shoe shop in Darjeeling for some time, and we never seemed to be particularly short of money. I suppose we were just living the ordinary sort of life of a working mother with two sons. But quite soon after the war my mother remarried—an Englishman in the British army in India, name of Stoppard.

A step-up to the sahib class?

Well, the lower-sahib class. I suppose, though I don't remember feeling in the sahib class—except perhaps towards the very end, when I was older. I went to an American school, but Indians went there too—all nationalities did, in fact.

And the family moved to England in 1946—anticipating independence?

No, my new father came from England, and was going back there now the war was over—simply as a soldier going home.

Do you think your mother would have stayed in India if she hadn't remarried?

I doubt it. I think we might have gone back to Czechoslovakia.

So you didn't really have any positive feelings towards England before you arrived?

Not quite: the first school I ever went to was an English convent, and English had always been my own language.

Your step-father left the army?

Yes—he was, and is, in the machine tool business, and this involved moving from place to place at first, as he moved up the machine-tool ladder. We lived in Derbyshire and Yorkshire, and somewhere else too, I think, before moving to Bristol round about 1950.

Privileged Boredom

But you were away at preparatory and a boarding grammar school—a 'privileged' education?

Well, the chief influence of my education on me was negative, and whether that had much to do with it being privileged is open to doubt. I left school thoroughly bored by the idea of anything intellectual, and gladly sold all my Greek and Latin classics to George's Bookshop in Park Street. I'd been totally bored and alienated by everyone from Shakespeare to Dickens besides.

Had you been expected to try for university?

I suppose in a notional sense everyone at Pocklington was. But don't get the wrong idea—it wasn't a school where everyone wore boaters and communicated in Latin, just a grammar school in a small Yorkshire town.

What age were you when you sold the books to George's?

For eighteen shillings, something like that . . . I was seventeen, and it took about another five years for me to start buying them back—not the same books, but books.

In between, you started in journalism?

Yes, this was while the family was still living in Bristol, so I joined the *Western Daily Press* straight from school, in 1954, living at home on £2-10s-8d a week.

Your ambitions were entirely journalistic?

Well, come 1956, when the British and French went into Suez and the Russians went into Budapest, then I wanted to be Noel Barber on the *Daily Mail* or Sefton Delmer on the *Daily Express*—that kind of big-name, roving reporter. Noel Barber actually got shot in the head in Budapest, which put him slightly ahead of Delmer as far as I was concerned.

You hadn't done any writing other than journalistic at this stage?

No, but it wasn't just news reporting. I did a lot of feature writing, and already in my second year I was being trusted with the odd colour piece.

I heard a malicious rumour that you tried for Fleet Street as a foreign correspondent, but were turned down for not knowing the name of the Foreign Secretary. . . .

Not a malicious rumour, but a mangled version of a story I told at the *Evening Standard* drama awards dinner a few years back. The job was actually on their 'Londoner's Diary,' and I got on very well with Nick Tomalin, bless his memory, who was then running it: but, yes, Charles Wintour did ask me about some politician I couldn't name, and whose identity seemed to me quite irrelevant to getting shot in the head at Budapest. So I stayed with the *Western Daily Press,* till I got sort of poached by the *Bristol Evening World* in 1958, and stayed with them for another couple of years. It was during this time that I started wanting to write for the theatre.

Why for the theatre, rather than novels or poetry, do you think?

Historical accident. After 1956 everybody of my age who wanted to write, wanted to write plays—after Osborne and the rest at the Court, and with Tynan on the *Observer,* and Peter Hall about to take over the RSC. In a sense I was writing plays for Tynan and Peter Hall.

And A Walk on the Water *was the first.*

Yes. I was on holiday in Italy, and it struck me that I was never going to start writing unless I did something active about it, so when I got back I handed my notice in, making sure I had two weekly columns for bread and butter while I was writing the play, which I did in the second half of 1960.

Had you been going much to the theatre?

I'd been reviewing plays as second-string almost from the first, because in provincial journalism the most junior and least competent person is, of course, the one who's sent to the outer edge of the suburbs to review *The Holly and the Ivy* put on by the Townswomen's Guild.

Writing in a Panic

How easy a play was A Walk on the Water *to write?*

I wrote it very easily in about three months, and I was astonished with myself—every day there was more done and less to do, and I hadn't stopped, and instead of getting harder it was getting easier. I was working in a sort of panic because—at my ripe old age it's hard to believe, but at that time it seemed incredibly important that I hadn't done any of the things by the age of 23 that I'd intended doing by the age of 21; so I was doing everything two years late, and really had to get down to it. I was living with a very nice family in Bristol, paying very little for my board and lodgings—in a sense, it was the good old days, from the point of view of life's complexity, though as it turns out the new days are good too.

It's an unusual kind of first play, isn't it? Not much that's autobiographical or seminal or whatever?

I don't think a first play tends to be that—it tends to be the sum of all the plays you have seen of a type you can emulate technically and have admired. So *A Walk on the Water* was in fact *Flowering Death of a Salesman*—though of course I didn't think that when I was doing it. My 'first' play—that is, the first play I regard as *mine,* after I'd cleared the decks with *A Walk on the Water*—was called *The Gamblers.* And that, I suppose, was really *Waiting for Godot in the Condemned Cell.* . . . (When I met Peggy Ramsay about that time, she said, knowing nothing about *The Gamblers,* that all young writers seemed to be writing first plays about people in condemned cells.) Anyway, it was eventually done by the Drama Department at Bristol University, round about 1965.

What was happening to you and to A Walk on the Water *meanwhile?*

I gave the play to the Bristol Old Vic, naturally, as I had lots of friends there, though I don't think I did anything with it for a while. But the whole thing was very amorphous, it was just a way of getting it assessed, as though there was never any possibility of it being performed. Ah yes, and then my life was changed. I asked someone at the Bristol Old Vic if they knew of an agent, and they recommended Kenneth Ewing, who handled the literary side of Fraser and Dunlop. So I sent off the play to him, and he didn't have my phone number or something, because I had one of those Hollywood-style telegrams that change struggling young artists' lives. I had never had ten quid in a lump sum before, and within a fortnight I was given a hundred pounds and Tennent's had an option on the play, and they were discussing various actors, all of whom were knighted. The option was for a year: a year later back came the play.

And in the meantime . . . ?

I was writing theatre reviews for *Scene* magazine, which lasted eight or nine months, and that of course got me to London. One room, scratching a living, not writing much apart from a few short stories— three of which Faber eventually published. Another one which they didn't particularly go for I turned into the radio play *M is for Moon Among Other Things*—the one about Marilyn Monroe's death. I was also hired by the *Daily Express* in some sort of showbiz category, but that got overruled by someone higher up. Fortunately, though, it was just about the time that *Scene* folded that I was managing the transition to living off playwriting, because *Walk on the Water* was bought by one of the commercial television companies. One television play then was worth about 150 weeks' rent to me.

What are your feelings now towards that play?

A great deal of gratitude and affection, and a certain amount of embarrassment. I don't think it's a very true play, in the sense that I feel no intimacy with the people I was writing about. It works pretty well as a play, but it's actually phoney because it's a play written about other people's characters.

Do you think it also distorted other people's attitudes towards your work because it was eventually produced on stage, as Enter a Free Man, *after* Rosencrantz and Guildenstern?

Yes, but again I could only be grateful because a very nice lady called Doris Abrahams bought a two-year option on it when I very much needed that sort of encouragement; it was just unfortunate that it didn't get put on till the very tail-end of the option, and by that time through no fault of hers or mine it was light years away from anything I was interested in.

Rosencrantz in Embryo

All this adds up to . . . what, four years, between the writing of that play and Rosencrantz and Guildenstern?

Yes, I began writing *Rosencrantz* in 1964. But that wasn't because I was in any sort of despair or sulks, I was just busy or lazy. I don't think I got too overwrought with the disappointments over *Walk on the Water,* though my memory *is* very good at erasing things I'd rather not remember. Also, very conveniently, just after *Scene* folded, and after *Walk on the Water* had been done on TV, Charles Marowitz was asked by some Germans if he knew any promising young playwrights, because the Ford Foundation was financing a kind of annual cultural picnic in Berlin—part of the general effort around that time to keep Berlin alive in every sense, I suppose. So between May and October they had this colloquium, which in 1964 was to be for young playwrights. We were fed and housed in great comfort and just asked to get on with it. Of course, it was quite incapacitating.

This must be the occasion Charles Marowitz describes in Confessions of a Counterfeit Critic—*one of the confessions being that he thought the early version of* Rosencrantz *you sketched out there was quite hopeless . . . ?*

Oh yes, what I wrote in Germany, if I remember—and I'm trying to forget—was just a sort of Shakespearian pastiche. It was Kenneth Ewing who gave me the idea, driving back from some abortive attempt to get ABC Television to commission a play from me—all my ideas were 'too downbeat,' they said. But he suggested that it should take place in England, and I remember writing a version—maybe the one Charles read—in which they got to England, and King Lear was on the throne . . . I mean, the whole thing was unspeakable. But it did contain some of the dialogue which still exists in the play.

Can you trace the progress of the play from that embryonic version to the one put on two years later at the National Theatre?

Not very adequately in terms of my intellectual process. What I do remember is that the transition from one play to the other was an attempt to find a solution to a practical problem—that if you write a play about Rosencrantz and Guildenstern in England, you can't count on people knowing who they are and how they got there. So one tended to get back into the end of *Hamlet* a bit. But the explanations were always partial and ambiguous, so one went back a bit further into the plot, and as soon as I started doing this I totally lost interest in England. The interesting thing was them at Elsinore.

*Were you still looking on it as a play about a play—*Hamlet—*or a play about these two characters . . .*

By this time I was not in the least interested in doing any sort of pastiche, for a start, or in doing a criticism of *Hamlet*—that was simply one of the by-products. The chief interest and objective was to exploit a situation which seemed to me to have enormous dramatic and comic potential—of these two guys who in Shakespeare's context don't really know what they're doing. The little they are told is mainly lies, and there's no reason to suppose that they ever find out why they are killed. And, probably more in the early 1960s than at any other time, that would strike a young playwright as being a pretty good thing to explore. I mean, it has the right combination of specificity and vague generality which was interesting at that time to (it seemed) eight out of ten playwrights. That's why, when the play appeared, it got subjected to so many different kinds of interpretation, all of them plausible, but none of them calculated.

What was calculated?

What was actually calculated was to entertain a roomful of people with the situation of Rosencrantz and Guildenstern at Elsinore. The chief thing that added one line to another line was that the combination of the two should retain an audience's interest in some way. I tend to write through a series of small, large and microscopic ambushes—which might consist of a body falling out of a cupboard, or simply an unexpected word in a sentence. But my preoccupation as a writer, which possibly betokens a degree of insecurity, takes the form of contriving to inject some sort of interest and colour into every line, rather than counting on the general situation having a general interest which will hold an audience.

Process of Solving Problems

So really Rosencrantz and Guildenstern *doesn't embody any particular philosophy but is a process of solving craft problems?*

That's absolutely the case *on a conscious level*, but one is a victim and beneficiary of one's subconscious all the time and, obviously, one is making choices all the time. And the kind of things which I personally enjoy, which I personally judge to be . . . quirky, and therefore interesting enough or funny enough or resonant enough to do the job of retaining an audience's interest, involve rather more than a simple matter of craft. *Why* do these things appeal to me? What is it about them that I find satisfying? There one starts to get into an area where a more interpretive attitude to the material is not irrelevant. It's difficult for me to endorse or discourage particular theories—I mean, I get lots of letters from students, and people who are doing the play, asking me questions about it, which seem to expect a yes-or-no answer. It is a mistake to assume that such questions have that kind of answer. I personally think that *anybody's* set of ideas which grows out of the play has its own validity.

With hindsight, do you think Rosencrantz *was more a play about, well, existential problems posed by bit-part characters in Shakespeare, or was it, maybe subconsciously, asking questions about more general, more 'real' philosophical problems?*

First I must say that I didn't know what the word 'existential' meant until it was applied to *Rosencrantz.* And even now existentialism is not a philosophy I find either attractive or plausible. But it's certainly true that the play can be interpreted in existential terms, as well as in other terms. But I must make clear that, insofar as it's possible for me to look at my own work objectively at all, the element which I find most valuable is the one that other people are put off by—that is, that there is very often *no* single, clear statement in my plays. What there is, is a series of conflicting statements made by conflicting characters, and they tend to play a sort of infinite leap-frog. You know, an argument, a refutation, then a rebuttal of the refutation, then a counter-rebuttal, so that there is never any point in this intellectual leap-frog at which I feel *that* is the speech to stop it on, *that* is the last word.

*That's curious, because I would have thought it could be said of quite a few of your plays, the more recent ones particularly, that they are solutions to problems—in a quite precise though often a very comic sense—*After Magritte, *for example,* Real Inspector Hound *or* Artist Descending a Staircase. . . .

If you're thinking of a situation as being a metaphor for a more general confusion then of course that's true of *After Magritte;* but that's not an intellectual play, it's a nuts-and-bolts comedy.

But isn't it true to say that most of your plays have a fascination with the eccentric in human behaviour, at least as a starting point? Aren't you more interested in that than in trying to explore the nuances of ordinary social activity?

What I try to do, is to end up by contriving the perfect marriage between the play of ideas and farce or perhaps even high comedy. Now, whether this is a desirable objective, or why it should be, is a matter which I'm not in the least interested in going into. But it *is* the objective, and to that end I have been writing plays which are farcical and without an idea in their funny heads, and I have also written plays which are all mouth, like *The Gamblers,* and don't bring off the comedy. And occasionally, I think *Jumpers* would be an example, I've got fairly close to a play which works as a funny play and which makes coherent, in terms of theatre, a fairly complicated intellectual argument.

How conscious are you before you start that this play is going to be a nuts-and-bolts comedy, and this other play's going to have philosophical complications?

Wholly. You see, I've only written four full-length plays, one being *Walk on the Water* which doesn't really count in this respect. Now the other three—that includes the new one, *Travesties*—are in this area of trying to marry the play of ideas to comedy or farce. At the same time, I don't think of myself, I don't think of any writer, as ploughing that narrow a field. *After Magritte* and *The Real Inspector Hound* are short plays and they really are an attempt to bring off a sort of comic coup in pure mechanistic terms. They were *conceived* as short plays. The one thing that *The Real Inspector Hound* isn't about, as far as I'm concerned, is theatre critics. I originally conceived a play, exactly the same play, with simply two members of an audience getting involved in the play-within-the-play. But when it comes actually to writing something down which has integral entertainment value, if you like, it very quickly occurred to me that it would be a lot easier to do it with critics, because you've got something known and defined to parody. So it was never a play *about* drama critics. If one wishes to say that it is a play about something more than that, then it's about the dangers of wish-fulfilment. But as soon as the word's out of my mouth I think, shit, it's a play about these two guys, and they're going along to this play, and the whole thing is tragic and hilarious and very, very carefully constructed. I'm very fond of the play because I didn't know how to do it. I just got into it, and I knew that I wanted it somehow to resolve itself in a breathtakingly neat, complex but utterly comprehensible way.

I find it very interesting, this combination of your not knowing what's going to happen and of knowing exactly what's going to happen—or exactly what you want it to come out like, anyway.

Well, for anyone who is actually familiar with *Hound*, I didn't know that the body was Higgs, and I didn't know that Magnus was going to be Puckeridge. I mean, as soon as I realized the body had to be Higgs and, later, Magnus had to be Puckeridge, as solutions to the problems in writing that play, it made sense of all the things I'd been trying to keep going. But it's a sort of risk operation, that particular play. *After Magritte* was worked out very carefully.

There's something equally careful about how many of your plays operate, yet one does wonder very much how particularly the more eccentric situations germinate.

Before *The Real Inspector Hound*, I wrote a sort of goon-show version of it, which had no kind of structure—it was just a situation of two people watching a whodunnit and getting involved in it. I wrote that in Bristol after *The Gamblers*, and then didn't finish it and kept it about, and brought it out again in 1967. But I have enormous difficulty in working out plots, so actually to use *Hamlet*, or a classical whodunnit, or another play (which I'm afraid I've just done again) for a basic structure takes a lot of the pressure off me.

I suppose even plays like Albert's Bridge *or* If You're Glad I'll Be Frank *also rely on . . . not so much familiar situations as familiar metaphors—painting the Forth Bridge, and the faintly ridiculous concept of a 'speaking clock,' in those cases.*

Yes—in fact *If You're Glad . . .* actually had its origins in a series the BBC were contemplating, which I don't think ever happened, about people in absurd jobs which didn't really exist, and the idea of doing one about the speaking-clock girl occurred to me then. For me, it is such a relief to get an idea! I know there are writers who are not going to live long enough to do justice to all the ideas they have, but to me it's like being struck by lightning—and I feel just as powerless to *make* it happen—even, as it were, by hanging about under trees in thunderstorms.

Visions and Revisions

Is your working method different when you know you're writing for radio rather than the stage?

Not at all. I mean the structure is obviously geared to radio, but I write the same way—in fact, overwrite, just as much for radio as for anything else. Once I've got an idea and I've got it worked out, I do this incredible ground plan for a play, and I always end up having to create a new first-act curtain, because my intended first-act curtain is an hour further on. Stepping on the tortoise in *Jumpers* was always, as far as I was concerned, going to be the first-act curtain. By the time my people had shut up, an hour and ten minutes had gone, and we were only half way there. And that tends to happen with my plays.

But the ground plan gives you confidence or something . . . ?

Yes, but it turns out to be almost irrelevant, because I am in this terrible self-imposed trap, where I feel I can't begin without knowing exactly what I'm going to do, and then the only way you know what you're going to do is by beginning. The play I've just finished, I started working on it and thinking about it round about March, and I vaguely said to the RSC I'd try and do it by the end of July, because I knew what the nucleus was. As it turned out, I couldn't get going before May, and between March and May I was just plodding about trying to make sense of the material, because I didn't quite know what to do with it. And I think it was June when I actually started writing this play which I'd said I could do by the end of July. But by simply *writing something*, in the space of half a second as you reach a certain point, you create the whole next two scenes, which you simply couldn't have reached after weeks of walking around just thinking—it's a ludicrous procedure and I never seem to learn from it. Yet it still seems to be necessary in a way, because one always feels one is writing oneself into a tunnel, and one might be going completely on the wrong track.

When it suddenly gels you then find yourself writing quite quickly?

Yes, it's always been smashing except this last time, as it happens, when I was still looking for answers all the way through. . . .

You write consecutively once you get started?

Yes, absolutely.

Do you find then that the first version goes through many revisions?

No, it goes through revisions when I'm doing it, in the sense that I tend to rewrite each page half-a-dozen times, four times or twenty times, so by the time I've done the first draft it's *been* revised so often on the way that the only thing to do is either to tidy it or to change it totally, if you see what I mean.

Do you talk to people whose opinions you trust while you're writing?

No.

Do you discuss what's probably going to be the final draft with the director or company you're going to work with?

No, I just do it and deliver it, like a parcel.

How disciplined and organised are you when you're writing a play?

When there's no pressure on me I'm not disciplined at all, but when I'm writing seriously I get up and write and eat my lunch in four minutes and write, stop when my wife gets home, and see the children for about two hours, 'be daddy' for two hours, and eat, and then I work from about nine until one or two in the morning, and go to bed and then do it again. The thing is that, through character-flaw, I always end up being late anyway, that's why I do it. It's not because I'm disciplined, it's because I'm panicked when I'm in the shit again. I bring the whole thing on myself by walking about the garden for two months thinking that I'm actually getting somewhere, and then abruptly I realize that I'm going to be incredibly late and inconvenience a great number of people. From that moment on, it's absolutely impossible for me to, say, put a plug on the hoover—*there's no time for that for god's sake, I'm late!*

A Writer for Hire

You talked earlier about Rosencrantz and Guildenstern *being very much a play for the middle 'sixties—do you feel yourself aware of a 'contemporary mood' while you're writing?*

No, I don't know that I could define such a thing. It was just that in that play the resonances happened to be in tune with the resonances associated with all sorts of other writers at the time.

You clearly don't feel yourself part of a 'movement' either, and your plays could hardly be called social or political. Does this mean you have no strong political feelings, or simply that they're not what you want to write plays about?

Look, can we clear a few decks to avoid confusion? I'm a professional writer—I'm for hire, if you like—as well as being someone who pursues his own path in his writing. Latterly I have been able to stick to accepting the kind of jobs which happen to lie on my own path, but in the past I've written all kinds of stuff, everything from 70 episodes of a serial translated into Arabic for Bush House, to a one-off spy thing for Granada. Furthermore, the plays which I do from pure choice are not all of a kind either. I find it confusing to talk about 'my plays' as though *Hound* and *Jumpers* were the same sort of thing. Obviously, the two have things in common—for example, *Jumpers* is a serious play dealt with in the farcical terms which in *Hound* actually *constitute* the play. Much the same is true of the play I have just finished, *Travesties,* which (and this is pertinent to your question) asks whether the words 'revolutionary' and 'artist' are capable of being synonymous, or whether they are mutually exclusive, or something in between. Okay. So forget the Arabs and *Hound* and whatever, and here I am as the author of *Jumpers, Travesties,* and of my next unwritten unthought-of play which we will, optimistically, assume represents perfectly the kind of theatre I am interested in. That's 'my plays.' Next—'political plays.' Well, here are some plays which I have seen or read in the last year or so and which I assume all go into your political bag: Hampton's *Savages,* Griffiths's *The Party,* Fugard's *Sizwe Bansi is Dead,* and his *Hello and Goodbye,* and for that matter the old one, *The Blood Knot* (I haven't seen the latest one yet), Hare's *The Great Exhibition*—and *Slag* if you like—and Brenton, again I haven't seen *Magnificence,* only the earlier ones, and there was another very good Griffiths—*Occupations*—and then the combined work, *Lay By.* Well anyway, regardless of how political or social any or all of these plays are as far as you are concerned, I'll proceed on the assumption that you wouldn't ask any of these playwrights why they didn't write political plays.

I'd have quibbles with one or two, but go ahead.

Well, there are political plays which are about specific situations, and there are political plays which are about a general political situation, and there are plays which are *political acts* in themselves, insofar as it can be said that attacking or insulting or shocking an audience is a political act (and it *is* said). There are even plays *about* politics which are about as *political* as *Charley's Aunt.* The term 'political play' is a loose one if one is thinking of *Roots* as well as *Lear*—I mean Bond's—as well as *Lay By.* So much so that I don't think it is meaningful or useful to make that distinction between them and *Jumpers*—still less so in the case of *Travesties,* and down to zero in the case of my next play but three which I'll call *XYZ.*

Well, I don't know yet about XYZ *or* Travesties, *but in terms of* Jumpers . . .

Jumpers obviously isn't a political act, nor is it a play about politics, nor is it a play about ideology. There is an element in it which satirizes a joke-fascist outfit but you can safely ignore that too. On the other hand the play reflects my belief that all political acts have a moral basis to them and are meaningless without it.

Is that disputable?

Absolutely. For a start it goes against Marxist-Leninism in particular, and against all materialistic philosophy. I believe all political acts must be judged in moral terms, in terms of their consequences. Otherwise they are simply attempts to put the boot on some other foot. There is a sense in which contradictory political arguments are restatements of each other. For example, Leninism and Fascism are restatements of totalitarianism.

Two Faces of Totalitarianism

I disagree profoundly. Doesn't this reduce politics entirely to theory, whether it's for better or worse, whereas one has got to take into account the actual effects on human beings of what it's done and is doing?

Exactly. The repression which for better or worse turned out to be Leninism in action after 1917 was very much worse than anything which had gone on in Tsarist Russia. I mean, in purely mundane boring statistical terms, which sometimes can contain the essence of a situation, it is simply true that in the ten years after 1917 fifty times more people were done to death than in the *fifty years* before 1917. The boot, in other words, was on the other foot, and how, but the point is not to compare one ruthless regime against another—it is to set each one up against a moral standard, a consistent idea of what constitutes good and bad in the way human beings treat each other regardless of class, colour or ideology, and at least my poor professor in *Jumpers* got *that* right. Even before I read Lenin it always seemed to me—well, curious, that while he was in a Tsarist prison, and in Tsarist exile, he managed to research and write his book on the development of capitalism in Russia, and receive books and magazines, and write to friends, all that, whereas—well, compare Solzhenitsyn.

People tend to think of Stalinism as being something else, a perversion of Leninism. That is an absurd and foolish untruth, and it is one on which much of the Left bases itself. Lenin perverted Marxism, and Stalin carried on from there. When one reads pre-revolutionary Lenin, notably *What Is to Be Done?* but also all the letters and articles in which he railed against the early Marxists who had the temerity to disagree with him, one can see with awful clarity that ideological differences are often temperamental differences in ideological disguise—and also that the terror to come was implicit in the Lenin of 1900. (Incidentally, artistic differences are also liable to be temperamental differences in artistic disguise. Perhaps we can get back to that in a minute). The great irony about Marx was that his impulses were deeply moral while his intellect insisted on a materialistic view of the world. His theory of capital, his theory of value, and his theory of revolution, have all been refuted by modern economics and by history. In short he got it wrong. But he was a giant whose shadow still reaches us precisely for the reason that, wrong as he was in detail, the force he represented sprung from a sense of universal moral justice. He realized which way things would *have* to go, and then he put together a materialistic theory which was quite irrelevant, like sticking scaffolding on a moving train. It was only a matter of time before somebody—it turned out to be Bernstein in 1900—somebody with the benefit of an extra fifty years' hindsight, would actually point out that Marx had got it wrong, but that it didn't matter because social justice was going to come through other means. Bernstein reckoned that the class war wasn't the way, that human solidarity was a better bet than class solidarity. And this argument between 'hards' and 'softs' constitutes a great deal of radical argument today. It is not an argument about tactics—that's just surface dressing—it's an argument about philosophy, I mean Bernstein stuck his banner on the grave of Kant. So I'd like to write a play—say, *XYZ*—which would pertain to anything from a Latin American coup to the British Left, and probably when I've done it I'll still be asked why I don't write political plays.

If you are, perhaps it would be because your plays—to date, that is—are so philosophically opaque that they don't really make clear statements. I'm thinking particularly of the philosophical element in Jumpers.

Opacity would be a distinct failure in the play. I don't think of it as being opaque anyway, and I consider clarity is essential. On the other hand, if you mean that the mixing up of ideas in farce is a source of confusion, well, yes, God knows why I try to do it like that—presumably because I *am* like that. Plays are the people who write them. Seriousness compromised by frivolity. It gets up a few people's noses, but that's not important. At the same time I'm making all this sound much more self-confident than I feel. The thing is, if my plays were the end products of my ideas, they'd have it all more pat, but a lot of the time I've ended up trying to work out the ultimate implications of what I have written. My plays are a lot to do with the fact that *I just don't know*. This is something I tried to bring to the surface in a

TV *One Pair of Eyes* programme, but to me it is even more evident in the thickets of dialogue. Few statements remain unrebutted. But I'm not going to rebut the things I have been saying just now. One thing I feel sure about is that a materialistic view of history is an insult to the human race.

Possibility of Political Art

Isn't there a danger that one just ends up with the conclusion that all political art is perhaps well-intentioned but impotent, so why bother?

The possibility of political art having a political effect in close-up, in specific terms, certainly exists, though I can't offhand think of an example of it happening, but it is in any case marginal compared to the possible and actual effects of, say, journalism. On that level, one *World in Action* is worth a thousand plays. Come to think of it, *Cathy Come Home* could be cited, though I don't know if it *changed* anything. Look, do you know who Adam Raphael is?

There are two, aren't there—one a BBC correspondent, one on The Guardian.

Right. The *Guardian* Adam Raphael is the one who broke the story on wages in South Africa. Within 48 hours the wages went up. Now Athol Fugard can't do that. God knows he can do things which Adam Raphael will never ever be able to do, but it is self-evident that the situation provokes a very important question, whether it is better to be Adam Raphael or Athol Fugard. But of course that sounds as though one is choosing between alternatives, whereas I am simply saying: one is doing a short-term job and one a long-term job. Both are important. I think I'd like to spell this out more because I usually cut corners and end up appearing to say that because art can't do what *World in Action* does, art is unimportant, plays are unimportant, and one might as well write *Pyjama Tops* as *Galileo*. The *Guardian* quoted me in 14 point bold quoting Auden saying that his poems hadn't saved a single Jew from the gas chambers, and ever since then I've wanted to pay homage to Auden, or his shade, with the rider that I was making a point about the short-term not the long-term. Briefly, art—Auden or Fugard or the entire cauldron—is important because it provides the moral matrix, the moral sensibility, from which we make our judgments about the world. Well, Auden and Fugard don't need to be told that, nor you, but that is ultimately the answer to your question—

What question?

The question about the impotence of political art—

Yes—and this is presumably why your plays tend to bear on life in an oblique, distant, generalized way—

Well, that's what art is best at. The objective is the universal perception, isn't it? By all means realize that perception in terms of a specific event, even a specific political event, but I'm not impressed by art *because* it's political, I believe in art being good art or bad art, not relevant art or irrelevant art. The plain truth is that if you are angered or disgusted by a particular injustice or immorality, and you want to do something about it, *now, at once,* then you can hardly do worse than write a play about it. That's what art is bad at. But the less plain truth is that *without* that play and plays like it, without artists, the injustice will *never* be eradicated. In other words, because of Athol Fugard, to stretch a point, *The Guardian* understood that the Raphael piece was worth leading the paper with, worth printing. That's why it's good and right that *Savages* has a long run in the West End. All kinds of people have said to me, how ridiculous to sit in the theatre and watch this, how pointless, how useless—what they were saying in effect was that Hampton's play wasn't going to save a single Indian, but that is to misunderstand what art means in the world. It's a terrible reason for *not* writing *Savages*.

At the same time, Hampton's plays, and Fugard's plays, are absolutely different from yours. You are neither Fugard nor World in Action.

Of course. Fugard writes out of his experience as a white South African living against the current in a white supremacist regime. I write out of my experience as a middle-class bourgeois who prefers to read a book almost to doing anything else. If you say, then Fugard is much more important, I'd say, yes, of course he is! He's very much more important than me, just as he's much more important than the gang of playwrights who think that waving your cock at the audience is a revolutionary act and makes a play 'political.'

Brains as Well as Balls

Have you read or seen much of what's been happening in fringe theatre?

I've read much more than I've seen, and perhaps that isn't fair to some of the fringe playwrights. For example, I've got a lot of enjoyment out of reading Brenton—I've only seen *Gum and Goo*—and I think of him as a very good, very funny writer, and of course he's a scatological writer, but the easy equation between being *scatological* and being *political* is one I resist, it's intellectually shoddy.

Presumably you didn't see the Powellite Measure for Measure.

No—but I don't mean this point to revolve around Brenton particularly, it's not fair to him—I'm talking about the general and ubiquitous equation between the sexual and socialist revolutions. When *Lay By* is playing the Haymarket to a house packed with stockbrokers and property developers I hope the authors turn out to have brains as well as balls. And of course they do. *Occupations* and *The Party* are plays I respect. So is *The Great Exhibition* by David Hare, which I love, in fact Hare is the kind of writer-craftsman who appeals to me most. I said something earlier about artistic differences often being merely temperamental differences, and you can see what I'm getting at now. But in the published text of the Hare play there's an epigraph in the form of a statistical table showing that down the ages the top ten per cent of the population owned eighty per cent of the property—I'm going by memory, but it's something like that. Now he only took the table down to 1960, and it so happens, because it's one with which I'm familiar, that it goes on to show that by 1970 a huge change had taken place—a much less unequal distribution. Perhaps the later figures only became available after the play went to press. *Statistically* they upset the argument, anyway, but the statistics are appended to a play which succeeds because it is a brilliant comedy which would fit comfortably in Shaftesbury Avenue (I can't think why it didn't transfer), and the West End is exactly the place where a political writer *should* put a play saying the Labour Party is a joke.

The point being—?

The point being that to me that play is 'important' because it is writing—comedy writing, as it happens—of a very high order, not because it is saying something 'important' about a statistical subtext. If Hare were a bad writer, the play would be totally unimportant. When I saw Bond's *Lear* I thought and still think that it contains a few things that are as good as anything in Shakespeare. Do you remember how the blind old man says how the holes in the ground 'cry out' before he puts his foot in them? And there's a line about somebody oversleeping on the morning after the battle 'because all the birds were dead.' Now that is probably the single image, the single line out of a whole year's playgoing, which I'll carry about with me till I'm dead, as I'll carry about, say, Auden's glacier knocking in the cupboard. Now I may be quite wrong about this, but I feel that that sort of response is the *least* important thing about the play as far as Bond is concerned. I imagine the thing which was supposed to make the experience rewarding was the overall statement about violence and power, which was simply a momentous restatement of something one walked *into* the theatre with.

You said that in Travesties *you asked the question whether the terms artist and revolutionary were capable of being synonymous—did you come to any sort of conclusion?*

The play puts the question in a more extreme form. It asks whether an artist has to justify himself in political terms *at all.* For example, if Joyce were alive today, he would say, juntas may come and juntas may go but Homer goes on for ever. And when he was alive he *did* say that the history of Ireland, troubles and all, was justified because it produced *him* and *he* produced *Ulysses.* Okay. So clearly one now has to posit a political prisoner taking comfort from the thought that at least he is in the country of Joyce, or of Homer, and to ask oneself whether Joyce, in moral terms, was myopic or had better vision than lesser men. And my answer to that question is liable to depend on the moment at which you run out of tape. Of course one feels uneasy in trying to work out questions that involve *oneself,* in terms of authentic geniuses, but it helps to clarify the issue. How do you measure the legacy of a genius who believed in art for art's sake?

Moving towards 'Issues'

Your plays are evidently at least moving *in the direction of 'issues.'*

Jumpers still breaks its neck to be entertaining as well, which was the intention, and it's still the way I tend to write things, though I think it's gradually becoming less so. With *Rosencrantz,* whatever lessons could be drawn from it, they were all just implied and not necessarily by me at that. *Jumpers* was the first play in which I specifically set out to ask a question and try to answer it, or at any rate put the counter-question.

The way you've been talking, am I right in thinking that you feel that it's your full-length plays which constitute your more important work, and the shorter the play the more occasional it is?

Yes, in practice. But I've been asked to do a short play now, and though I've no idea what I'll do, if anything, there's absolutely no reason why it shouldn't be a serious play. I think actually that it probably isn't a matter of length, it just happens that at the time when I wrote the short plays my inclinations were slightly different.

Writer at Rehearsal

How far do you involve yourself in the first production of your plays?
Wholly.

And does the play itself undergo any change in the process?

Some, yes. One day when I was out for ten minutes, Peter Wood cut a scene in two and played it backwards, and it was better. So we kept it. That was in *Jumpers*.

Normally you're there all the time to make sure things like that don't happen?

No, I sit there to *do* things like that if they're necessary. I'm very free about that sort of thing as long as I'm there, and pretty rigid about it if I'm not. I think of rehearsal as being a very important part of getting the play right. Of the directors I've worked with, I had very good rapport with Robert Chetwyn, and with Peter Wood, and that is the main thing—it's not that somebody is born to direct your plays, or that they particularly understand them. I always feel it's like what Evelyn Waugh said about the Second World War, that the great thing was to spend it among friends. Getting a play on is so awful, the important thing is to spend it among friends.

We've talked about how accessible audiences find your work—how accessible do actors find it?

Sometimes something needs explaining—sometimes it's the case that something I'd thought to be crystal clear turns out to be difficult to understand. But there's never been a serious problem.

From the stage directions in your printed texts, you appear to have a very clear idea of what you want from your set. Is this after the first production's happened, or do you write with a very clear idea of what you want scenically?

I write with a very clear idea—not necessarily the right idea. I wanted the critics at the back for *Inspector Hound,* and we did it that way, but it's always worked much better with the critics at the front. I had this idea for a great big mirror upstage, all sorts of rubbish like that, so the answer is—I do, but it goes wrong.

Talking of Inspector Hound, *can I ask about the elements in the plays that one might call recurrent private jokes—matters of nomenclature, in particular, like all those Moons, not to mention the moon?*

I'm afraid the answer to that, though I'm happy to give it, is wholly devoid of interest. When I was in Bristol I went to see Paul Newman in *Left-Handed Gun,* and at one point of this film there's a reflection of the moon in a horse-trough. They're all drunk as far as I remember, and suddenly they shoot the reflection of the moon, the water explodes, and Newman is also shouting the word Moon, which is the name of one of the characters in the film. About this time I was writing the first draft of *The Real Inspector Hound,* and I needed a name for one of these critics. At a certain point in an early draft—I don't think it's in the play any more—the name of this character was cried out in the same sort of spirit, so I called him Moon. And for one reason or another, Moon is a very good name for the sort of person I write about quite a lot—obviously, he could be called Blenkinsop for you.

Another Moon Called Boot

And how about all the Boots?

When I was on *Scene* magazine I was reviewing plays, and I was also interviewing actors and playwrights, and it seemed to me that it oughtn't to be done by the same person, which I now no longer believe—I think it *ought* to be done by the same person. But at that time I felt that critics ought to come down on pulleys from the cumulus and review a play and go back, so I decided to have another name. I've always been attracted to the incompetence of William Boot in Evelyn Waugh's *Scoop*—he was a journalist who brought a kind of innocent incompetence and contempt to what he was doing. I'd always thought that William Boot would be quite a good pseudonym for a journalist, so I used it, and got quite fond of Boot as a name, and that was all. I think the thing is, so much of one's work has to do with free association that it would be odd if one didn't bring the same sort of concern to the naming of characters. In the original version of *Jumpers,* which was a half-hour television play, Bones was the name not of the Inspector, who didn't exist, but of the husband. So it's not really a matter, as you see, of a particular character having to have a particular name, it's just that the name itself must be right. All I know is that if you're actually writing a play and somebody ought to be called Boot and is called Murgatroyd, it's impossible to continue.

One could even call some of your work surrealist, in the associative sense of the word. Take that image at the beginning of After Magritte, *was that worked out tortuously backwards, or did it somehow* happen *and then have to be explained?*

It was based on fact for a start—somebody I know had a couple of peacocks in the garden, and one escaped while he was shaving. He chased it and he had to cross a main road to catch it, and he was standing in his pyjamas with shaving cream on his face holding a peacock when the traffic started going by. That was one of those moments when somebody tells you something and you realize that in due course it's going to be useable, so I built it up forwards and backwards between the first image and the last image.

Is even the moon-landing motif part of the associative process?

No, that's just something which I happened to think at the time. Years and years ago, before a moon-landing seemed imminent at all, I thought, I *felt,* that the destruction of moon mythology and moon association in poetry and romance, superstition and everything, would be a sort of minute lobotomy performed on the human race, like a tiny laser making dead some small part of the psyche. And this perception or pseudo-perception was something that I would want somehow to write about.

Coming almost full circle, was that in the back of your mind when you wrote A Separate Peace, *where the main character opts out in rather the same way as the wife in* Another Moon Called Earth?

Well, that second piece was written specifically to go with a half-hour film which I helped to make about international chess masters and grandmasters for the Chess Congress at Hastings in about 1965. So I actually had to think up some kind of play which was about exclusion, about disappearing into oneself, about finding a substitute for reality. As you can see, it's quite a loose analogy, but as far as I can recollect my only concern was that I should come up with a play which at least suggested what we were saying about chess-players.

You don't think there's a danger that all these Boots and Moons and the other elements which are . . . well, dramatic conveniences for yourself as playwright, might prove confusing for audiences, who are going to start looking for all sorts of other resonances?

No, I don't think so. I don't think of an audience as consisting of readers of *Theatre Quarterly,* if you see what I mean. I just think it's curiously important to call people by the right name in any sort of fiction. Which sounds like an excellent topic for your next interview.

Jumpers Author Is Verbal Gymnast

Mel Gussow

Jumpers had its American premiere in Washington, D.C., in February 1974 before moving to Broadway in April. By then *Travesties* was already in rehearsal in London and Stoppard was jetting back and forth across the Atlantic to attend to both plays. The American *Jumpers* was a decidedly more athletic version, which at first pleased Stoppard: "In England you can ask a guy to do Horatio for you, but you can't ask him to do a cartwheel. Here a guy jumps 12 feet in the air, twists around twice, lands, and says 'What shall I do next?' It's too bloody marvelous!" But by the time *Jumpers* reached Broadway it had fourteen jumpers (rather than London's eight), a secretary who stripped while hanging by her teeth, and as many music and light cues (250) as a big musical. In retrospect Stoppard would say that the Broadway version was "elephantine in every department—save for happy memories." In New York for the Broadway opening, Stoppard was at some pains to spell out "what the play says" while also talking up the show's spectacle.

A conversation with Tom Stoppard, in common with his play *Jumpers* (which opened last night at the Billy Rose Theater), is heady—full of verbal acrobatics and intellectual cartwheels.

"My objective has always been to perform a marriage between a play of ideas and a farce," he began. "As to whether this is a desirable objective, I have no idea. It represents two sides of my own personality, which can be described as seriousness compromised by my frivolity, or ... frivolity redeemed by my seriousness."

From the *New York Times*, 23 April 1974.

Then he attempted to describe his artistic process. "The only way I really work," he said, "is to assemble a strange pig's breakfast of visual images and thoughts and try to shake them into some kind of coherent pattern."

The image that led to *Jumpers* came to him about three years ago. In his imagination he saw "a troupe of gymnasts making a pyramid and there being a gunshot and one gymnast being blown out of the pyramid, the rest of the pyramid imploding on the hole that he left. I had this piece of paper with this dead acrobat on the floor and I didn't know who he was, who shot him, or why."

Pondering the who's and why's, contemplating the nature of existence and morality, he began writing a play about an "abstract proposition—moral values are purely social conventions or, alternatively, they refer to some absolute divinity."

"I didn't calculate it as such, but this whole thing of gymnasts and standing on one's head and doing somersaults is a fairly good metaphor for philosophical activity." By "jumpers" he means both acrobats and "jumping to conclusions."

As for himself, Mr. Stoppard is a man torn by ambivalencies. "I tend to write about oppositions and double acts," he said. "I identify emotionally with the more sympathetic character in the play who believes that one's mode of behavior has to be judged by absolute moral standards.

"At the same time I don't have to get anyone else to write the other character for me, because intellectually I can shoot my argument full of holes. This conflict between one's intellectual and emotional response to questions of morality produces the tension that makes the play."

Asked if he conceived of philosophy itself as a balancing act, he said, "I think that Wittgenstein said that philosophy wasn't a subject; it was an activity. Most of the propositions I'm interested in have been kidnapped and dressed up by academic philosophy, but they are in fact the kind of propositions that would occur to any intelligent person in his bath. They're not academic questions, simply questions which have been given academic status.

"Philosophy can be reduced to a small number of questions which are battled about in most bars most nights. Linguistic philosophy doesn't even have that distinction. That should occupy the position in life of collecting the labels off triangular pieces of cheese. There's a word for people who do that. And they trade cheese labels across continents. It doesn't do anybody any harm, but why would you want to have a professor in it? When I started reading books on moral philosophy, I was just amazed at how many people were writing the same book.

"I've always thought," he added, "that the idea of God is absolutely preposterous, but slightly more plausible than the alternative proposition that, given enough time, some green slime could write Shakespeare's sonnets. And then I started reading to make sure that my profound thoughts were not going to be refuted by any first-year philosophy students. It turned out that they *were* the propositions of first-year philosophy students."

While indicating that he was "impressed" by philosophers personally, he said that he often found their books "unconsciously hilarious." "There are things in my play which people innocently suppose to be my kind of bizarre version of academic discourse, that I'm doing a Mel Brooks on it, when, in fact, occasionally, I hardly had to change a thing."

Just as he might think of philosophy as being an "activity," his plays are sometimes criticized as simply intellectual exercises. To the charge, he said, firmly, "My plays are so near the knuckle of life. . . . "

He laughed, and admitted that art was not the best means to social action. "If you looked out of your window and saw something that you really felt must be changed, something you felt was a cancer on society and you wanted to change it *now*, you could hardly do worse than write a play about it."

He made it clear that he himself has no revolutionary designs. "I'm an English middle-class bourgeois, who prefers to read a book to almost anything else. It would be an insane pretension for me to write 'poems of a petrol bomber.'"

Then he simply added "I think that art provides the moral matrix from which we draw our values." Talk about the revolutionary aspects of art led him directly into the subject of his new play, *Travesties*, which opens in June at the Royal Shakespeare Company in England.

Travesties deals with Lenin and Joyce and Tristan Tzara, the Dadaist, all of whom lived in Zurich in 1917. "There's a question worth asking, can the artist and the revolutionary be the same person or are their activities mutually exclusive? How would you justify *Ulysses* to Lenin, or Lenin to Joyce?"

Mr. Stoppard said that in preparation for *Travesties*, he did considerable research on Lenin and Joyce, but to forestall attacks on his facts, "I've taken the precaution of setting the play within the memory of an old gentleman who cannot be totally relied upon for accuracy."

Briefly, he returned to the subject of *Jumpers*. "What the play says—and this is going to sound so turgid in print—is that if the status of goodness is a matter of convenience and social evolution, then it is open to be changed into a reverse direction where casual murder might be deemed good."

Without pausing, Mr. Stoppard switched discourses in midstream, his seriousness compromised by his frivolity. "Did I tell you," he said, "that there's a nude lady in *Jumpers*—and singers and dancers?"

'Call Me the Thinking Man's Farceur'

Stanley Eichelbaum

Stoppard's plays enjoyed a long and happy association with the American Conservatory Theater in San Francisco under the direction of William Ball. Not only did *Rosencrantz and Guildenstern Are Dead* have a three-year run, but *Jumpers* had its ACT debut just months after its Broadway opening. By the time he returned to San Francisco for the ACT production of *Travesties,* Stoppard could joke, "I feel like a house playwright." In December 1974, Stoppard arrived in time to oversee the final ACT rehearsals of *Jumpers* and met with journalists from several Bay Area publications. While saying that he had been happy with the New York production, Stoppard noted that the ACT was "using fewer jumpers, which I prefer." In all of these conversations, Stoppard denied that *Jumpers* was written to be elusive or obscure and went to some lengths to dismiss the impression that his play was absurdist, telling his interviewers, "It's not absurdist in the way of the Theater of the Absurd, with a capital 'A.'"

Playwright Tom Stoppard is here from London to enjoy the sights and attend the West Coast premiere of his mercurial comedy, *Jumpers,* which ACT is presenting Tuesday night at the Geary.

Taking in everything around him at Trader Vic's, Stoppard lunched yesterday on consomme and beef jardiniere while being interviewed about his play, a challenging intellectual exercise mixing verbal

From the *San Francisco Examiner,* 11 December 1974.

77

gymnastics and stage acrobatics with a hard-to-pin-down murder mystery.

It was originally performed by the British National Theatre in 1972. The first American production, earlier this year, ran two months at Washington's Kennedy Center and on Broadway. William Ball asked to do it next and Stoppard agreed, having had warm relations with ACT since Ball's staging of *Rosencrantz and Guildenstern Are Dead,* which remained in the repertory for three seasons.

The 37-year-old author talked earnestly about *Jumpers,* rejecting the often-held idea that it's a highly elusive work containing too many layers of abstract propositions to be fully understood.

"You don't write a play to be elusive," said Stoppard. "I don't intend anything to be obscure.

"It isn't a play which reduces to easy little paraphrase. It's partially a whodunit, partially a play of ideas and partially a farce.

"Everything in it is absolutely logical, though it's admittedly quite bizarre, like the opening moment of a girl stripping on a trapeze.

"But it isn't nonrealistic. It suggests that real life can rise to surprising and bizarre effects. I don't mean absurd—not with a capital A, like Ionesco—because these are real people talking in a real room."

Stoppard's title, *Jumpers,* refers not only to acrobats who perform on stage but to the human failing of jumping to conclusions about moral values and social conventions.

"The play actually derived from an image of a pyramid from which one of the jumpers is shot out," he said. "I didn't know who the jumper was. Or who shot him. Or why. That's how it started.

"I really like theater which ambushes you now and again. I try to write from ambush to ambush."

Stoppard came to playwriting via journalism. He was born in Czechoslovakia and was taken to England by his widowed mother in 1946. He was Tomas Straussler until he assumed his step-father's name, Stoppard, and went to work for a newspaper in Bristol.

"I had a desire to write for the theater ever since the renaissance of English drama with *Look Back in Anger.* Everybody my age wanted to write plays.

"As a reporter, I wrote with a certain facetiousness and I've never stopped loving comedy. If you write a tragedy, it's difficult to know what you've got because silence in the theater is a very ambiguous sound. Laughter isn't ambiguous at all.

"My ambition has always been to combine a play of ideas with farce. That's what I'm like, frivolity redeemed by seriousness. Call me, if you like, the thinking man's farceur."

Stoppard is married to a physician who is medical director for British Syntex. His wife will join him here later this week for conferences at Syntex headquarters in Palo Alto.

"She'll be at the premiere of *Jumpers,* though I expect I won't sit with her, since I'll be nervously pacing the lobby."

Tom Stoppard Eats Steak Tartare with Chocolate Sauce

Ross Wetzsteon

The praise and abuse heaped on *Travesties* were almost equally extreme. It was hailed as "a masterpiece of serious wit" and "a miraculous display of verbal fireworks" or dismissed as "inveterate trifling" which is "ultimately about nothing at all." Clive Barnes celebrated "the sheer intellectual shimmer of this remarkable play" while Kenneth Tynan dismissed it as a "triple-decker bus that isn't going anywhere." Eleven days before the play's Broadway opening, Charles Marowitz published a lengthy piece in the *New York Times* under the headline "Tom Stoppard—The Theater's Intellectual P. T. Barnum." On opening night, Stoppard was—at first—in no mood for conversation, but he sharply countered his interviewer's suggestion that the play gives equal weight to Joyce, Lenin, and Tzara without choosing sides. Beyond revealing where he stands on such questions, Stoppard also makes some unequivocal assertions about the significance of the first act curtain.

"I'm afraid it's not in the cards today," Tom Stoppard said, nervously taking a pack of Larks out of his shirt pocket.

"Uh-uh, luv," wagged a finger at the door of the dressing room. "The firemen are here."

"Oh hell. Where can we go? Never mind." He replaces the pack of cigarettes, laces his fingers—a fireman peers into the room, disappears. "I don't know whether this is an apology or an explanation,"

From the *Village Voice*, 10 November 1975.

Stoppard says with a nervous, sad smile, "but we're opening tonight and I have presents to buy and tickets to take care of and it's just not in the cards today, a deep discussion of the state of the English theatre. Follow me."

Stoppard stands abruptly and leads the way down a short corridor to the back of the auditorium. The director and cast and technicians are working on sound levels—they have only four hours to go until the opening night curtain.

"Oh Hell!" After only one puff, Stoppard spots another fireman and quickly squashes a cigarette in an ashtray on the floor at the head of the aisle. The sound levels are suddenly much too loud and we can hardly hear each other. "Follow me," Stoppard says, and we go backstage again. He nervously fingers the pack of cigarettes, puts it back in his pocket, and sits down, his fingers entwined between his knees.

"I'll have to be bitty," he apologizes, again with that sad smile, "but if you're happy, I'm happy."

I'm far happier than I would be with "a deep discussion of the state of English theatre," and "bitty" isn't a bad style for this "intellectual P. T. Barnum," as Charles Marowitz has called Stoppard, this pinball playwright who shoots off ideas and watches them bounce crazily around and light up in garish colors, this burlesque philosopher who dresses theories in baggy pants and knocks logic for a pratfall; this word-wizard and delight-mongerer who understands that the true function of comedy is to help us define what should be taken seriously.

I'd seen *Travesties* in London a month earlier, and found it an astonishing advance in maturity over Stoppard's previous work, far funnier for one thing, but also wise where he'd been merely clever before, humane where he'd been cold, exuberant where he'd been frantic. A fantasy of what might have happened if Joyce, Lenin, and Tzara had actually met (they all lived in Zurich during World War I), as told by a nearly senile British civil servant (played by John Wood with manic radiance), *Travesties* asks, in Stoppard's words, "whether the words 'revolutionary' and 'artist' are capable of being synonymous, or whether they are mutually exclusive, or something in between." Throw in a parody of Oscar Wilde and a lawsuit over a pair of pants, obscene limericks and Beethoven's "Appassionata," "Every Little Breeze Seems to Whisper Louise" and Lenin's prose style, and you don't have to ask him why he called it *Travesties*.

I was interested, though, in knowing if he'd written it with Wood in mind. "Oh, absolutely," he says. "He has amazing control of diction—incredible clarity and speed—and I wanted the role played with his high definition and his virtuosity, both technical and emotional." (The New York production, fast-paced as it is, seems a shade slower than the breakneck pace of the London production, a shame, since one of the virtues of Stoppard's work is the dazzling speed of his sleight-of-mind. The merest hint of sluggishness would be as fatal to this play as razzmatazz would be to *Waiting for Godot*.)

I asked Stoppard what other changes he was making for the New York production. "Mainly we've had to adjust to a different shaped stage," he said—we'd moved back out to the auditorium, but he still couldn't find a place to smoke—"this huge widescreen Cinerama we have here. In an odd way it's meant that I've had to make the narrative line clearer. I've rewritten some parts, just on the story-telling level, so it's a little more explicit."

Did that imply he thought New York audiences were less sophisticated than those in London? On the contrary, "audiences are much sharper here, much. They've read more. They pick up things. They understand my plays better. Where can one smoke in this place? No, it's just the shape of the stage. And the bookcases move in different ways, with winches instead of stagehands, that kind of thing. That's the only reason for the changes."

Anyway, he went on, his texts never stand still. "You write a play and you have the impression everything is clarity itself, but there'll always be those small mysteries hiding in the script. You find them all the time. They're even emerging now, even years after I wrote it."

He wrote the play, Stoppard said, as part of "an ongoing debate with myself over the importance of the artist." It seemed to me that one of the strengths of the play, one of the signs of his maturity, was that he gave equal weight to Joyce, Lenin, and Tzara, that he allowed each of them to speak without choosing sides. Stoppard only partly agreed. "Equally *just*, I hope, but not equal *weight*. Of course I don't want to give any of them shallow arguments and then knock them down. No, you have to give the best possible argument for each of them. It's like playing chess with yourself—you have to try to win just as hard with black as you do with white. But while my sympathies may be divided in that sense, I find Joyce infinitely the most important. Are we talking of historical significance or of quality? Tzara's work, for instance, was momentarily interesting but ultimately worthless. Joyce's evolution means more to me than Tzara's revolution."

But Tzara's flamboyance takes up more space on stage . . .

"That's true, but when they have that argument about art at the end of the first act, notice that Joyce has the last word. I wanted him to murder Tzara, and he does."

Some critics feel Stoppard's work is too facile, too gimmicky—intellectual in the pejorative sense, arid, unfelt, not revelatory but merely skipping like a pebble over the surface of ideas.

This can't be exactly what Stoppard wants to talk about on opening night, but his nerves—"one is *always* frightened, *always*"—seem to welcome almost any distraction. "What happens in my plays is a kind of marriage of categories. It's not my objective in the sense that I calculate it—it just seems to be what I'm doing, the way things come out. But I want to marry the play of ideas to farce. Now that may be like eating steak tartare with chocolate sauce, but that's the way it comes out. Everyone will have to decide for himself"—he smiles and spreads his arms in an amiable gesture of vulnerability—"whether the seriousness is doomed or redeemed by the frivolity.

"The old man's speech is much different now," he goes on abruptly. "I've rewritten large sections of it—but you'll see. Now your comparison to Shaw"—I'd called him the heir to Shaw in a report from London last month—"it's very flattering, but frankly I get a different feeling from him entirely. His people have their feet on the ground. They walk into habitable rooms." Stoppard suddenly stands up, then just as abruptly sits down again. One wonders if Shaw ever experienced this nervousness. "His characters say sensible things to each other. They exist in a real world."

But I'd been referring to their shared understanding that ideas in the theatre can be both explicit and entertaining, that, in fact, one could enjoy steak tartare with chocolate sauce.

"You're very tolerant of me, I must say, all these bits and pieces, but I just remembered"—Stoppard gives that sad smile again, as if in amiable apology for a hopeless situation—"I have to order some flowers over the telephone and even in this day and age that takes precedence over being interviewed."

He returns in a minute, obviously relieved to have gotten that off his mind.

I wonder if the media barrage—interviews, photo sessions, opening night, all of it—isn't rather intimidating.

"It's *very* intimidating, yes, but I do it out of . . ." he pauses, the intellectual seeking articulation for contradictory feelings, "I do it out of . . . obligation and gratitude.

"But back to your question about being too intellectual," he goes on immediately. "I feel that all the serious questions of classical philosophy—the old debate about perception and the nature of the object seen, for instance—most such academic philosophy is simply the organized version of the random thoughts of the ordinary man lying in a bathtub wondering if he can turn off the tap with his toes. Follow me."

Abruptly we're back in the auditorium, where the cast is rehearsing the curtain call. "I want it brisk, but not . . ." the director seeks the right word, " . . . not *Olympian.*"

"You use more music in this play than ever before . . ." I begin, and Stoppard suddenly becomes animated. "Yes, yes, yes! I have cloth ears," he says excitedly. "I have no understanding of music at all. That was all inserted by the director." And now he can hardly contain himself, talking about someone else's work. "Tzara's entrance—that entrance to the tune of 'Louise'"—he almost bounces in his seat as he reaches out and slaps my knee, hard, three times—"That entrance! I worked over a year on this play! Over a year! And precious moments like that have almost nothing to do with what I wrote! Peter Wood took my play as a starting point and created these *precious magic moments.* I mean the way Bennett flutters his hands in the dance scene at the end—it's one of my favorite moments in all of theatre! I mean can you explain it? *I turned my bowels over* for a year on this play, and these things have nothing to do with what I wrote! Nothing to do with it!"

In love with *Travesties* once more, he laughs delightedly, almost uncontrollably, no longer nervous, no longer intimidated. Tom Stoppard doesn't need a cigarette anymore.

Tom Stoppard

Oleg Kerensky

Rather than talking to reporters as part of public relations for the opening of a production, Stoppard spoke to Oleg Kerensky as part of an interview intended for book publication. Perhaps as a result, Kerensky found Stoppard to be a very difficult interviewee who was reluctant to participate at all. But having agreed, however grudgingly, Stoppard applied himself to the task at hand and, in fact, rewrote most of the interview himself. Although Arthur Miller has often taken that kind of care to clarify his remarks, Stoppard was the only one of the fourteen playwrights Kerensky dealt with to take so much interest in the exact wording of the interview. Talking to Kerensky while still writing *Every Good Boy Deserves Favour,* Stoppard looks back at the genesis of *Travesties* and *Jumpers.* Although Stoppard had indicated elsewhere something of his sympathies in *Travesties,* his remarks to Kerensky contain his most unequivocal assertions that what prompted *Jumpers* was his desire "to write a theist play."

Stoppard mentally divides his plays into the 'real' ones, which are about something other than what they appear to be about and which take a long time to write, and the mere entertainments, which he can do very quickly. *Dirty Linen,* for example, was written in about three weeks, and the *New-Found-Land* section was done while the main part was being rehearsed. 'It's easy to write about MPs in committee but hard to write about art and society. *Travesties* took about nine months to write, and that's about par for the course. It's full-time writing—I

From *The New British Drama: Fourteen Playwrights since Osborne and Pinter* (London: Hamish Hamilton; New York: Taplinger, 1977).

go to bed worried and wake up worried for the whole of that nine months. And for a long time I'm not certain that I will ever finish. I've already been writing my latest play in my head for several months.'

. . . .

Travesties arose because Stoppard had heard that Lenin and Tzara were in Zürich at the same time, because he wanted to write a play for John Wood, and because he wanted to say something about the role of the artist in society. 'James Joyce came into the play at a late stage, after I'd started working, because John Wood didn't look a bit like Lenin and I thought he could play Joyce. But Lenin, Tzara and Joyce had to be roughly equal parts, and I wanted to write a large part for Wood. So I started looking for a seat to hold my three-legged stool together. I came across Henry Carr as a role for Wood—later on I discovered that they even looked alike.

'Once I had this group of people to manipulate, I used them to get various things off my chest. At first there was no narrative line, but then I discovered that Joyce and Carr were mixed up in a production of *The Importance of Being Earnest.* That gave me the linking theme. I couldn't write an inconsequential Dadaist play. Instinctively I'm out of sympathy with Tzara and that kind of art, and I had to think very hard to give Tzara good arguments in the play. My prejudices were all on Joyce's side—I utterly believe in his speech at the end of Act I on what an artist is. I used to have a slight guilt feeling about being an artist, but I don't any more. When I tried to visualize a completely technological world without culture, I realized that one does not have to apologize for being an artist. It took me years to reach that understanding.'

Jumpers had its origin in a television play of Stoppard's, *Another Moon Called Earth,* about a woman in bed while her husband is writing a history of the world in the next room. 'I wanted a device enabling me to set out arguments about whether social morality is simply a conditioned response to history and environment or whether moral sanctions obey an absolute intuitive God-given law. I've always felt that whether or not 'God-given' means anything, there has to be an ultimate external reference for our actions. Our view of good behaviour *must* not be relativist. The difference between moral rules and the rules of tennis is that the rules of tennis can be changed. I think it's a dangerous idea that what constitutes 'good behaviour' depends on social conventions—dangerous and unacceptable. That led me to the conclusion, not reached all that willingly, that if our behaviour is open to absolute judgement, there must be an absolute judge. I felt that nobody was saying this and it tended to be assumed that nobody held such a view. So I wanted to write a theist play, to combat the arrogant view that anyone who believes in God is some kind of cripple, using God as a crutch. I wanted to suggest that atheists may be the cripples, lacking the strength to live with the idea of God.

'I never studied philosophy formally, and I like to think that philosophers and logicians operate at a much deeper level than I can. My philosophy is the sort of philosophy that anyone can think out in their bath-tub, but perhaps I can put these speculations into dialogue and epigrams better than most. I read a lot of moral philosophy in preparation for *Jumpers*—some of it is taken straight from modern philosophical works. I'd never read Wittgenstein before, and I read him several times without understanding lots of it—it's like reading poetry.'

Stoppard does not have any interest in word games and puzzles, outside his work as a playwright. 'I don't do crossword puzzles. But the way language and logic can be used or misused amuses me—it's a wonderful garden to enjoy. At one time I thought perhaps I enjoyed playing with the English language because I came to it late; I used to compare myself to Nabokov and say it was like suddenly finding oneself on top of a mountain and looking down, instead of laboriously climbing up as most people do when they learn a language from childhood. But then I discovered that Nabokov had spoken English from childhood and anyway I myself had never been literate in any other language. English was the working language at my schools in India. I think I'd probably have been interested in language just the same, if I'd been a Czechoslovak writer instead of a British one.'

It is tempting to speculate whether Stoppard's Czechoslovak origin is in any way relevant to his concern for human rights behind the Iron Curtain and his recurring interest in problems of identity. If so, it can only be unconscious as he left Czechoslovakia when he was one and does not remember his father.

Stoppard first started writing stories and plays when he began to get bored with journalism. At first his energies were entirely devoted to becoming a first-class journalist; then he started to look for other horizons. He explains his preference for plays, rather than other forms of writing, by saying that everyone was writing for the theatre in Britain in the late 1950s. Also, he thinks plays get more concentrated attention. 'The impact of a novel is dispersed, it's not dangerous enough. Nobody concentrates on a television play in the way they do in the theatre—one is always being distracted. So I'd probably have preferred the theatre even if everyone else hadn't been writing for it. And I don't mind writing for an élitist audience, if that is what the audience turns out to be. I find it crucial to be at rehearsals—there is no notation for writing down what one intends to happen on the stage. You may think that my stage instructions are detailed, but they are a basic minimum to me. I don't say my plays have got to be done the way I want them—I once saw *Rosencrantz and Guildenstern* in Italy, played in perspex boxes and with a woman as Rosencrantz—and I loved it. But if I'm at the rehearsals, the play works according to my prejudices. If I'm not there, it either becomes half of what I want—and that is awful—or it becomes something utterly different. That can either be awful or superb.'

Tom Stoppard, Nonstop: Word Games with a Hit Playwright

Jon Bradshaw

Stoppard followed the recondite intricacies of *Travesties* with *Dirty Linen,* an unpretentious "knickers farce"—which, Stoppard says, is "what used to be called a 'romp' in the good old West End." The play evolved from a commitment Stoppard had made to contribute to Ed Berman's 1976 season of "plays with any American connection of the writer's choice" in commemoration of the American Bicentennial. The only American connection turned out to be a fifteen-minute sketch called *New-Found-Land*—dealing with the naturalization of an American (Ed Berman) as a British subject—which Stoppard sandwiched into the middle of *Dirty Linen.* The play (or plays) opened as a lunchtime entertainment at Inter-Action's Almost Free Theatre on 6 April 1976, the day Berman was naturalized. American journalist Jon Bradshaw spoke to Stoppard in late 1976 after *Dirty Linen* had become the first lunchtime play to transfer to the West End and just before another production of the play, also directed by Berman, opened in New York. In contrast to his wariness with some interviewers, Stoppard is clearly at ease with Bradshaw in a series of conversations in London pubs and at Stoppard's home. In ebullient form, Stoppard intersperses wisecracks with substantial discussions of *Rosencrantz and Guildenstern Are Dead* and *Dirty Linen* and concludes with a considered response to the charge that his work is "all style and no substance."

From *New York,* 10 January 1977.

The Quality Inn is an inferior hostelry in the upper reaches of Regent Street. Two men entered the inn and took a booth toward the back. The taller man, a playwright, carried a large leather bag. For reasons which later escaped him, the shorter man, a journalist, assumed it was filled with plays; he had been drinking seriously since noon and his perceptions were not what they had been before lunch. The playwright wore a blue imitation-leather suit, purple shoes emblazoned with red stars, and a black-and-white striped scarf into which was knitted in red the word *travesties*. The journalist was certain of that. He drank his tea. The tea was rank and bagged. Lifting his hand, he summoned a waiter.

"May I have a drink?" he said.

"Only if you have something to eat."

"I don't want anything to eat."

"Suppose *I* have something to eat," said the playwright. "Can he have something to drink?"

"No, it's against the rules."

"Suppose I have something to drink," said the journalist. "Can *he* have something to eat?"

"I don't understand," said the waiter.

The journalist pushed the tea bag through the murky tea.

"Well, where shall we begin?"

"Why don't I give you a prepared statement?" the playwright said. "Actually, I'm quite prepared for interviews. I'm always interviewing myself. Or at least I used to. I don't have to interview myself anymore because people come and do it for me." He grinned. "Mind you, they don't do it as well as I do.

"I must tell you," he continued. "There's something you should know right away. I'll say *anything* to an interviewer, but somewhere in the middle of the piece, there ought to be a warning, like on cigarette packets. A warning which states: This profile is in the middle truth range. Don't inhale. And that's the point, since a profile shows just *one* side of somebody...a very good term for this particular *kind* of journalism."

"And which side did you intend to show?"

"The outside. That's what I like about interviews. Now, I suppose you'll want some sort of background. The facts. The wheres and whens?"

"Yes, I suppose. But don't exaggerate."

"Oh, I'm very good at giving boring interviews," he said. "I can say, yes, my name is Tom Stoppard and, yes, I'm 39 and, yes, I left school at seventeen and joined the *Western Daily Press* as a junior reporter in 1954 and joined the Bristol *Evening World* in 1958 and, yes, I began to write *Rosencrantz and Guildenstern* in 1964. I'm very good at that. No problem. Wait while I get some cigarettes and I'll tell you some more."

He walked off to the back of the restaurant. The facts, to dispense with them immediately, were more than a little surprising. He was born in Czechoslovakia in 1937. Both his parents were Czech. He had an older brother. Shortly before the outbreak of World War II, the four of them were sent to Singapore, quite the wrong place to go since shortly after, the Japanese invaded it. The Stoppards were evacuated to India. Stoppard's father remained behind and died in Japanese captivity.

They spent the rest of the war in India—in Calcutta and in Darjeeling, where Stoppard attended an American multiracial school. In late 1945 his mother married an Englishman serving in the British Army who early in 1946 brought them to England. "My stepfather's name was Stoppard," the playwright said, returning to the booth. "My father's name was Straussler, like the composer with *ler* at the end." He smiled. "As you can see, Tomas Straussler sits before you."

"Is that all?"

"Yes, I'm afraid that's it. I have never starved, never lived in a garret, and I've never had TB."

The playwright ordered another cup of tea. "When I left school," he said, "I wanted to be a great journalist. My first ambition was to be lying on the floor of an African airport while machine-gun bullets zoomed over my typewriter. But I wasn't much use as a reporter. I felt I didn't have the right to ask people questions. I always thought they'd throw the teapot at me or call the police. For me, it was like knocking at the door, wearing your reporter's peaked cap, and saying: 'Hello, I'm from journalism. I've come to inspect you. Take off your clothes and lie down.'

"But I wasn't much good at it and I never got to Fleet Street. Early on in my career, I had an interview with Mr. Charles Wintour, the editor of the *Evening Standard*. At one point, Mr. Wintour asked me if I were interested in politics. Thinking all journalists should be interested in politics, I told him I was. He then asked me who the current home secretary was. Of course, I had no idea who the current home secretary was, and, in any event, it was an unfair question. I'd only admitted to an interest in politics. I hadn't claimed I was *obsessed* with the subject.

"But I'm through with all that now. I gave up journalism and became a playwright."

"But you have no objections to seeing journalists who have come to inspect *you*?"

"No, but I'm wary of them. Do you see what I'm saying?" The playwright paused to light a cigarette. "I feel I should preface this with an epigram, which is: 'Nothing is more studied than a repeated spontaneity.' And on that note I'll repeat what I said to you the other day. You see, the unstated supposition to any interviewing situation is that I know the answers to the questions you're asking. And there are certain kinds of questions to which I do indeed know the answers. If you ask me how tall I am, I'll say six foot one and tomorrow if you ask me again I'll say the same thing... unless, of course, I've grown. But if you ask me what I think of Virginia Woolf, then the answer would have a different *status*."

"What *do* you think of Virginia Woolf?"

"Well, in my opinion, Virginia Woolf was the tallest woman writer of the twenties."

"Are you quite sure?"

"Yes, yes. My information is that Katherine Mansfield was only four foot eleven and Edith Sitwell was only five foot three. But Virginia Woolf was six foot eight, a fact not commonly known." The playwright laughed. "Actually, life would be very simple if writers *were* judged by measurable criteria. Now as a matter of fact, I don't know if I'm six foot one, because I haven't measured myself lately. But then I would be being merely inaccurate, which is a different kind of a mistake. Do you see? I often give a frivolous answer to a serious question, which is a kind of a lie. I don't lie about my age or the number of bathrooms in my house, but if you ask me whether I write comedy because I am too insecure to make a serious statement, well, that's a complex question and rather than getting into it, it's much easier to say yes. One doesn't tell lies. I now have a repertoire of plausible answers which evade the whole truth. It just goes wrong. The truth slips away and becomes something you probably won't mean tomorrow."

"You could, of course, have a prepared statement and when a newshound knocked at the door you could slide it out to him," said the journalist.

"Yes, or it would be very funny to have the answers written on cards and do tricks. You could say to the interviewer, 'Now listen, take a card, any card. Okay? Don't tell me what it is. Okay? Now ask me a question. Right. Now, look at the card. Got it?'"

The two men paid the bill and left the restaurant. "You know, if every card said 'maybe,' you could get away with that," the playwright said.

The large stone Victorian house is situated near a busy traffic circle in Buckinghamshire. Tom Stoppard has lived here for four years with his wife and four children. During the week there are a nanny and a secretary in attendance. As the two men entered, little shrieks of welcome emanated from down the hall and the four children came rushing in. The journalist was introduced and the two men retired to another room.

"This is really a parlor sort of room, which I very rarely use," said the playwright. He seemed concerned. "I can put you into a more interesting room if you like."

Observing a bar in the corner, the journalist assured him the room was more than adequate—grand, even, in its way. Barnaby, the seven-year-old, came in.

"Daddy," he said, "when is Mr. Bradshaw leaving?"

"I suppose just as soon as we can get rid of him," his father said.

"Get *rid* of him?" said Barnaby.

Since the two men were going to a performance of *Dirty Linen,* an early dinner was served in the spacious kitchen. Miriam, the playwright's wife, served spaghetti. (Miriam, a doctor, author, and business executive, has become something of a British-television personality answering questions on popular medicine.) Everyone ate together at a large round table. Having set out the food and wine, Miriam sat down and said, "Tom, Mr. Bradshaw's not asked a question for some time."

"He's going to ask the questions later," said the playwright. "First he's collecting the incriminating domestic evidence."

Looking up from his plate, Barnaby watched his father eat spaghetti. "Daddy, why do you twist your fork like that?" he said.

"Because if you kept the fork still and twisted yourself," said the playwright, "you'd get dizzy and fall into the spaghetti."

After dinner the two men drove up to London. During the trip the playwright recalled the success of his first play. "In 1965 I began work on a novel called *Lord Malquist and Mr. Moon,*" he said. "I just couldn't write it. Time passed and I finally started it two days before it was due. I worked out that if I wrote 30,000 words a day, I could still get it done in time." It was about this time that he also began work on *Rosencrantz and Guildenstern Are Dead.* "I believed my reputation would be made by the novel. I believed the play would be of little consequence. They both appeared in the same week in August of 1966. I remember taking the train back to London from Edinburgh, where *Rosencrantz* had opened at the Edinburgh Festival. I looked through the pages of the *Observer*. There was no mention of the book. But there was a photograph of me with a caption which said: 'The most brilliant dramatic debut since Arden.' And I thought to myself, 'I didn't know Arden had written novels.' But, of course they were referring to the play. When I went to bed that night I remember thinking that some monstrous hoax had been perpetrated on me. The novel, on the other hand, did very badly. It sold about 688 copies and I'm told it did very well in Venezuela. I'm very big in Caracas, you know."

"In Caracas?"

"Well, not exactly *in* Caracas. Near Caracas."

It began to rain and slowing down, the playwright turned on the windshield wipers. "I became a playwright," he said, "almost as the result of a historical accident. I began writing during a period when young writers in England wanted to be playwrights. In the late fifties, the playwright was the hottest thing in town. It's true. I promise you. Pinter, Osborne, Arden, and Wesker were the four hoarse men of the new apocalypse. Now, that's a truthful answer, in a limited way, as to why I write plays."

"And the rest of it?"

"Well, when I seriously consider why it is that I write plays, it has nothing to do with the social history of England or with what other people were writing around 1958. I'd rather write for the stage than television, for instance, because in a theater one has the full attention of one's audience, whereas watching television one tends to glance at the newspaper, to talk, or to answer the telephone. I'm not terribly keen on having my plays performed in that sort of situation. And I'm not terribly attracted to writing novels because their impact is dispersed over the time it takes someone to read them. And could I trust my readers to lock the doors and take the telephone off the hook? I could not. There is also the fact that I like theaters as places. So one begins to see that my plausible answer turns out to be very much like a lie.

"*Rosencrantz* came about in a curious way. I was riding back from one of the commercial television stations with my agent, where I had failed to convince them that I was *the* person to write an *Armchair Theater*. We were talking about a production of *Hamlet* at the Old Vic. He said there was a play to be written about Rosencrantz and

Guildenstern after they got to England. What happened to them once they got there? I was attracted to it immediately.

"The play had no substance beyond its own terms, beyond its apparent situation. It was about two courtiers in a Danish castle. Two nonentities surrounded by intrigue, given very little information and much of that false. It had nothing to do with the condition of modern man or the decline of metaphysics. One wasn't thinking, 'Life is an anteroom in which one has to kill time.' Or I wasn't, at any rate. God help us, what a play that would have been." He paused to light a cigarette. "I think I've actually seen one or two of those plays," he said. "But *Rosencrantz and Guildenstern* wasn't about that at all. It was about two blokes, right?

"But there you go. There's a deep suspicion among serious people of comic situations. The point is that good fun is merely frivolous. There was something I said the other day which bears repeating. The trouble is that I think I said it to you. Never mind. I think I used to have a redeeming streak of seriousness in my work and now I have a redeeming streak of frivolity. That's a neat way of putting it and I wouldn't say it represents the *precise* truth of the matter. But that is the tendency.

"I tend to see everything through a comic prism. *After Magritte,* for example, sprang from a friend's story about the morning he was shaving when he saw from the bathroom window his pet peacock leap over the garden hedge and make off down the road. Peacocks being rare birds, he dropped his razor and, barefoot and lathered, he pursued it, caught it, and returned with the peacock under his arm. Now, I tend to write plays about people who drive by in a car at that particular moment. They see a man in pajamas, bare feet, and shaving foam, carrying a peacock, for about a third of a second. They never see him again. They never quite understand what it is they've seen. They probably wouldn't even agree on what it was.

"You see, I know what I'm after. And it's like this. I'm stuck with the kind of plays I write. I'm stuck with the level I write on because I enjoy humor, I'm good at humor, and I enjoy it being performed and laughed at—ironic juxtapositions, all that sort of thing. And that's what I've got to do. Because if I decided to write a modern Greek tragedy in blank verse I'd just write rubbish. You see, I want to demonstrate that I can make serious points by flinging a custard pie around the stage for a couple of hours. In other words, I want to write plays that are just funny enough to do their jobs but not *too* funny to obscure them. My line at the moment would be to try to reduce weighty preoccupations about the way the world is going to an extended exchange of epigrams with a good first-act curtain."

"Your plays aren't peopled by what one would call *real* people. Why don't people interest you as much as words?"

"I don't know. I don't know. I mean you're wrong actually to put it in quite those terms. I'm not a lexicographer. I'm not interested in words as such, I'm interested in ideas. But there's no other way to express an idea except in words. It's a distinction worth making. I'm not being pedantic. I'm not James Thurber, who, if he couldn't get to sleep, thought up 93 words beginning with *pqu* or something. That's not it at all. Couldn't care less. Never do crosswords. Don't care."

The car crossed the Hammersmith cloverleaf and moved into central London. "It doesn't interest me in any way to create *characters*. In *Dirty Linen*, the Chairman is off the shelf and Miss Gotobed is off another shelf. She's not a *real* character. What interests me is getting a cliché and then betraying it. Miss Gotobed is a busty lady who triumphs in the play and she's sharper and brighter about a lot of things and that's fine but it doesn't mean she's a real character at all. In fact, it probably means that she's *less* real than anybody else.

"Incidentally, it's worth pointing out that you make it sound as though I belong to some rather exclusive little club who write plays which aren't about real people. Without making too much of it, it *appears* that my plays which aren't about real people go down well with enormous numbers of real people. Now you tell me why that is."

"Well, perhaps characters in a play are never *real.* Have you met anybody who's reminded you of Oedipus Rex lately?"

"Only my father. God, I should say immediately into this tape recorder that it's not true. I have a weakness for wisecracks which I don't sometimes have the tact to withhold. I always think that mere untruth is a very poor reason for restraint. Let me rephrase that. Accuracy is a high price to pay for truth. End of epigram." The playwright laughed and then in a solemn voice said: "This epigram has been brought to you by Hitachi.

"You know, the kind of joke I enjoy the most is a tautology. When I was at school we used to listen to the Goon show and I remember they were doing a sketch on colonial India and there was this joke. One of the Goons, Spike Milligan, I suppose, said, 'And then the monsoons came, and they couldn't have come at a worse time, bang in the middle of the rainy season.' Now, that to me is a perfect joke. My kind of joke is a snake in a funny hat eating its own tail. Tautologies, right? And for reasons which may be very uninteresting indeed, I'm very fond of them."

"You do speedwriting, I suppose?"

"Yes, if I'm given enough time."

"How long have you been a pedestrian?"

"Ever since I could walk."

"And how do you see yourself in the scheme of things?"

"*Je suis, ergo sum.*"

"I *thought* so. It's a theme that runs throughout your work."

The two men walked hurriedly up Great Newport Street. It was still raining and they were late for *Dirty Linen*. "It's raining," the playwright said. "Let's duck into the nearest theater."

Entering the crowded theater, the playwright was recognized by several of the lingering astute and a flurry of whispers rose in his wake. The two men retreated to the upstairs bar.

"How many times have you seen *Dirty Linen?*" said the journalist.

"Twelve," said the playwright, "and it gets better every other time."

Moments later, the bell rang and the two men took their seats. The playwright took pen and paper from his leather bag in order to make notes on the performance. It was a habit of his to stop in from time to time to assure himself (and the actors) that matters were running smoothly. The houselights went down. The play began and one was soon immersed in jokes—tautologies and puns, wisecracks and japes, *non sequiturs,* absurd conceits and epigrams, followed about an hour later by the curtain and much applause. A man sitting two seats away turned to his wife and said, "Is that the *end?*" The two men returned to the bar.

"*Dirty Linen* sort of grew like Topsy, really," the playwright said. "Ed Berman, the director, would have been perfectly happy if I'd turned in a 25-minute sketch, which is all I'd intended to do because I didn't have any ideas and because I couldn't think of a sketch relating to his own particular needs, which were for a season of plays about America or something to do with America. I ended up using an idea I'd saved for some other occasion and that idea was to have a play about a committee of very high-powered people. I was thinking of the archbishop of Canterbury and the prime minister, the equivalent of Einstein, some guy doing nuclear physics, a theologian, a philosopher, and they were going to have this committee meeting on some topic worthy of their brain power and there was going to be this staggering bird, who was there to sharpen the pencils and pass the water carafe around and I was going to have her correcting them on points of theology and nuclear physics in a very bland sort of way.

"I hadn't developed the idea beyond that single notion of dislocating the category of dumb blondes, you see. Finally, out of despair—you know, the usual deadline trouble—I began writing that play in the form of a committee meeting to debate Ed Berman's application for British citizenship. Got sick of that, decided to hell with Berman's American problem, and just wrote *Dirty Linen*. And then, you see, because there is a God and he *does* look after writers, I realized that all I had to do was to have an adjournment, put in fifteen minutes about America, and I'd solved Berman's problem as well. And the whole thing is a nonsense, of course, little more than an extended joke."

"What are you doing next?"

"What next? Well, I've written a sort of play which involves six actors and a symphony orchestra. The setting is contemporary, political in its implications, to do with human rights, and the treatment is tragicomic. The idea, which was suggested by André Previn, appealed as much as anything to my incipient megalomania, I think. I just love the idea of having a hundred musicians in a play. And I'm very in awe of conductors. Apart from Evel Knievel, I think the conductor of a great orchestra is the most awesome figure on earth.

"You see, ultimately, before being carried out feet first, I would like to have done a bit of absolutely everything. Really, without any evidence of any talent in those other directions, I find it very hard to turn down offers to write an underwater ballet for dolphins or a play for a motorcyclist on the wall of death. That's why I did this thing with André Previn. No one ever asked me to write a play with a symphony orchestra before. Probably no one ever will again."

The theater was empty now but for a few of the actors who had come up to the bar to chat with the playwright and to have a drink before going home. "Are you bothered much with urgent requests from people seeking *meaning* in your work?" the journalist said.

"Not often, but often enough to be irritating," he said. "You see, plays are written to entertain, they're *theatrical*. I don't want to be disobliging or churlish to people who are invariably nice and are paying me a real compliment in asking academic questions about my plays. But I do insist on making the point that they aren't written to be studied and discussed. No plays are written to be studied and discussed any more than pictures are painted to be discussed. The lit-crit industry is now approaching the dimensions of ITT. It reminds me of a very good footnote to an edition of Goethe's letters. Goethe was saying something like 'And now, I fell in love for the first time.' And in the footnote, the editor said: 'Here Goethe was mistaken. In 18...'" He laughed. "You know?"

"What about the style of your work? You've been accused of being all style and no substance," said the journalist.

"Not quite. In my own work, I think if you took away the style, the gift for putting things in certain ways, if you took that away and re-wrote everything so that it was pedestrian, but said the same thing, then you would have a residue of a certain number of things worth saying, but not worth listening to. I don't think I would say that of, say, Oscar Wilde. I think Wilde was *motivated* by style, which is a differ-ent thing. With Wilde, style was not merely the means, it *was* the end. In my own work the distinction between style and substance is never quite as clear as an academic might wish it to be. I'm not a writer who doesn't care what things mean and doesn't care if there isn't any meaning, but despite myself I *am* a kind of writer who doesn't give a fair crack of the whip to that meaning. The plays tend to give an impression of effervescence and style and wit for their own sake and thereby obscure what to me is the core of the toffee apple."

"The toffee apple?"

"A toffee apple, American readers, is a sort of hot dog, taken from Sanskrit.... *Tof* meaning hot and *Ap,* a sort of dog."

"Are you prepared to stand by that?"

"Well, I write fiction because it's a way of making statements I can disown. And I write plays because dialogue is the most respectable way of contradicting myself."

"Not bad," said the journalist. "May I quote you on that?"

"There's no point in being quoted if one isn't going to be quot-able," the playwright said.

A Playwright on the Side of Rationality

C. E. Maves

In January 1977 Stoppard had come to California to look in
on the West Coast premiere of *Travesties* at the Mark Taper
Forum in Los Angeles and to deliver a lecture at the University of California at Santa Barbara (a visit memorably recounted by Kenneth Tynan in his *New Yorker* profile later in
the year). Just two months later, Stoppard was back in San
Francisco to sit in on rehearsals for the American Conservatory Theater production of *Travesties* and take part in a question-and-answer session sponsored by the ACT as "An Evening
with Tom Stoppard." In conversations with various Bay Area
journalists, Stoppard went to some pains to distinguish his
style of theater from "anarchic or unstructured art."

Tom Stoppard ordered Campari over ice and talked about complexity.

"If a play has an easily compressible meaning, it's a failure. I used
to hear writers say, 'If I could tell you what it means, I wouldn't have
written it.' That always sounded pretentious to me, but experience
teaches you that it's the truth."

Born in 1937, Stoppard looks a lot younger. With his tousled
black hair and amiably rugged features, he might well be a senior rock
idol or rugby captain. Instead, he is quite possibly the finest living
British dramatist.

He is in San Francisco for the American Conservatory Theater
production of his latest play, *Travesties,* which will open Tuesday night
at the Geary.

From the *Palo Alto Times,* 25 March 1977.

"It's sort of three-legged, and the three legs are Lenin, the political revolutionist; Tristan Tzara, the artistic revolutionist; and James Joyce, the artistic evolutionist. The three legs are held together by Henry Carr," who was a minor British official in Zurich when that improbable trio gathered there in 1917.

The Campari arrived, and I asked Stoppard where he got the plot for *Travesties*.

"Its historical nugget was mentioned to me by a friend back in 1960. It seemed like a fruitful idea, so 14 years later I wrote a play about it."

The occasion for all this chat was a San Francisco press luncheon with Stoppard and the play's director, Nagle Jackson. Another reporter wondered if Stoppard has any special feeling for San Francisco and for ACT. "Haven't you noticed? I'm the house playwright!" he answered.

He is relaxed and very candid about his personal relationship to his latest play. "I have Tzara the Dadaist argue against Joyce the traditionalist, and a lot of the audience decides that Tzara is right. Actually, I empathize with Joyce, though I don't necessarily give him the last word. The play is a dialectic; it just happens that I'm on his side."

And what side is that? "The side of logic and rationality. And craftsmanship. There's a correlation between craftsmanship and art— craftsmanship is what crystallizes art. I have enormous admiration for well-made plays. I'm much more like Terence Rattigan than," he searches for examples, "Cocteau or Arrabal."

What about Samuel Beckett? "The early plays of Beckett are significant for me in that they didn't rely on elaborate theatrical paraphernalia. They redefined minimums, they show us how much can be done with little."

Are there any new plays in the works? "I'm writing one for television with the provisional title 'Professional Foul.' That's a term from football," by which he of course means soccer. "It's about . . . ethics."

Is he at all interested in films? "I've written the script for an adaptation of Vladimir Nabokov's *Despair*. Rainer Fassbinder is directing it, Dirk Bogarde is in it, and it starts filming in Munich three weeks from now."

Stoppard ordered papaya for dessert, and I asked "Do you think you're at the *Hamlet* stage of your career, or maybe at *The Merchant of Venice* stage, or maybe even back at the *Henry the VI, Part III* stage?"

Tom Stoppard laughed. "That's wonderful. I sometimes think," he said in dodging the Shakespearean comparison, "that I'm at the *Gammer Gurton's Needle* stage. *Travesties* was difficult to write, and I feel it's as good as I can do. Perhaps, as they say nowadays, I've already 'peaked.'" One sincerely doubts it.

So Often Produced, He Ranks with Shaw

Stanley Eichelbaum

During "An Evening with Tom Stoppard" sponsored by the American Conservatory Theater on 27 March 1977, the playwright responded to questions about *Jumpers, Dirty Linen,* and *Travesties,* about influences on his work, his techniques of writing, and his advice for a young writer. Confronted by one questioner who was "interested in knowing where your ideas come from," Stoppard quipped, "I wish I knew where they come from; I'd move there." Agreeing with another member of the audience that his plays are nonlinear, he explained that even though "*Travesties* is a play about real people in a real place at a real time," it does not use a historical treatment, "a linear one, putting the events in the right order," because "I don't think it tells the truth." Moments later when another questioner asked "How do you feel about that argument between Joyce and Tzara?," Stoppard shot back, "I can answer you categorically; I'm on Joyce's side." The give-and-take of the ACT session formed the backdrop for Stanley Eichelbaum's conversation with Stoppard the next morning. While he may not relish questions about the meanings of his plays, Stoppard not only affirms that he personally agrees with Joyce's position in *Travesties* but also asserts that "consciously or not, I loaded the play for him." Having told Maves the previous day that within the dialectic of *Travesties* the author agreed with Joyce but "didn't necessarily give him the last word," Stoppard establishes a certain dialectic as an inter-

From the *San Francisco Examiner,* 28 March 1977.

viewee by telling Eichelbaum that as the author of *Travesties* he had "given Joyce the last word."

As you might expect, Tom Stoppard is a verbal man. And though he'd rather not be asked about the meaning of his plays, he doesn't shy away from the question.

"I suppose I could be like other playwrights and say, 'If I could tell you, I wouldn't have written the play,'" said the British writer when I asked him how he felt about explaining himself, as he did last night at the Geary in "An Evening With Tom Stoppard," in which he read from his work and replied to audience questions.

"I don't like to be evasive," he continued, "but experience tells me it's quite an honest answer to say that I don't exactly know what it all means. If there were a way to summarize a play in 12 words, I think it would be a failure.

"It's not the first time I've done a stage appearance. My only concern about lectures and readings is that people have to put up with my rambling monologue. I'm happy, though, to do it for ACT, since I am, after all, the house playwright."

Stoppard's joke was no exaggeration. He is indeed a favorite with ACT audiences. William Ball's production of *Rosencrantz and Guildenstern Are Dead* remained in the repertory for three seasons. Ball then staged *Jumpers,* another big success. Now, Nagle Jackson has directed *Travesties,* which opens tomorrow night at the Geary.

"You'll be seeing a fuller version of the play—the fullest text, in fact, since *Travesties* opened in London in 1974. I tend to fiddle with my plays once they're on. It's nice to find a director like Nagle who's assimilating everything. I've looked in on the Geary production and a number of lines hit me as completely new—as if I never heard them before in my life.

"I've just been in Vienna to see a German production, and it had a very different feel. The middle-European sensibilities took over, particularly in respect to Lenin and his wife. The truth of their predicament was much more tangible."

Vladimir Ilyich Lenin is a pivotal character in *Travesties,* a comedy that juggles history to bring together Lenin, James Joyce and Tristan Tzara (the father of Dadaism) for a discussion of revolutionary politics and art.

The play is very Stoppardian, in that it's reinforced with intellectual ideas, but unfolds as a frolicsome charade, in this instance, through the foggy reminiscences of a retired British diplomat, Henry Carr, who recollects meeting Lenin, Joyce and Tzara in Zurich during World War I. Then there's Carr's involvement in an amateur production of *The Importance of Being Earnest,* which results in a parody of Oscar Wilde's comedy.

How did Stoppard ever arrive at such a curious mix of history and fiction?

"It began with the historical nugget of information that Lenin, Tzara and Joyce were residents of Zurich in 1917," he replied. "It seemed a fruitful situation, particularly since Lenin had no use for the kind of art represented by Dada, which is one of the few things Lenin and I agree on.

"Joyce, on the other hand, is an artist I can respect and sympathize with. I happen to be on his side, which is why I've given Joyce the last word. Consciously or not, I loaded the play for him. He stands for a stream of literature that the Dadaists derided in their non-art. And Lenin belongs in the play as another sort of revolutionary. He's like all serious political revolutionaries who tend to have an artistic taste that's utterly bourgeois.

"*Earnest* didn't get into it until comparatively late. I've always felt that *Earnest* was part of our consciousness. It's a play everyone knows, like *Hamlet,* which I used in a similar way in *Rosencrantz.*"

Despite the popularity of *Travesties,* audiences consider it a challenging, even difficult play. In reply to this, Stoppard said, "I don't set out to write plays that are hard to understand. My plays may have a fragmented look, but they're very traditional plays.

"Everything is logical and rational. I have no interest in anarchic or unstructured art. I'm rather conservative and have much more in common with Terence Rattigan than, say, Jean Cocteau. I believe in craftsmanship. It's what crystallizes an art form."

The 40-year-old author hasn't written many plays, yet has outdistanced all of his English contemporaries, including Pinter, in popularity. He has a new hit on Broadway, *Dirty Linen,* and his work is so frequently produced in this country, he ranks with Shaw and Shakespeare.

However, none of his plays has been made into movies. "I'm always asked about the screen rights," he said. "But nobody's been able to give me an idea of the kind of film they want to make."

Stoppard has nevertheless written his first screenplay, *Despair,* from a 1930 novel by Vladimir Nabokov. He calls it a black comedy.

The film will be shot in Germany by Rainer Werner Fassbinder. "He hasn't previously worked with an English script," said Stoppard. "Dirk Bogarde will play the lead, and production starts in Munich in three weeks."

The Politicizing of Tom Stoppard

Milton Shulman

After years of responding to questions about why he was not
more political, Stoppard had to deal—after the premiere of
Every Good Boy Deserves Favour in July 1977 and the televising
of *Professional Foul* in September 1977—with questions about
the "politicizing of Tom Stoppard." Stoppard had also published lengthy articles in the *Sunday Times* about Soviet mis-
treatment of political dissidents and in the *New York Review of
Books* and the *Daily Mail* about the Czech government's suppression of the Charter 77 movement. Although such public
outspokenness on political issues clearly represented a new
departure, Stoppard insisted in his interview with Milton
Shulman, the theater critic of London's *Evening Standard,* that
he "was always morally, if not politically, involved" and that
"there was no sudden conversion on the road to Damascus."
The interview was published in the *New York Times* three days
prior to the first American airing of Stoppard's television play
Professional Foul. Stoppard discusses his involvement with Amnesty International and the genesis of *Professional Foul* and
Every Good Boy Deserves Favour.

Tom Stoppard writes like a mathematical philosopher who really wants
to be a clown. His verbal equations balance out on the side of absurdity and his logical calculations tend to be springboards to nonsense.
His most famous plays—*Rosencrantz and Guildenstern Are Dead, Jumpers*
and *Travesties*—have established him as a specialist in philosophical
farce. He can use a syllogism like a custard pie and give logical positivism the status. But his intellectual frivolity has naturally made Mr.

From the *New York Times*, 23 April 1978.

Stoppard suspect in the eyes of those who believe that great dramatists ought to be committed to more serious social and political issues. Critic Kenneth Tynan has described him as a cool, apolitical stylist, and to prove his point quotes Mr. Stoppard as having once said that his favorite line in English drama comes from Christopher Hampton's *The Philanthropist:* "I'm a man of no convictions—at least, I think I am."

Interviewing Mr. Stoppard about his latest TV play, *Professional Foul,* I asked him what he thought of Mr. Tynan's implied charge that he preferred to float above the battle rather than take an uncomfortable position in the moral trenches.

"I suppose that line must have chimed for me in some way or I wouldn't have quoted it several years later. Sixteen years ago, when I first started writing plays, one was surrounded by artists who were making positive statements about social and political questions. But they did not seem to be aware of the difficulties involved in solving those questions.

"I had a reaction against making heroes for plays who had positive points of view and no qualifications about them. And I became quite good at seeing the other side or, to rephrase that, I became a terrible hedger. But I was always morally, if not politically, involved. Other people always try to put writers in some overall context and try to make sense of their work in that way. But obviously one doesn't see oneself in some intellectualized cosmos and then perform accordingly. I haven't the faintest idea what my main preoccupation will be this time next year. But whatever it is, it won't be because I consider it to be the appropriate preoccupation for a man who is deemed to be a certain sort of writer with certain appropriate preoccupations."

Nevertheless there is such an obvious shifting of creative gears in Mr. Stoppard's last two important works—*Professional Foul* and *Every Good Boy Deserves Favor*—that one is entitled to ask what created the change. Seen last year in Britain—one on television and the other for just a one-night stand in a large concert hall—these plays do not hedge, quibble or equivocate about the issue of human rights. *Professional Foul* is about a professor of ethics who goes to Prague for an academic convention and there loses his intellectual detachment when he becomes involved with a former Czech student trying to make a statement about individual freedom. *Every Good Boy,* which integrates in its production the London Symphony Orchestra under André Previn, concerns a victim of Russian K.G.B. brutality who finds himself in the same cell as a genuine lunatic who has fantasies about conducting a symphony orchestra.

"There was no sudden conversion on the road to Damascus," said Mr. Stoppard. "I know human rights have been around for a long time and I have always been concerned with the daily horrors that I read in the newspapers. But it was really only a coincidence that both these plays about human rights should have been written about the same time. For some time I had been involved with Amnesty International, the worldwide human rights organization. The BBC had been asking me to write a TV play for them and Mark Shivas, a BBC producer who had worked with me on a London magazine many years ago, had told me he would be interested in any ideas of mine. Amnesty International had decided to make 1977 Prisoner of Conscience Year and I thought a play on TV might help their cause.

"For purely technical reasons, I have never been very fond of television but I thought that on a subject like this a TV play would have more impact than a play for the stage. After all, on TV you would get a large audience on a single night. In a theater, the impact would be spread over weeks and months. And that's assuming the play is good enough to last. So I phoned Mark Shivas in the middle of 1976 and promised him a play about persecution behind the Iron Curtain, to be delivered at the end of the year. But when the deadline came I had written nothing and had nothing in mind."

It was, oddly enough, a week's trip to Moscow and Leningrad that unlocked the idea for *Professional Foul,* which takes place in Czechoslovakia. Except for a day trip to East Berlin, it was Mr. Stoppard's first visit behind the Iron Curtain.

"I was accompanying a friend of mine who works for Amnesty. Instead of a Cook's tour, which I thought I was taking, one thing led to another and I came in contact with a number of Russians concerned with human rights. I met Irina Orlov, the wife of Yuri Orlov, who had been arrested three days before. She told us how eight K.G.B. men searched their flat and when she tried to get help—she is entitled to two witnesses by law—she had her arm twisted behind her back. It was a very unpleasant experience in many ways, trying to talk to people who were on a precipice and simply didn't know if they were going to be there for breakfast the next morning. I am sure I was followed. A chap took my photograph in the street and the thorough search they gave me at the airport was rather frightening."

It is this atmosphere of menace in congenial surroundings that Mr. Stoppard seeks to evoke in *Professional Foul.* His professor of ethics finds himself in a flat in Prague just as the former student he has come to visit has been taken away by security police. It is this experience that determines him to read a lecture on human rights at the Conference rather than the purely theoretical paper he had come to present.

"As a matter of fact I felt much more vulnerable in the Moscow hotel I was staying at than in the flats of any dissidents. It was the Ukraine Hotel which was, I think, built in the 1950's but had a pre-1914 look about it. Everyone took it for granted that the rooms were bugged. When I got back to London I heard a marvelous story about a group of Russians on New Year's Eve who raised their glasses of champágne and toasted their bug. 'Here's to the unseen listener!' they shouted. A couple of minutes later the phone rang and there was silence on the other end of the line. But after a moment or two they heard the pop of a champagne cork from their silent caller and the phone was then put down."

Coupled with this experience in Russia, Mr. Stoppard early in January, 1977, heard about the arrest of a playwright, an actor and a journalist in Prague because they attempted to deliver to the Czech Government a document asking it to implement for the Czech people the human rights that had been called Charter 77 and was signed by 241 people. One of the men arrested was Václav Havel, a playwright whose work Mr. Stoppard very much admired.

"I came across his plays in 1967 and I have always felt a real affinity with Havel's point of view," said Mr. Stoppard. "They were plays which I would have liked to write. They are very playful plays. One of them, for example, is about a bureaucracy that suddenly introduces a completely new language which Havel invents. The metaphor is worked out in a wonderfully witty way and exactly appealed to my taste."

The third element that stimulated him into writing a play about repression in Prague was the fact that he was born in Czechoslovakia in 1937. The family moved to Singapore when he was five and when the Japanese invaded, he, his brother and mother were evacuated to India. His father remained behind and died in Japanese captivity. His mother married a Major Stoppard of the British Army in 1946 and Tom's name, which had originally been Straussler, was now that of his stepfather's. He was educated in an English minor public school and his formal schooling ended at 17 when, without a university education, he took up journalism.

"I'm as Czech as Czech can be," he said, in a voice whose slight foreign undertones hint that he was not born in England. "So you can see that with my desire to write something about human rights, the combination of my birth, my trip to Russia, my interest in Havel and his arrest, the appearance of Charter 77 were the linking threads that gave me the idea for *Professional Foul.* I wrote it in three months and it was ready for transmission in September, 1977."

Professional Foul has already been seen twice on British TV and a third showing is soon to be scheduled. It received unanimous praise from the critics and even the Communist paper, *Morning Star,* grudgingly conceded that it was "fast, entertaining, intellectual footwork." It has already won the British TV critics' award as the best play of 1977 and has been nominated for the best play of the year award by the prestigious British Academy of Film and TV Arts.

Once the play was in production, Mr. Stoppard mothered it like a protective hen. He was in on all discussions about casting with Mark Shivas, the producer, and Michael Lindsay-Hogg, the director. During the rehearsals, he actually visited Prague for the first time since his childhood and to everyone's relief there was no need to change anything in the script because Mr. Stoppard felt that in mood, clothes and atmosphere they had got it right.

"I have always been suspicious about writing for television because I miss the writer's ability to control the frame," the playwright said. "On the stage, I have a total picture in my mind about how something is going to look. But when I write for television I'm completely at sea because I don't know whether during the scene I'm writing, the viewer will be looking at my hero's left nostril or the four walls of the room. I write TV plays as though they were stage plays. You know the camera is just sitting there, and there are no instructions about how to use it. That's why I like to be around during the shooting to see what is happening to my situations and dialogue in terms of the accompanying image."

The decision to cast Peter Barkworth as Anderson, the professor of ethics who undergoes a violent change of conscience in Prague, seemed rather odd since Mr. Barkworth is not readily identifiable as an academic type. His most famous role was as Edward VIII in a play about the Abdication and his well-bred features have an uncanny resemblance to that handsome King who gave up a throne for love. Usually Mr. Barkworth is seen as a banker, stockbroker or socialite. Why, then, did Mr. Stoppard feel he was right for the part?

"I had just finished the text of *Professional Foul* and in my script I had typed in the instructions that Anderson, the professor, was about 60. That same evening I was watching a TV play in which Barkworth had a leading role. As I sat watching him, I thought to myself, 'He is so wonderful I really ought to write a play for him.' After about 10 minutes, I began to think 'Well, Anderson could be about 55.' Then I thought to myself, 'What the hell does it matter what age he is?' By the time the TV play was finished, I decided I had to have Peter Barkworth in the part of Anderson. Then, of course, when it came to the rehearsals, there was Barkworth plodding around saying, 'I'm a bit worried. It does say 60.'"

Mr. Barkworth had no need to worry. He has just been declared the best TV actor of 1977 by Britain's TV critics for his portrayal of Professor Anderson.

KGB to Blame in the End

Martin Huckerby

After a single performance at the Royal Festival Hall on 1 July 1977, *Every Good Boy Deserves Favour* was revived at the Mermaid Theatre on 14 June 1978. Set in a Soviet psychiatric hospital used to confine both political dissidents and psychotics, the play climaxes in the release—by a KGB officer—of a dissident who had almost died on hunger strike. The play reflected Stoppard's experience of totalitarian regimes in real life. After the Czech regime had unsuccessfully tried to bribe dissident playwright Václav Havel with an exit visa following international outrage that erupted over his arrest, Stoppard claimed in a February 1977 letter to the editor of *The Times* that "the Czech Government now has to choose between two opposite embarrassments; to pursue the logic of repression, or to climb down." By making the KGB officer in *Every Good Boy* a philologist, Stoppard intended for the release to hinge on a semantic quibble that the KGB was transparently using as a face-saving device after it had made the embarrassing decision to climb down. However, numerous observers mistakenly regarded the KGB officer as merely bumbling and saw the dissident's release as a bureaucratic bungle rather than the outcome of a test of wills. This briefest of interviews contains the most explicit indication of Stoppard's intentions for the much-misinterpreted ending of the play.

Tom Stoppard's play with music by André Previn, *Every Good Boy Deserves Favour*, is running successfully at the Mermaid Theatre, but there

---

From *The Times*, 17 August 1978.

is one slight difficulty: people keep misunderstanding the meaning of the climax.

At the Russian psychiatric hospital where the play is set the inoffensive dissident, who refuses to recant, is allowed out because the KGB colonel deliberately confuses him with a genuine madman. The final anguish is caused by the dissident having to decide whether to go along with that ploy in order to gain his freedom.

Stoppard admits that when the play was first performed, at the Festival Hall last year, the ending was ambiguous. Plenty of critics came to the wrong conclusion, suggesting that the dissident was responsible for the confusion and was duping the KGB.

The play opened at the Mermaid in June and Stoppard has been fiddling with it ever since. "I really thought we had it licked for the Mermaid. I'm baffled that a substantial number of people still misunderstand the ending."

Earlier this month he was working on it again while doing rehearsals with new actors for the cast at the Mermaid, but he confessed that he did not really know how to resolve the difficulty.

Every Good Boy starts a tour in the United States this month, with Previn and the Pittsburgh Symphony Orchestra providing the music. No doubt plenty of Americans will also get the wrong message.

The South Bank Show

Melvyn Bragg

While addressing political issues, *Every Good Boy Deserves Favour* and *Professional Foul* seemed unlikely to betoken a sea change in Stoppard's career because both appeared, in different ways, to be one-off affairs. *Every Good Boy Deserves Favour* initially received a single performance with the London Symphony Orchestra on 1 July 1977; as a television play, *Professional Foul* was broadcast on 24 September 1977. Further, both works were occasional pieces. *Professional Foul* was written for Amnesty International's Prisoner of Conscience Year; *Every Good Boy Deserves Favour* was written in response to André Previn's invitation to "write something which had the need of a live full-size orchestra on stage." Even after *Every Good Boy* (rescored for a chamber orchestra) was revived at the Mermaid Theatre for a three-month run in the summer of 1978, a piece requiring an orchestra had to seem more an anomaly than a harbinger of future work. For those seeking to find the method in Stoppard's direction, the stage play was, still, the thing. And on the West End stage in the autumn of 1978, the farcical one-act *Dirty Linen*—still running after a thousand performances—seemed to provide an easy answer to a question being asked by Stoppard detractors: "Tom Stoppard: serious artist or siren?" When *Night and Day* opened on 8 November 1978, it was Stoppard's first full-length stage play since *Travesties* (1974). The play was naturalistic, journalistic, and political, and John Barber of the *Daily Telegraph* announced that it "makes all Stoppard's other plays look like

Transmitted on London Weekend Television, 26 November 1978 (recorded 22 November 1978).

so many nursery games." Two weeks later, London Weekend Television taped an interview with Stoppard as part of an hour-long "South Bank Show" devoted to his work. The program begins with videotape of the new West End production of *Night and Day,* including the opening encounter between Wagner and Ruth (performed by John Thaw and Diana Rigg). To provide a contrast with Stoppard's earlier work, the program brought John Stride and Edward Petherbridge to the LWT studios to recreate their roles in the coin-tossing scene that opens *Rosencrantz and Guildenstern Are Dead.* After discussing the "linguistic skills and dramatic audacity" of such plays as *Jumpers* and *Travesties,* moderator Melvyn Bragg speculates on "a change in Stoppard's work ... not from less to more serious, or from more to less complicated, but a change in his personal commitment, and, especially, in its dramatic expression towards naturalism." To highlight that change, Bragg turns to the moment in *Night and Day* when Wagner discovers that fellow journalist Milne is "the Grimsby scab," prompting Milne's blistering attack on Wagner's "abusive vocabulary" and the leftist ideological jargon used by "the house Trots." Videotape of the scene, with Peter Machin as Milne, immediately precedes Bragg's first question to Stoppard.

BRAGG: That extract from *Night and Day,* and the play, *Night and Day* itself, seems to represent a different sort of play from the play you were writing about ten years ago and the play that people most easily associate with you. Do you think it is a different stage in your writing? Do you think it is a change?

STOPPARD: It is different in a sense but it's not the consequence of any act of principle or policy. I wanted to write a play about journalism in some way. I had no idea what to do; I don't have a lot of ideas for plays. I'm desperate for anything to write a play about and I was a journalist in the provinces for some years so I had something which I felt I ought to make some use of—not because I was a journalist only but because I've just been interested in journalism. And I spent a long time wondering how to write a play about journalism: you know—"a day in the life of the *Western Daily Press*"?—what do you do? And *Night and Day* came out the way it did because it came out the way it did. Driving down the M-4, suddenly I thought, "Oh. It's got to be abroad. Got it."

BRAGG: Did *Jumpers,* for example, come out the way it did, with such a stroke?

STOPPARD: Well, no play, obviously, arrives in any real completeness. Most plays are a pulling together of various threads, some of which only turn out to belong to the same play quite late on in the day. *Jumpers* was more that sort of a business. I wanted to write *Jumpers*—as indeed any play I've written—because I wanted to write about something abstract. I wanted to write about an idea. Thereafter I have enormous difficulty in constructing some sort of vehicle for this thing to travel in—some logical coherent interesting story where I can use my internal debate. And *Jumpers*...the *story* just made its own demands finally.

BRAGG: When you were writing his speeches—George's—they're very long, they're quite complex ideas, and one of the early speeches, for example, about God (not "Is there a God?" but "Is God?")—were you worried about taking that on, on a stage?

STOPPARD: Yes; pass me the play—I can't remember exactly what he says. I'm now post-rationalising. I don't remember how this speech got written; I honestly don't. The main thing about it is that one of me has a thought which may or may not be profound and the other me has got to find quite a mundane and—one would like to think—a funny way, a witty way of saying it. I have a sense of humour, variously described by my friends, associates and critics as "brilliant," "tacky," "undergraduate," you know, and it's a bit of each maybe; I just like jokes and I quite often work quite close to the line of the cheap joke. There's always one where my family groans and says "oh God, please take it out" and I say "no I won't—I love it." Then at the other end there are jokes which nobody understands except me [*laughter*]—which is another problem. In between, one tries to get the ones which I like and they like.

[Extract from *Jumpers* of Michael Hordern delivering George's lengthy speech beginning "Secondly!...To begin at the beginning: is God?" and ending "to begin at the beginning: *is God?* Leave a space."]

STOPPARD: The whole thing is to do with my being the beneficiary of an irrepressible sense of humour and, at the same time, being a victim of it. So the consequence is that when you have a speech like the one Michael just did for you, you are left with two possibilities. One is that you have compromised your seriousness by an excess of frivolity; and the other is that you've redeemed an over-seriousness with a welcome streak of wit.

BRAGG: It's just on the surface that *Jumpers* which seems to bring . . . not bring to a conclusion but seems to be in the mainstream of your plays where you were dealing with verbal extravagances, in a way, with philosophical ideas running underneath them, with fireworks all along the way. Were you there doing something that you would describe as much more theatrical than the one you are up to now?

STOPPARD: I am quite hot on the theatricality of theatre. It's not quite such a tautology as it sounds because there are kinds of theatre which aren't theatrical in that colloquial use of the word. And I enjoy other people's plays which are not theatrical in the sense that I'm using the word; they're nearer literature than theatre. For me, theatre is not literature; it's an event.

BRAGG: Are you therefore saying that once you take a play into the theatre you abandon the things that *must* occupy you when you're alone here writing it in the first place.

STOPPARD: I'm shamelessly empirical about the theatre and I want the *equation* to work. I mean, writing a play is to write some kind of equation; it's got to be an elegant equation. When you start working with actors, and a director, and the designer, and sound cues—all kinds of other variables enter the equation and you have to—I don't know the verb for this, not being a mathematician—but, if it were English, rather than maths, you'd have to parse these pieces, so that the equation remains elegant and comes out to the same answer.

Rehearsing a play is more or less the best time in my life. I just love it. I don't mean that it's all wonderful and happy. But I just like the experience in spite of the un-wonderful moments. And, as I say, in this period I am very empirical. Now, on a given occasion, there's an equation to be got right and that's what I'm there for. I'm not there to say "Ooh! I've been at Iver Heath for *so long* and I've taken *enormous* trouble with this play and this is what you are going to do, folks." What for?

There's all kinds of considerations which I haven't even mentioned. For example, by the time you open a play you are very close to the people you're working with—even the ones you've never met before, let alone Peter Wood, who is one of my closest friends now for years.

BRAGG: He's the director.

STOPPARD: He's the director of *Night and Day* and, indeed, *Jumpers.*

And you're sort of a family of a kind. You're closer to some people than others, but you've worked together, and you have a great... I have a great feeling and respect for the actors. I like actors a lot and I'm impressed by what seems to me to be a mad courage just to go on there at all. In the end they're going out on a limb for you, every night. I'm back in Iver Heath watching "The Muppets"; and they're out there doing it. And I'm not going to say "No. This is what I wrote; you go out there and do it." I just don't feel like that so I don't do it like that.

BRAGG: You've used the words "equation" and "elegant" in what you've been talking about... and "empiricism." But some people say, well, you are dealing *in* equations, in abstractions, and not really with human nature—that plays shouldn't be about equations, they should be about quests and searches and explorations of character. And what would you say to that?

STOPPARD: Were I interviewing you as the author of these plays, I would have put that slightly differently—I think—that what *is* remarked upon is that the plays have some difficulty in being about the people that inhabit them, rather than about the ideas which those people express. And that is a consequence of my own first interest, you see. I mean, I'm no good at character; it doesn't really interest me very much. What, however, mostly saves me is that the *actor* is interested in character and *is* a character. Even in a play which is as scrupulously inhuman as *The Real Inspector Hound*—I mean, that play, you know, it's a sort of mechanical toy; it actually is a play which is being built to go, "Brrn, chink, clonk, klump." And it does. And I like it for that. It's about a couple of critics watching a sort of Agatha Christie play and one of them ends up dead. And I wrote the critic, mea culpa, without love, you know. He had to do certain things, he had to parody certain things, he had to get inside the wrong machine and end up dead. And it was an inhuman joke, really. The only thing is, is that when this play is done—the first time it was done, Richard Briers played this critic—I was saved, or scuppered, or whatever, by Richard Briers. When he died, people cared about him, and the equation is somehow maintained. In *Night and Day* the question doesn't really arise; I mean the question would be less pertinent to a play like *Night and Day*.

BRAGG: It would seem to me that with the television play, *Professional Foul,* you changed direction, you went for a much more realistic situation, of a philosopher going to a conference in Prague. He's also going to a football match and being taken up by a train of events which led him to have to make a moral decision which was parallel to the moral questions he was talking about in his own philosophy.

STOPPARD: The subject matter of the play determined the form of the play as much as the television medium determined it. It wasn't something I wanted to do a music hall about. *(interrupting himself)* It's all back to front!—what actually happens is you sit here with this tape on the desk, and say "What do I do? What do I do?!" You don't think, "You know, in two years' time, I'll be here with Melvyn saying, 'Well, what I thought I'd do is . . .'" It's all lies, you see.

I mean, I wanted somebody to go to Prague for some purpose. I began—I thought I'd have—these bizarre ballroom dancing competitions. I suppose there's still a streak of my *Travesties* weaknesses there. I thought I'd have ballroom dances as well, you see, as well . . . instead of gymnasts or something. So I was going to have ballroom dances going there.

And at the same time I'd always sort of had a vague idea that there was some sort of play to be written about the suspension of moral conduct on the sports field. I am fascinated by matches. I remember when I was at school—it's in the play—that when you play football, and the ball goes into touch, you *know* who touched it last, and you don't try to pretend that *he* did if *you* did. It just never occurred to you to do it. And yet, you know, we all are sitting there watching everybody being applauded for trying to steal some dishonourable advantage. And you know perfectly well, that when both players claim the throw-in for themselves they both know whose it actually is. Now, what is going on? There is a complete suspension of code.

[Extract from *Professional Foul* with McKendrick talking about yob ethics.]

I wanted to write a play about somebody going to an eastern European country in a state of innocence and just getting too close to a totalitarian system and just having a slight taste of what it's like.

BRAGG: It's very—can I just interrupt for one moment—because that's about the fourth time or fifth time in the interview that you've determinedly contradicted something and then gone back and affirmed it.

STOPPARD: I know, yes.

BRAGG: It's interesting, because is it something that you will not say, "Now that's a perfect answer: I wanted to write a play about the man who did thus...went in a state of innocence..." You denied vigorously five minutes ago that you had anything in mind at all. So which is right?

STOPPARD: No, I didn't *intend* to do that. You were asking me why *Professional Foul* turned out to be a relatively straightforward look at a certain series of events. And I was trying to explain that I didn't sit here thinking, "This one is going to be a straightforward look at some events." I began as always with an abstract thought: some innocent from a free society goes to a totalitarian society and just sort of gets dirty. And that's an honest answer. What I was saying was, that having got that far, I didn't know whether he was a ballroom dancer or a moral philosopher.

BRAGG: Why did you opt for a moral philosopher?

STOPPARD: Because as you get further into it you have to integrate the internal profound subject matter with the narrative subject. You've got to actually make them the same thing. You'd think this was fairly obvious and you'd discover it earlier than I did. But, in the end, you're better off not having a play where people are actually talking about ballroom dancing while, as it were, being used to demonstrate moral truths. It's better if they—it's just a better—what is it?—it's just a better ... sandwich, or something. What a wonderful metaphor. But it's better in some way if you integrate the deep subject matter with the top subject matter so that if somebody is going to be in Prague to tell me something about moral absolutes then it doesn't do any harm if his profession is moral philosophy.

[Extract from *Professional Foul* with Pavel Hollar talking about the collective ethic coming from the individual ethic.]

STOPPARD: The fact of the matter is that in *Jumpers* I felt as strongly about writing a play about a man who really believed that good and bad were absolute moral truths as I did about a man going to Prague to lecture on moral philosophy and finding his comeuppance in a sense. I felt equally strongly about the internal subject matter of both plays. As you said, in the former case, there was so much mayonnaise on it that it was very hard to taste the roast beef at all.

BRAGG: I didn't say that, alas; you said that.

STOPPARD: I'm trying to ... no, I won't say that. And as you say, you know, the equation was different then, and the kind of entertainment value of the piece perhaps just got too strong for its internal subject matter. I'd agree. I prefer *Professional Foul* to *Jumpers* but the interesting thing to say about that is—and the implications for me are horrifying—is that compared to writing *Jumpers, Professional Foul* is a doddle. I mean, the difficult thing is to write *Travesties* and *Jumpers*. To write about ordinary men in an ordinary airplane having an ordinary conversation and then again in the hotel room ... what can I say? I can just tell you the truth. *Travesties,* you know, at this desk at 9 A.M. (actually that's a lie, 9:30, 10) but by 11 A.M. actually writing—five minutes for lunch, stop when the children come home from school, start in at 9 or 10 at night, work till 1 or 2 in the morning and do the same thing the next day—seven, eight or nine months, I forget. *Professional Foul,* which I suspect you prefer as a play and I suspect that you may be right, once I knew it wasn't ballroom dances, I mean I was *there* in three weeks. Now, what do you make of that?

BRAGG: Well, what do you make of that? That's the question.

STOPPARD: Well, as I say, I find it very alarming because, you know, I don't know what to *say* about it. I just don't know what to say about it. It's an anomalous ... there's a contradiction there which is very worrying for me. I mean, people liked *Professional Foul* a lot, and I began to flinch from their congratulations which invariably took the form of "at last you've taken this giant step forward," you know. Well, I'm not trying to place too much importance on how long a play takes to write because that's to oversimplify, because after all, you know, you can write a rotten play in 28 months and a very good one in 28 days if you're writing the right play at the right time, and so on. But there's something in that; you know, I worked bloody hard on *Travesties* and found it *extremely* difficult to do and Henry Carr's opening speech—I mean, the paper I threw away must have been about that high. And writing *Professional Foul* was just kind of a joy and a pleasure, you know; obviously I worked just as hard but for a much shorter period of time.

BRAGG: What about this play, *Night and Day,* which is your first full-length stage play for a while. What made you choose this particular subject which is to do with journalists in Africa embroiled in what might be a revolution or a coup or a civil war—not quite sure of which at different stages—in Northern Africa and also to do with the issue of the closed shop in journalism and to do with the freedom of the press. What made you go for this complex of issues?

STOPPARD: I wanted to write a play about journalism, but I had nothing to write about, if you see what I mean. When the NUJ closed shop controversy blew up, I was passionately interested in it. I felt and thought all kinds of things which bore upon that question and they sort of pop up in the play—I hope not like pieces of toast in somebody else's toaster—but they are there, around. I had always felt that no matter how dangerously closed a society looked like it was getting, as long as any newspaper was free to employ anybody it liked to say what it wished within the law, then any situation was correctable. And without that any situation was concealable. I felt that very strongly; I feel it strongly now. I am passionate about this. It's the one thing that makes a free society different from an unfree one. It's the crucial thing. It's the last thing to go. While you've got it, you're in a situation where you can get better. Once you've lost it, it can only get worse. So, then it was no longer a play about journalism—it was about something else again. Now, having got that far, I still have nothing to write on another level. Who is in this play? You know: Who are they? Where do they come from? What sex are they? How old are they? Why are they there? Who, you know, what do I care? Same old problem from the moment I began writing plays. And, bit by bit you invent some sort of a vehicle to put your play in about journalism.

Now, I'd be leaving out something terribly important if I were not to say immediately that I *also* wanted to write a play—another play you understand, *Day and Night,* about a woman, not exactly falling in love, but having an instant love reaction to somebody just-like-that. It didn't stay like that, but *Night and Day* is also a play about this woman and a young reporter. It's about something which is not journalism at all. And I've been discreetly telling people that my play is about journalism. I discovered pretty shortly after starting rehearsal that this play wished to be more about that woman and that young man than I had realised.

BRAGG: You've spoken of your own commitment to a free press, and that's represented most forcibly in the play by a young 23-year-old reporter called Milne who's stumbled into Africa and discovered himself to be in the middle of a marvelous scoop, rather like Boot in *Scoop*—I think there are one or two affinities with the war novel there. And the character played by Diana Rigg, the mine owner's wife, falls in love with him while he is telling her about the freedom of the press. Now these two things, her falling in love with him, and him declaring his idealistic commitment, they go together very well. But did you see it ... how did that scene come about? It's another of these impossible questions, but there you are, how did that scene come about?

STOPPARD: In some odd way you've actually put your finger on *exactly* the right part of the play to enable me to answer this question adequately. Peter Wood susses things out in my plays which somehow I've just left to look after themselves. And when he read the play, the thing he liked most was *exactly* what you've just described: that a young man is actually talking about "x" but "yz" is going on all the time. And I didn't do it. As a matter of fact, I just said, "she's there, she's on the stage, and he's speaking his bit." And it's a part of the production which I like as much as anything else, perhaps, because Peter realised something which I hadn't realised which is that you can't just sort of say later, "Well, you know, she fell in love with him." He decided on the moment where this would actually happen and worked with the actor with such persistence and detail just on the one tiny moment of that whole scene—to make it happen *then.*—

BRAGG:—when's that?—

STOPPARD:—I'm not going to tell you. He'll never do it right again if I told you! And I sit there, knowing that I am the beneficiary of what's happened to that scene.

[Extract from *Night and Day* of that interchange between Milne and Ruth. The scene begins with Peter Machin as Milne saying, "Dick wants union membership to be a licence to practise" and ends with Diana Rigg as Ruth saying, "No. I like you to talk."]

BRAGG: Diana Rigg and Peter Machin in *Night and Day* by Tom Stoppard at the Phoenix Theatre in London. As much a play of ideas in its way as is *Jumpers* but using a more naturalistic style. On the whole the critics have been very favourable but not unanimously enthusiastic. Bernard Levin and Peter Jenkins, for example, stood aside from a majority and expressed considerable disappointment. For what it's worth, I think it will come to be regarded as Stoppard's most important play to date.

A Playwright in Undiscovered Country

Hugh Hebert

The week after speaking to Hugh Hebert, Stoppard was going to have four plays on stage in London when *Dirty Linen, Night and Day* and *Undiscovered Country* (an adaptation of Schnitzler), were joined by his newest play, *Dogg's Hamlet, Cahoot's Macbeth.* Despite the wealth of new work, the burning question was, still, how the apolitical wordsmith of *Travesties* and *Jumpers* had become the socially committed playwright of *Every Good Boy Deserves Favour* and *Professional Foul.* Faced with claims that the change in his work seemed as radical a transformation as the conversion of St. Paul on the road to Damascus, Stoppard was greeted by a certain incredulity when he sought to explain that the common thread connecting plays as seemingly disparate as *Jumpers* and *Professional Foul* was their concern with moral questions. Stoppard also offers one of the clearest indications of his own sympathies in the discussion of journalism in *Night and Day.* In that play the photographic journalist George Guthrie maintains that "information, in itself, about anything, is light" in response to Ruth's assertion that by being killed while trying to get a story, journalist Jacob Milne "died for the product."

As he talks in his study, a door behind Tom Stoppard opens, revealing one end of a billiard table, and a bevy of potential purchasers, ushered by an estate agent. The Stoppards are selling their house, and one of

From *The Guardian,* 7 July 1979.

the might-be purchasers mutters that he'd prefer to have a full size billiard table.

Stoppard's is two-thirds size, the room is smallish for its purpose, and you need a short cue. The man who installed it told him the last table he'd delivered, the owner had something he called his fridge shot. You had to open the fridge door to get enough room to make it.

More Chekov than Stoppard—all that billiards, and the sense of impending evacuation of the big, white slightly squirearchical house. But there's nothing to be read into that. By next week Stoppard will have four plays running in London at the same time, and all of them—even his adaptation of Schnitzler at the National—bear his inimitable hallmark.

All that's changed in the five years since *Travesties* is the kind of product he's stamped it on. *Dogg's Hamlet, Cahoot's Macbeth* starts its previews next week at the Collegiate Theatre—the first production of Ed Berman's British American Repertory Company—and it should, if rumour is right, give a glimpse of both kinds of Stoppard.

Dogg's Hamlet includes his 15-minute version of the WS masterpiece done as a school play, which should give us Stoppard the vivid wordsmith and striker of theatrical sparks. *Cahoot's Macbeth* stems from the experience of one of Stoppard's Czech theatrical friends who, banned from public performance, took a mini-*Macbeth* round the private homes of Prague with five actors and a suitcase.

Unseen, it would seem to offer the Stoppard of the past two years, the concerned playwright, the usually vivid wordsmith, and hammer of regimes, from the National Union of Journalists to the Kremlin, that are seen to suppress basic freedoms.

The difference is between *Rosencrantz and Guildenstern Are Dead* or *Travesties,* or *Dirty Linen,* and, in contrast, his television *Professional Foul* or his Previnised work for full orchestra and actors, *Every Good Boy Deserves Favour.* Between the hallucinogenic trip on words and pure ideas, and the more conventional intoxication of good causes.

But as Stoppard tells it, there was no conversion, no road back from the Damascene. Years ago, accused of failing to face head-on the problems of the world, he over-reacted with a bon mot about having "the courage of my lack of convictions." But his truthful feeling at that time, he says, was "not that I had no convictions, but that a lot of my work connected with the same sort of areas of interest as more overtly social plays, but did so in much more generalised terms."

In the past two years the plays have become more specific, and for specific reasons, *Jumpers* and *Professional Foul* both have professors of moral philosophy as their protagonists. *Jumpers* (1972) is a comic farce, full of brilliantly, entirely theatrical inventions. *Professional Foul* (1977) is about a real place—Prague—and real dilemmas, written within the constraints of television and realist conventions.

But both, says Stoppard, address themselves to the same moral questions. "Both are about the way human beings are supposed to behave towards each other."

"*Professional Foul* had to be realistic . . . because whether the audience is aware of it or not, and on the whole they aren't, the effectiveness of dangerous theatrical devices on the stage depends on them being difficult to do in the physical situation you are working in.

"Once you have a camera and editing facilities, I lose all interest in trying to astonish people by what actually happens, because anything *can*."

The dangerous theatrical devices, and the free-flowing style that went with them, in *Jumpers* and *Travesties,* have been abandoned in the next of his big stage plays, *Night and Day,* still running at the Phoenix, because *Night and Day* is a West End play, and for that purpose "you can't have 15 acrobats" (though he does have a Jeep drive on stage).

It's about the mores, and some would say the morons, of Fleet Street, and he wanted to write "a story telling play, you know, one which didn't suddenly stand on its head and start to rhyme."

Stoppard has a great admiration for the press in the abstract which reaches its apogee in his admiration for the foreign correspondent writing his story while bullets ricochet off his Olivetti portable. "I was very interested in the idea of people risking their lives for what was, in the real world, a commercial enterprise.

"After all, if you were selling Leyland cars, and you felt you could sell six Morris Marinas in Managua if you could just get through to the showroom . . . I mean, you wouldn't think, I'll get into a crouch and just run in a zig-zag manner to the Leyland dealer, and I'll sell six more Marinas. But a guy who's working for a newspaper, at the end of one of those lines of connection, is merely working for a different set of shareholders. In a sense. Obviously he's not.

"But whatever conscious level it's done on, the person in the play who says that information, in itself, is light—about anything—does speak for me."

Which he says is a *Boy's Own Paper* kind of sentiment (and mixed with a total aesthetic distaste for some of the popular press) that nevertheless expresses a reality.

Night and Day lacks what the Stoppard fan has most eagerly come to expect: the verbal glitter that in *Jumpers* and *Travesties* always seemed more than that; a running commentary on language itself. A bit of that is back on stage in *Undiscovered Country*, where it is always possible to blame the boredom on Schnitzler and credit the wit to Stoppard.

For instance, at one point there is a Schnitzler bit where the character says that yearning is good for the economy of the soul, and human relationships should be orientated more towards yearning for people than towards habit. The final Stoppard version runs: "In an ideal world, more and more people would see less and less of each other."

Stoppard says "I don't want to feel of myself that I now exist to scan the political victims of Eastern Europe, and then reach for my pistol. That's not how I see myself." *Professional Foul, Every Good Boy Deserves Favour, Cahoot's Macbeth* have all, in the past couple of years, found him scanning in that way, but by incident rather than design. And the Schnitzler adaptation—an equally incidental, or accidental, task—is a reminder that the Stoppard touch is intact.

When Peter Johns produced his camera, Stoppard brought out his. Some months before, he had taken a whole series of shots of three cigarette lighters, posed on the window sill, so that they looked as though they were giant megaliths in a landscape of lawn and dark, blue-green trees. After Paul Nash, rather than *After Magritte.* He wanted to try different exposures and apertures. But, Johns points out, it's a fully automatic camera.

"I know," says Stoppard. "But it offends my sense of elegant economy to have a control and not to use it—it must be for something."

Stoppard's Intellectual Cartwheels Now with Music

Mel Gussow

Just prior to the New York opening of *Every Good Boy Deserves Favour,* Stoppard talked about the distinction he makes between his "plays of ideas" and his "entertainments." Stoppard's most recent work, *Dogg's Hamlet, Cahoot's Macbeth,* had opened in London at the Collegiate Theatre on 17 July 1979 after a six-week tour of provincial theaters. On the day before the London opening, Stoppard was still making last-minute topical additions to the play and director Ed Berman indicated that Stoppard planned "to update the piece—daily if necessary—to keep it current with recent developments in Prague." That process continued not only with the production Berman brought to Washington, D.C., in September 1979 and to New York in October 1979, but in further topical allusions Stoppard added to the play—redubbed *Mackoon's Hamlet, Cahoot's Macbeth*—for a production at San Diego State University in November 1981. Talking to Mel Gussow about the individual origins of *Every Good Boy* and *Night and Day* and his adaptation of a Schnitzler play as *Undiscovered Country,* Stoppard emphasizes that his plays "don't break rules" but are "real play[s] about real people." In terms reminiscent of a similar declaration by T. S. Eliot, Stoppard asserts that he is "a conservative in politics, literature, education and theater."

With the opening tomorrow night of *Every Good Boy Deserves Favour* at the Metropolitan Opera House New Yorkers will have an opportunity

From the *New York Times,* 29 July 1979.

to see the political and musical side of that acrobatic English play-wright Tom Stoppard. This "play for actors and orchestra" by Mr. Stoppard and André Previn, the conductor and composer, is about a Russian dissident who is confined in a hospital room with a madman who thinks he has a symphony orchestra at his disposal. Right now Londoners have a choice of four Stoppards. *Night and Day,* now starring Maggie Smith, who is scheduled to head the cast when the play comes to Broadway next season, is a current success on the West End. Mr. Stoppard's adaptation of Arthur Schnitzler's *Undiscovered Country* is a major production in the repertory of the National Theatre. The author's political cartoon, *Dirty Linen,* is a long-running comedy hit. A new play, *Dogg's Hamlet, Cahoot's Macbeth,* a combination of two short Stoppard works, has just opened to generally positive reviews, inaugurating the new British American Repertory Company (BARC), which plans to tour the package to America.

This exceptionally busy Stoppard season marks the culmination of 18 months of nonstop activity, which also included writing the screenplay for Otto Preminger's film version of Graham Greene's *The Human Factor.* Stepping momentarily off the assembly line, Mr. Stoppard talked about the cross-currents of his rapidly flowering career.

This career has taken him from *Rosencrantz and Guildenstern Are Dead,* his backstairs look at the castle at Elsinore which was a Broadway hit in 1967, through the philosophical headstands of *Jumpers* and the literary cartwheels of *Travesties* into what could be considered his mature, socially conscious phase. This is the Tom Stoppard of *Professional Foul* (a television drama about censorship and suppression behind the Iron Curtain) and *Night and Day,* a play about headline journalism and African insurrection. Asked if these latest works represented a new attitude, if he were in fact taking himself more seriously, he held fast to his cherished inconsistency. It was suggested that perhaps his career paralleled that of Woody Allen—as a humorist ripening into a serious artist. He smiled at the notion. If anything, he saw his career as representing the opposite of Mr. Allen's. In his words, "The boot is on the other foot."

He said that *Rosencrantz* was intended as a comedy, but claims were made by others as to its weighty philosophical and intellectual content. Trying to clarify the situation, he said, "All along I thought of myself as writing entertainments, like *The Real Inspector Hound* and plays of ideas like *Jumpers.* The confusion arises because I treat plays of ideas in just about the same knockabout way as I treat the entertainments."

For him, playwriting is an intuitive occupation. He acknowledged his natural gift for dialogue but underscored the fact that ideas for plays can come with agonizing slowness. Sometimes a push or a deadline helps. As a former journalist and quondam critic, he seems to thrive under artificial pressures.

He described the individual origins of his recent works. In the case of *Every Good Boy,* it was the offer—to write a theatrical piece for full orchestra—that was tempting. "I wasn't sitting there saying I want to write about a Russian dissident. I had to write a play for a small number of actors and a large orchestra. At first I decided that it would be about a zillionaire who had his own orchestra; after supper, the musicians would troop in to play. Then I thought, he could be a zillionaire who thinks he has an orchestra.

"Once the orchestra was in his imagination, he didn't have to be a zillionaire, he could be a lunatic. Coincidentally, I read about people locked away in asylums for political reasons. Suddenly the subject matter seemed appropriate to the form: the dissident is a discordant note in a highly orchestrated society.

"*Night and Day,*" he said, "was written for Michael Codron, who is a commercial West End producer—and that fact dictated the ground rules. "A play with 15 acrobats would be of no value to him," Mr. Stoppard said. He decided to write a "storytelling" play, one with a direct narrative line. In contrast with past Stoppard, *Night and Day* is a real play about real people. His chosen subject: journalism. "I've always wanted to write a play about journalism," he said. He explained his three-step progression: "I don't have a lot of ideas. I've been a journalist. It's absurd not to write about journalism sooner or later." He had no shortage of material—25 years of stored-up impressions, anecdotes and withering remarks. "My primary problem," he said, "is not what the play should be about on the abstract level, but who are the people in it—their gender, their age—and where are they?" Conceiving *Night and Day,* he asked himself, "Are they in Africa or in the reporter's room in Bristol?" He chose Africa. "I was interested in people endangering their lives in what is ostensibly a commercial enterprise." When it was suggested that it might not be clear which character represented his point of view, Mr. Stoppard replied: "I don't write plays with heroes who express my point of view. I write argument plays. I tend to write for two people rather than for One Voice. Rosencrantz and Guildenstern were two sides of one temperament. When I start writing I find it difficult, except on simple questions, to know where I stand—even in *Travesties* in the argument on art between James Joyce and Tristan

Tzara. Temperamentally and intellectually, I'm very much on Joyce's side, but I found it persuasive to write Tzara's speech. Faced with the problem of writing a scene, I found things to say for Tzara. In *Jumpers*, George Moore represented a morality that I embrace, but both Moore and Archibald Jumpers spoke for me. This is also true of *Night and Day*. There are various things said by various people that I agree with. The things I write are not consistent enough to keep an interview tidy."

Asked to define his role as playwright, Mr. Stoppard said: "In general terms I'm not a playwright who is interested in character with a capital K and psychology with a capital S. I'm a playwright interested in ideas and forced to invent characters to express those ideas. All my people speak the same way, with the same cadences and sentence structures. They speak as I do. When I write an African president into a play, I have to contrive to make him the only African president who speaks like me." What if you write an American play, he was asked. Mr. Stoppard replied: "All the Americans would have to be educated at Sandhurst or Christchurch—Rhodes scholars discussing John Wayne." Doesn't that limit you? "It limits me in areas in which I'm not interested in expanding."

One area that does interest Mr. Stoppard is adaptations—on stage as well as in films. Asked what motivated him to adapt Schnitzler, he responded in the negative. "What it wasn't was a long interest in Austria and Austrian drama in general and Schnitzler in particular.

"What it was—while rehearsing *Night and Day* in a church hall in Chelsea, I saw a copy of a literal translation of *Undiscovered Country* on Peter Wood's table. I was just being nosy. They had asked somebody to adapt it, but he pulled out. My interest was partly because Peter Wood would direct it and John Wood would act in it. Once I read the play, I agreed with Peter. It was remarkable, a play completely unknown in England, and worthy to stand with Ibsen and English contemporaries." He stressed that for him the choice was accidental. "I might have found myself doing whatever was on Peter Wood's table— Molnár, Feydeau, little known Ibsen."

Because he does not speak German, he worked closely with a German-speaking student. "I started by doing an obsessively faithful first draft—accurate but actable." Then he began asking himself, "What would I have done if I were writing this play." The final version is "considerably shorter" but "very faithful in most respects. It is a bit titivated," he admitted. "For someone like me who enjoys writing dialogue but has a terrible time writing plays, adaptation is joy time. It's a craftsman's job, not 'my soul speaks through Schnitzler.' You go around with a bag of tools doing jobs between personal plays."

His new play, *Dogg's Hamlet, Cahoot's Macbeth,* is an original, with a double assist from his old collaborator, Shakespeare. As is often the case with Mr. Stoppard, this is a melding of past efforts. The first half, *Dogg's Hamlet,* is itself an amalgam of two sketches—a short working-class vaudeville skit called *Dogg's Our Pet* in which odd words are substituted for others (for example, "gymshoes" means "excellent"), and *Dogg's Hamlet,* a 15-minute condensation of *Hamlet,* which was supposed to be staged on top of London buses. At first he had thought about writing a five-minute *War and Peace.*

For BARC's tour, the director Ed Berman wanted Mr. Stoppard to create a second matching piece. For a long stretch the playwright was idealess. Then he thought he would write a play about Ernest Hemingway. "I was very taken with his writing when I was a late teenager. I know a great deal about him. So...elegant economy strikes again! Then I realized, I knew a great deal but I had nothing to say about him." Shelving Hemingway (perhaps Hemingway at Oxford is in his future), he remembered Pavel Kohout, the Czechoslovakian playwright. Kohout had written him a letter about his private, 75-minute living-room version *Macbeth,* staged in defiance of an official edict preventing some citizens from working in the theater. In Mr. Stoppard's show, Kohout becomes Cahoot, and the production is interrupted by an inspector who seems to have wandered in from *The Real Inspector Hound* and a moving man who wanders in from *Dogg's Hamlet.* Trying to explain the relationship of his *Hamlet* and *Macbeth,* he said, "The first play can be done without the second but the second cannot be done unless you've seen the first one first."

Because Mr. Stoppard's plays are becoming more political, it seemed appropriate to ask him about his politics. In some quarters he has been criticized as right-wing. "I try to be consistent about moral behavior," he said. "Let other people hang labels. It's a tactical distortion to label certain attitudes right or left. I'm a conservative with a small c. I'm a conservative in politics, literature, education and theater. My main objection is to ideology and dogma—Holy Writ for adherents." Turning to theater, he said, "My plays don't break rules. If you take the orchestra away from *Every Good Boy,* it is a series of scenes telling a coherent story." When he was reminded about the naked lady on the flying trapeze in *Jumpers,* he said, "That was a real naked lady on a real trapeze, not just a collage of intriguing images. I don't write

Terence Rattigan plays but I think I have more in common with Rattigan than with Robert Wilson. We attempt to be coherent tellers of tales. In *Travesties* a lot of odd things happen, but the crucial thing is that the whole play is filtered through the memory of an old man—and the audience knows it." Then he offered one final thought: "Plays are events rather than texts. They're written to happen, not to be read."

This Time, Stoppard Plays It (Almost) Straight

Robert Berkvist

In Washington, D.C., for the American premiere of *Night and Day*, Stoppard had the opportunity to counter the perception that his play was a scathing attack on journalism. Stoppard had injected himself into a 1977 "journalists' closed shop" controversy with a letter to the editor of *The Times* arguing that an unclosed shop creates a state of affairs "called freedom of expression" and a closed shop results in an "absence of freedom of expression." Claiming that "very few people think about journalism on the level of social philosophy," Stoppard insists to Robert Berkvist that those characters in *Night and Day* who argue for the importance of freedom of the press "utterly speak for me."

Tom Stoppard, verbal gymnast, master of the mind-bending pun and the literary backflip, whose plays are notorious for standing logic on its head and history on its ear, has put aside his bag of tricks for a while. Not that the still youthful British playwright doesn't indulge his love of linguistic Ping-Pong in his latest venture, *Night and Day*, which opens Tuesday at the ANTA with Maggie Smith in the leading role. This time around, however, Mr. Stoppard is playing it relatively straight. In fact, he admits almost sheepishly to having written "one of those beginning, middle and end plays with one set and eight characters, including a woman who's falling for somebody."

Night and Day takes place in a newly independent African nation, Kambawe, where a British mining engineer and his wife are caught

From the *New York Times*, 25 November 1979.

up in the first rumblings of a civil war. Kambawe's autocratic president is being challenged by a rebellious army officer, and the countryside is crawling with trigger-happy soldiers and war-happy journalists. When the journalists settle down at the engineer's house for the duration, complications ensue—some of them romantic, some tragic.

Linear plot? Love story? Is this the Stoppard who wrote *Rosencrantz and Guildenstern Are Dead, Jumpers* and *Travesties,* and the recent, extravagantly zany *Dogg's Hamlet, Cahoot's Macbeth?* If so, has he suddenly decided to hang up his madcap and become a different kind of playwright?

Mr. Stoppard, looking weary and a bit rumpled, pondered the question over a jug of morning coffee in his Washington hotel room. Across the street at the Kennedy Center, where *Night and Day* was being polished for its Broadway opening, preparations were underway for a midday rehearsal at the Eisenhower Theater. A substitution was being made in the cast, which also features Joseph Maher, Paul Hecht and Peter Evans, and Mr. Stoppard planned to attend in case the director, Peter Wood, called for adjustments.

"I'm a writer of comedy," he said at last, taking short, nervous puffs at one of the cigarettes he chain-smokes but doesn't inhale. "My favorite noise is an audience laughing in the theater. There also is a side of me which makes me want to prove I can do things which nobody is really asking me to prove at all. I'd written plays which by certain standards were described as being bizarre or fantastic. I'd also been told repeatedly, by actresses and others, that I hadn't ever written a really good part for a woman. Quite separately, I had decided I'd like to write a play about journalism, and I felt I owed a play to Michael Codron, a West End producer who had put on a play of mine called *The Real Inspector Hound* in 1968.

"Well, when I finally got round to doing it, I knew quite clearly I couldn't write a West End play which required 14 acrobats. There's a certain amount of down-to-earth plumbing about these things, and such a play would be impossible to stage in the commercial theater. I was also thinking that I wanted to demonstrate I could actually write a story-telling number, one in which people don't suddenly jump through flaming hoops and recite a poem."

Eventually, the elements meshed and the result was *Night and Day,* which opened in London a year ago and is still running there, having starred in turn Diana Rigg, Miss Smith and now Susan Hampshire. "The best thing that can happen to a playwright," Mr. Stoppard said, "is to discover that two plays he's been thinking about can actually be the same play. That way, with some luck, you can wind up with more than the sum of the two parts. Journalism was an interest of mine, I wanted to write a ... love story, really, and finally the arcs intersected."

Some observers have interpreted *Night and Day* as a scathing attack on journalism. Was that his intention? "The extraordinary thing is that the opposite is the case," he said, shaking his head wonderingly. "I'm a lover of and an apologist for journalism. The play actually is saying that the aspects of journalism which one might well disapprove of are the price we pay for the part that matters, and that the part that matters is absolutely vital. Ruth, the engineer's wife, expresses her withering scorn for journalists, true, but one meets people all the time who feel that way about certain kinds of journalism. Very few people think about journalism on the level of social philosophy, or examine it for its importance.

"I characteristically write plays for two voices," he went on. "Obviously I try to be as persuasive as possible on both sides. Unusally for me, there are things said in this play which utterly speak for me, things very much on the side of free journalism. I think information about anything is its own justification. As one of the characters in the play says, 'Information is light.'"

Mr. Stoppard says he chose to write about journalism mainly because he himself once worked as a reporter, columnist and critic. "I have to use everything I've got," he explained. "Unlike some writers, I don't have a long list of ideas for plays that I'm waiting to get to. On the other hand, I don't use my own experience in any direct way in the play at all." He began his career as a general assignment reporter with the *Bristol Evening World* in 1954, he recalled, covering "the courts, the inquests, city hall."

"In the afternoon I'd be writing up the meeting of some city planning committee and then perhaps be sent off to the suburbs to review an Agatha Christie play being staged in a church," he said. "I thought it was extremely exciting." He still regards the profession as "an adventure" and is particularly fascinated by the "curious question" of the war correspondent who fights for the privilege of being sent into an arena in which he stands a good chance of being wounded or killed. It is one of the questions he addresses in *Night and Day,* along with the responsibilities of the "popular press."

"At first I admired the sense of excitement whipped up by popular journalism," he said, "but now I find I read most of the mass circulation papers with a sense of despair that grown men can feel it's a worthwhile way of life to present news in that form, and that infinitely greater numbers of people wish to read it. I find that depressing and baffling. The other side of the coin is that there's an equally substantial body of British journalism which to me is an absolutely vital part of our society."

There are those who feel that Mr. Stoppard's recent work—his television play, *Professional Foul,* and the stage plays, *Every Good Boy Deserves Favor* and *Cahoot's Macbeth,* all of which concern freedom of expression in Iron Curtain countries—signals a change of direction on his part, a new seriousness of purpose. The critic Kenneth Tynan has speculated that "history has lately been forcing Stoppard into the arena of commitment." On the other hand, Mr. Stoppard himself has declared, "I'm not impressed by art *because* it's political. I believe in art being good art or bad art, not relevant art or irrelevant art." Does he now see himself as having assumed a newly political stance?

"That's just not the way it looks from my end of the telescope at all," he said, after a long pause. "*Jumpers* has got the same subject as *Professional Foul.* They're both about professors of moral philosophy, but the treatment is entirely different. *Jumpers* is a farce, while *Professional Foul* is a sort of realistic look at a real situation. I've just written the next thing I wanted to write. Even with these four plays—I'm including *Night and Day*—which do address themselves in a more direct way to topics of the day, even with them behind me, I have no sense whatsoever that a fifth play would be a natural successor. For all my sense of purpose tells me now, I might write a play in which an English duchess comes through the French windows with a basket of begonias and a tennis racquet and announces that the butler is dead in the library. I'm just not sitting here thinking, 'From now on, I'm such and such a kind of writer.'"

Mr. Stoppard, who is 42, says he is still learning about playwriting and that "the things that make a piece of drama work" are still mysterious to him. When he is working on a play he writes every day, after seeing his children off to school ("There are four of them, aged 5 to 13"). He writes in longhand and revises each speech until he is satisfied with it; only then does he go on to the next one. As a result, he says, his first drafts tend to be fairly close approximations of the final product, subject to the valuable modifications suggested by the play's cast and director. "They are the ones who save the play from being a kind of rigid construct," he said, smiling. "You have to grate-fully receive the contributions of your colleagues."

As a result, Mr. Stoppard says it is not unusual for him to continue making script revisions long after one of his plays has opened. "I rewrote perhaps a half-dozen pages of *Night and Day* while we were rehearsing in England," he said, "and, in fact, revised a section of the second act three or four months after the play had opened."

His biggest problem as a playwright, he says, is deciding how to populate his work. The ideas come first and the characters follow, often slowly: "My plays, generally speaking, derive from a desire to discuss and dispute a certain subject. My plays are not about the inter-action of character. Another kind of writer might say, 'I've got this marvelous idea for a play,' and what he means is that he's thought up this wonderful grandmother and grandfather and their granddaughter who works in a baker's shop and marries a soldier. Now, he thinks, what can they talk about? I have the opposite problem. I want to write a play about journalism or art or morality—*but who the devil are the people?*"

He laughed, stubbed out his cigarette and promptly shook an-other from the nearly empty pack. The time of greatest anxiety, he went on, is "getting as far as page one." In the case of *Night and Day*, he said, he had been driving home one day when he decided— "though I couldn't explain why"—that the setting for the play had to be a foreign country. "Suddenly, for the first time, I felt I had one piece of solid ground for my extremely abstract play about journalism, that it would not take place at a provincial newspaper office or in a publisher's boardroom. I worked from that point onward, choosing an African setting because I wanted a plausible locale where British reporters could be covering some kind of war."

Once he had the context, he said, the rest came more easily and he finished the first draft in four months. *Travesties*, on the other hand, took him nine months to write, while his much admired 80-minute television play, *Professional Foul*, poured forth in less than three weeks. "I write because I want to get out of jail, really," he said. "I find the whole thing so anxious that I think of it as being rather like a sentence that you have to serve. So I just keep going. You're frightened of losing it, you know, afraid that it may escape from you at any time. So every hour you put in, you've trapped a bit more of it—even if it's three lines in a day and a half, which it often is. You scratch away at it."

He is not scratching away at anything new, at present, having been fully occupied by revisions and rehearsals of various productions of his work, including his screen adaptation of Graham Greene's *The Human Factor*. He has been asked to write a children's book and the idea appeals to him. Other than that, he says, he looks forward to a period of inactivity, "a time to fill up a bit."

He stood up, stretched and walked to the window where he stood looking out at the gray clouds hanging over the capital skyline. "I don't know," he said quietly. "In a funny kind of way, I haven't got any great desire to write plays at all anymore. At the moment, it doesn't seem important that I write plays. I'm in a different state of mind. I'd like to leave myself receptive. I'd like to be struck by lightning, so to speak, but I'm not going to go around looking for storms. I'm tired, I've been living in hotels, I miss my children. Of course," he said, brightening, "in a little while, when I'm back in my own house with my family and my books, everything could be quite the other way around."

Tom Stoppard and the Politics of Morality

Daniel Henninger

After its American premiere in Washington, D.C., in October 1979, *Night and Day* moved to New York, where it opened on 27 November 1979. At the time, American hostages were still being held in Iran and a line in *Night and Day* began getting applause from Broadway audiences apparently frustrated about America letting itself be "pushed around." Prompted by that phenomenon, the arts editor of the *Wall Street Journal* conducted a telephone interview with Stoppard about the playwright's views on American foreign policy, Russian imperialism, and the moral perceptions of a child. In the middle of the trans-Atlantic conversation, Stoppard suddenly interjected: "You know, I must say that I've never been asked to talk about any of these things with a journalist before. This is a very unusual kind of interview." When his conversation with Henninger turns to the conflict between ideological rigidness and individual freedom, Stoppard offers as his own position statements that are at times remarkably similar to those of Pavel Hollar in *Professional Foul*.

A funny thing happened on Broadway not long ago: An audience began applauding a character's dialogue. The play was Tom Stoppard's *Night and Day*. The Russians had not invaded Afghanistan at the time of this performance, but the embassy hostages had been languishing for some time in Tehran. The United States was full of nervous political talk, and *Night and Day*, like Mr. Stoppard's other recent plays, contains a fair amount of talk about politics.

From the *Wall Street Journal,* 1 February 1980.

The play is set in the imaginary African nation of Kambawe, recently independent and on the brink of civil war. Western reporters are arriving to seek an interview with Kambawe's elusive President Mageeba, and reporter Dick Wagner asks a local British mining executive named Carson how he thinks Mageeba will fare against the revolutionary opposition.

"I think [Mageeba is] going to go in with air strikes and tanks and lose half of them in a week," says Carson, "and appeal to the free world about Russian interference. I also think that the British and the Americans will protest, and all the time they're protesting the Russians will be interfering the stuffing out of Mageeba's army, until Kambawe is about as independent as Lithuania...."

That didn't get the applause, but it set up the audience for what was coming. Wagner asks Mageeba if he will seek military aid from the U.S. and Britain. "I'd be a fool to do that," Mageeba replies. "Your record of cowardice in Africa stretches from Angola to Eritrea [Ethiopia]." At this, sharp applause burst from pockets of the audience, the exchange having apparently tripped the frustration of people who thought then that America was letting itself be "pushed around." A call to the stage manager later revealed that Mageeba's line had indeed been producing this reaction during the play's run, though not every night.

In a telephone interview from his home in the English village of Iver, Mr. Stoppard was asked if Mageeba's charge of cowardice expressed his own point of view. "If instead of 'cowardice' he'd used a word like 'short-sightedness,' that would have more nearly expressed my feelings," Mr. Stoppard said. "I haven't made a study of international affairs. I'm simply reacting as a newspaper reader, and obviously there's a point of view that Russian imperialism has been allowed to have too easy a ride. That seems a very plausible proposition to me."

Plausible propositions are the philosopher's pathways to truth, and for some time now Tom Stoppard, who is 42, has been turning philosophical arguments into dramatic art to reveal truths bearing on the relationship between the individual and society. In Mr. Stoppard's mind the core of these truths is personal freedom. The lines about Russia in *Night and Day* are incidental to the play's purpose, which is to argue the case for a free press. But one of the most effective ways to dramatize freedom of opinion and conscience is by writing about their absence; as a result, Marxism has been taking its lumps in Mr. Stoppard's recent work.

Professional Foul, a play written for TV and shown here in 1978, has among its characters a Czech dissident, Pavel Hollar, who has written a doctoral thesis on Thomas Paine and John Locke. He is employed in Prague as a cleaner of toilets. Hollar beseeches a visiting British professor of moral philosophy to smuggle out his thesis for foreign publication and desperately summarizes the paper to persuade the professor of its value.

"The ethics of the State must be judged against the fundamental ethic of the individual," Hollar says earnestly. "The human being, not the citizen. I conclude there is an obligation, a human responsibility, to fight against State correctness. Unfortunately that is not a safe conclusion." After the visit, Hollar is arrested.

Mr. Stoppard next wrote about Soviet prison hospitals in *Every Good Boy Deserves Favor*. Alexander, a political prisoner, is being held in a hospital run by a Doctor of Semantics. Early on, Alexander's young son, Sacha, recites the pristine logic of the laws of geometry to a teacher, who in turn explains the Soviet logic of his father's detention.

Teacher: "Open the book. Pencil and paper. You see what happens to anti-social malcontents." Sacha: "Will I be sent to the lunatics' prison?" Teacher: "Certainly not . . . The asylum is for malcontents who don't know what they're doing . . . They know what they're doing but they don't know it's anti-social . . . They know it's anti-social but they're fanatics . . . They're sick." Sacha does not believe this. He is terrified.

"It seems to me," says Mr. Stoppard, "that the point of view which these plays express is one which would be recognizable not merely to intellectuals but to an intelligent child—that something is self-evidently wrong."

"One of the things which complicates argument at the moment for me," he continued, "is that people are so clever that, paradoxically, they can be persuaded of almost anything. For example, if one were to say to an intelligent child the following: 'Life in East Germany is very agreeable, and there's a wall around it to keep people in,' the child would say, 'There's something wrong here.' But if you said it to a professor of political science or of political history, you'd have a much better chance of persuading him that what you said isn't nonsensical."

Thus Mr. Stoppard's characters are often smart people adept at smart talk, Harlem Globetrotters of the intellect, passing around an argument. A Stoppard play delights the mind; it makes us laugh. But the unfunny subject of the recent plays (all available in readable texts from Grove Press) is repression, and, by the plays' ends, Mr. Stoppard has used events and the pressure of conscience to force his clever characters—and us—to see, as a child would, that "there's something wrong here."

Mr. Stoppard in his recent work has undoubtedly done an effective job of lampooning the left. In *Night and Day,* for instance, he spiked the doctrinaire Fabian socialism of the British reporter Dick Wagner, who on a matter of pro-labor principle wires back from Africa that his paper is using a nonunion freelance writer in Kambawe. Result: The union walks out, making it impossible to publish Wagner's interview with President Mageeba.

But Stoppard says he is not so much interested in hanging Marxeism out to dry as he is in showing how ideological rigidness sits heavily on individual freedom. "If you take any ideology you like," he says, "which might be labeled Marxism or Islam or conservatism, what happens is that people justify their actions by referring to a 'holy book' of principles, as though these principles had a preexistence of their own and stood as an endorsement of any action. If an ideology becomes too rigid about applying the lessons of that book, one finds inevitably that the result is unfairness.

"Surely," he says, "the truth is the other way around. However inflexible our set of beliefs, whether it's mine or the ayatollah's, however authentic their existence may be, the truth is that they owe their existence to individual acts between individuals, which themselves are derived from an individual's intuitive sense of what is right and wrong."

Values based on an intuitive sense of right and wrong would serve pretty well as the pragmatic ethic of a decent politician. James MacGregor Burns, in his biography of Franklin Roosevelt, suggested that FDR believed "men can live together only on the basis of certain simple, traditional ethical rules."

Pairing the beliefs of a playwright and a President seems odd at first, but I think that has more to do with our prevailing view of the cultural role played by American writers. Our novelists and playwrights tend not to write about political ideas anymore (indignant letters to the *New York Times* excepted), and most that do suggest strongly that politics is an instinctively immoral enterprise. Tom Stoppard seems to view public and private morality as more complicated and interesting than that. He is using the special revelations of drama to help us understand the recurring tension in modern societies between politics and personal freedom.

Double Acts: Tom Stoppard and Peter Wood

Ronald Hayman

In 1972 Peter Wood directed the National Theatre premiere of *Jumpers* by Tom Stoppard, beginning a remarkable working relationship between the two men. Stoppard credits the selection of music in virtually all his plays to Wood and claims that some of the theatrical moments he likes best in his own plays were devised by Wood. In a joint interview, Stoppard and his long-term director discuss the way they work together in rehearsals. Stoppard contrasts his own "reluctance to be over-explicit" with Wood's "fear that the audience isn't being given enough information." Focusing on *Night and Day,* they reveal that Stoppard added a crucial speech for Wagner as a result of the director's sense of the need for further interaction between two of the characters.

In 1958 there was not much precedent for what John Dexter told Arnold Wesker after reading *The Kitchen:* "It needs a middle section. I don't know what it is, I don't care what it is, except it's got to be quiet. Now go away and write it."

Today it is less unusual for a director to ask for substantial rewriting, and to work closely with the writer, rather as a film director does, on the revision or completion of the script. Sometimes the collaboration develops into a long-term partnership. Dexter directed the first five of Wesker's plays, and the partnership spurted back into life for *The Old Ones* in 1972, and in 1976 for the American production of *The Merchant.* Since co-directing Pinter's *The Collection* with him in 1962,

From the *Sunday Times Magazine,* 2 March 1980.

Peter Hall has directed all his new plays, while Pinter has directed most of Simon Gray's. Michael Blakemore's partnership with Peter Nichols lasted from *A Day in the Death of Joe Egg* (1967) until *Privates on Parade* (1977), and Lindsay Anderson's with David Storey from *In Celebration* (1969) to *Life Class* (1974).

Since 1972 Peter Wood has directed all Tom Stoppard's full-length plays. Michael Rudman has directed all Michael Frayn's from *Alphabetical Order* (1975); Robert Kidd has directed all Christopher Hampton's.

In all these cases the director has indubitably influenced the writer's development, though it would be hard to analyse how. Conversely there are playwrights whose careers have patently suffered because they have never had such a symbiotic relationship with one director. The most obvious case is John Osborne, who would never do any rewriting or even cutting. His recent plays might have stood a better chance of being staged if he had had a strong enough director first to work with him on the text and then to champion him.

The best partnerships, like the best marriages, are those in which the interdependence is limited and invisible. But the stresses in the relationship are considerable, and the divorce rate high. Directors hardly ever seem dependent on one playwright, but playwrights can come to seem dependent on one director, and naturally don't like to. Arnold Wesker has had more success abroad than in England as a director of his own plays; Tom Stoppard says he sometimes comes home "as high as a kite" with the idea of directing, "but when we move from the rehearsal room into the theatre, I feel out of my depth in a way that has nothing to do with simply learning various techniques." Peter Wood kept the opening moment of *Night and Day* "a complete secret, so that he'd have the thrill of seeing the curtain go up and seeing $3\frac{1}{2}$ ft. of dry ice looking at him."

There are many areas of possible collaboration between writer and director. Some of it is tacit. The mere presence of the author in the rehearsal room affects the actors, who tend to become more guarded and less creative, until he becomes as close an ally as the director. Before this can happen the director has to overcome the anxiety that his authority will be undermined or that the actors will be confused if two people talk to them about how to interpret the text.

As yet there have been all too few experiments in cross-fertilisation between creativity of actor and the author. Until comparatively recently most actors had little chance to do anything beyond what they were told by the leading actor or autocratic director. Even today they have relatively few chances of inventing dialogue or influencing the development of a story, but one of the director's functions now is to mediate between the two kinds of creativity. Though improvisation is now widely used, we still have very few companies like Joint Stock which operate on the assumption that author and actors should get together before the script is even begun, let alone finished. But it is something that there is now so much more fluidity around that pivotal relationship between playwright and director.

Tom Stoppard and Peter Wood

STOPPARD: A good deal of the work ends up in areas where we've reconciled each other to a middle way of doing something. This may be to do with *my* reluctance to be over-explicit and *his* fear that the audience isn't being given enough information. I like to get the shock of finding things out, and in some cases Peter saves me from their *never* finding out.

WOOD: With *Night and Day* I took refuge in an imaginary character called Rupert, so that I could say: "Yes, I absolutely understand this, but I don't think Rupert does." I'm constantly aware that you can't do in a play what you can in a book—turn back the page to find out what has happened to make this happen.

STOPPARD: I think partnerships are based on compatibility of temperament more than of intellect. One finds a person's temperament and personality agreeable or not, and there are some great directors with whom I don't think I'd feel at home. Peter and I possibly err on the side of rehearsals being—

WOOD: Too jokey—

STOPPARD: They're almost too much fun, really, sometimes.

WOOD: But the performers must feel free to risk looking foolish or their suggestions sounding inept, or whatever. They must have that sense of ease.

STOPPARD: There's a certain kind of actor who doesn't feel that he's rehearsing at all, the way we work. My plays for me—in my head, before anyone gets hold of a text—make a certain quality of noise, which rises and falls at certain places, and slows and speeds up at certain places, and much of our rehearsal consists of my trying to explain what this noise is like, and trying to make the actors make this noise; and then Peter and the actors working from the other end, show me how the action can speed up in a different place, and not get loud there, but get very quiet, and it's my turn to be shown an alternative orchestration for these voices.

WOOD: For me, to begin with, it was terribly formidable, because I'd never worked in rehearsal with the author there every day. I didn't know how delightful it was until we'd been rehearsing about three weeks, and Tom didn't come one morning, and I was mortally insulted. It was like an actor not coming to rehearsal. Because it's all there in one room, all gathered together and interacting in some very exciting way. You don't think: "I'll ring Tom later." There's that ready interpretative voice which enlarges your understanding of the line. Over and over again I've had immense light suddenly vouchsafed on a line or a moment I'd totally underrated when I read it.

STOPPARD: It's an event rather than a text that one is trying to convey. Text is merely an attempt to describe an event. I have very vivid recollections of being shown where there was a gaping hole in the text—at least once in *Night and Day,* and at least once in *Travesties,* and probably in *Jumpers* too. We've gone into rehearsal, and even—in the case of *Night and Day*—opened out of town, with a text that didn't include a two or three minute section which ultimately, without exaggeration, is the part of the play which I feel most pleased about.

WOOD: It was a great thrill when you phoned me on the Sunday between the two weeks at Wimbledon, and said in that comfortable way you can: "I've written a bloody good speech for Wagner."

STOPPARD: We opened the play without that scene in which he and she for once have the stage to themselves. By one devious route or another it was Peter who alerted me to its absence.

WOOD: It started with my saying: "There's nothing for Carson and Ruth." And you said: "I know about that," and that appeared very early in rehearsal. I just feel an emotional need to know this or that about X or Y. It's visceral.

STOPPARD: I find I don't actually know what you mean until I've forced you to give the actual dialogue, as though it were written for the worst possible kind of television cops and robbers, and then I find it from that—get a sense of what vaguely he feels should be happening at that moment, what isn't happening.

WOOD: A good example—talking over the telephone I say: "This lady goes through this play as a ball-breaker, mowing down everybody before her. Until that man can make her say 'Ouch', there's no play." But Tom's instinct was that Ruth wouldn't say ouch out loud, at least not yet, and not to Wagner. So he wrote the speech for Wagner, and her reply comes out as "If you're waiting for me to say 'Ouch', you're going to get cramp." So my offer was taken up but turned upside down in a way that refined it.

Trad Tom Pops In

David Gollob and David Roper

Acknowledging that "some critics have condemned Tom Stoppard's work for its innate frivolity," *Gambit* devoted a special issue to the playwright in an attempt to "redress the balance" so that "Stoppard's position as a serious contemporary artist should not be obscured." Stoppard had been stung by a lengthy profile Kenneth Tynan had published in the *New Yorker.* Appearing in 1977 prior to Tynan's untimely death, the profile seemed to bear the authority of a dying man's parting curse in its accusation that Stoppard was "withdrawing with style from the chaos." Stoppard would have to confront that charge again and again until eventually he claimed that the Tynan profile "seems to be the one thing on earth that everybody has read." The *Gambit* issue contains the most extensive interview Stoppard has given on his plays of the late 1970s. Asked whether the more overtly political content of *Professional Foul, Night and Day,* and *Every Good Boy Deserves Favour* signifies "a kind of movement from withdrawal to involvement," Stoppard affirms the continuity of his work, insisting that *Professional Foul* and *Jumpers* share many of the same concerns. In particular Stoppard rejects an equation between "serious, involved, engaged playwriting" and his use of a more naturalistic form. The interview contains Stoppard's fullest account of what he was seeking to do in *Professional Foul* and a substantial explanation of his concerns in *Night and Day.*

Thirteen years on and *Rosencrantz and Guildenstern* are still very much alive. *The Real Inspector Hound* is still nosing around, though *Dirty Linen*

From *Gambit*, 10, no. 37 (Summer 1981).

has finally come off, after an almost interminable hanging at the Arts Theatre in London. All round the world, in France, in Canada, in the States, the plays that first established Stoppard's reputation as a comic playwright with a message continue to delight, tease, and draw audiences.

But lately Tom's work seems to have modulated away from the glitter of Wildean disengagement, biting into the more meaty domains of freedom of expression in Czechoslovakia and freedom of the press in the embattled U.K. More matter with less art? Or a desire for art that matters more?

However you look at it, there is a distinctly politically conscious cloud darkening the later plays, and when Tom kindly consented to be interviewed by *Gambit*, I thought this would be an interesting area to probe around in, especially as the late Kenneth Tynan's article on Stoppard was lying in front of me, inviting questions about what Tynan had called Stoppard's shift from withdrawal to engagement.

GOLLOB: Let's plunge in . . . with a bathing anecdote. This is an apocryphal anecdote about A. J. Ayer going swimming with some other philosophy dons at a men only bathing area on the Cherwell. They are frolicking around starkers when all of a sudden these girls go by in a punt. All reach for their towels in a mad rush to cover their private parts except for Ayer who covers his head. Do you know the story?

STOPPARD: Yes, and the story is a lot older than Freddy Ayer.

GOLLOB: Is it?

STOPPARD: Yes, I mean I suppose it may have happened to somebody sometime but I'm not even sure that it did. It's a story told about Oxford dons, sometimes about a particular one and it's usually set in a sort of Edwardian England when I suppose naked men were even more shocking, but let's assume it happened to Freddy as well and—I'll take the supplementary if you like.

GOLLOB: I grabbed this little anecdote because I'd like to explore the role of the disinterested play of the intellect in your work and ask you if we should see the thematic darkening and return to naturalism characterized by your most recent work—*Night and Day,* for example—as a kind of movement from withdrawal to involvement, as some have put it . . . as if you were covering your cleverness in order to force it to serve a more serious moral purpose. In other words, is this your response to the kind of criticism that has been levelled against you by people like Tynan and Walter Kerr: that *Travesties* is, for example a 'three decker bus going nowhere' or Kerr's description—'an intellectual hummingbird unable to light anywhere'... Were you consciously reacting to this kind of criticism of insubstantiality?

STOPPARD: Not consciously, as I was about to say. If it is a response, it's a deeply subconscious one. All that I'm aware of is that I had practical reasons for writing *Professional Foul* which is the first more or less realistic play I've written for ages, and is so, as far as I was concerned at the time of writing, because I knew I was writing for television. The attraction of unexpected, unnatural, or 'unnaturalistic' things happening on a stage is precisely that they *are* happening on a *stage*. The surprising effects depend partly on the audience's barely conscious knowledge of the limitations of a stage. A lot of things I like very much as pieces of staging in *Jumpers* or *Travesties* would be more or less pointless if you were making a movie of either of those plays. When I came to writing a play for TV I felt something of the same thing. I should make it clear that I'm speaking with hindsight knowledge now—in sitting down to write a play one doesn't really examine all these options—but I do know that I just thought, without even having to bother to think about it, that *Professional Foul* ought to be naturalistic, and that TV is best for that sort of play, and that its impact should be to do with human relationships and the way things are said and to whom they're said and not to do with the sort of ambushes I like to or did like to set up on a stage.

And then, *Night and Day,* the last stage-play I've written, is also a naturalistic play. I had a perfectly sound explanation for that as well, and a very mundane one. It was a play which I wrote for Michael Codron because I'd promised him a play ten years previously, and there were a number of considerations which were more or less self-conscious ones, to do with one set, and not too many actors, so that Michael Codron would be able to do it as a West End manager. I mean, giving him a play which started with fourteen acrobats wouldn't have pleased him. And because it was a play about journalism, one of the few times I've ever drawn on my own experience, even secondhand experience, because I didn't work on Fleet Street, I wanted to do a naturalistic play.

I was also interested by the way journalists tend to ape their fictitious models. It's a certain way of behaving which derives from 'tough' films. Of course, in naturalism there is a reciprocal thing between the model and life, and in thinking yes, yes, a play about journalists of some sort, again without a great deal of thought, I fell into a way of thinking about the material which led to a naturalistic play. Sorry to be so garrulous, but your question contains a lot of elements and I don't want to shortchange you ....

GOLLOB: Can I just try and focus it a bit? I located something that intrigued me in your critical preface to *Every Good Boy Deserves Favour* and *Professional Foul* where you describe an incident when Vladimir Bukovsky having been released from the Soviet Union attended a rehearsal of this play about him. There was a certain moment of malaise or embarrassment when the real thing, the real life issue came into contact with this very wonderful entertainment. I was wondering if this was a kind of fulcrum for you, seeing that you have mentioned *Professional Foul* as a naturalistic play, whereas *Every Good Boy* in its very playful way also dealt with a serious issue.

STOPPARD: The embarrassment which you refer to when Bukovsky attended a rehearsal wasn't really to do with the playfulness or otherwise of *Every Good Boy*. As a matter of fact, when he came we weren't doing one of the playful parts. Ian McKellen, one of the actors involved, playing one of the more serious characters, was in fact doing the least playful speech in the piece. So the feeling of unease which I got—which Ian got: as far as I can remember he couldn't carry on—wasn't to do with the discrepancy between the mood of the art and the mood of the real situation which this man represented. No, it was to do with the discrepancy between art and life full stop. And I think one would have felt the same thing if *King Lear* had been based on fact and Gloucester had wandered in—the same sort of embarrassment would have ensued. You know, what we were engaged in was a sort of artifice, and one knows that it's an artifice, I mean the whole *point* of it is that it is an artifice, not the point of the piece but the point of us being there together, was to simulate something, not to live it. And it was that discordance which suddenly went 'clang!'

Every Good Boy is about a serious subject. It's not a naturalistic piece, it's an odd sort of a piece that was defined by the situation it was to be performed in and by the people it was to be performed by, namely the orchestra. I can sum up this whole area of question, without necessarily suggesting it should be fore-closed, by saying it is not the case that one examines the nature of a subject matter and thereupon decides on using a certain kind of form ... Let me just think a minute . . . Let me just start that again. The equation which I would disavow is that any serious, involved, engaged playwriting is equated by this author with naturalism—no. The plays which I've written more recently which tend to be naturalistic and also tend to engage themselves with serious immediate matters are not exhibiting a relationship between those two facts ... as far as I am honestly aware ... if I can just add a rider to explain more fully what I mean.

See, at bottom, *Professional Foul* and *Jumpers* can each be described as a play about a moral philosopher preoccupied with the true nature of absolute morality, trying to separate absolute values from local ones and local situations. That description would apply to either play, yet one is a rampant farce and the other is a piece of naturalistic TV drama.

GOLLOB: *Professional Foul* also seems to bear certain similarities with the existentialist drama, the Sartrian theatre of situations, in the way that the central character becomes more aware of his global situation in terms of other men at grips with, engaged in the problems of life. He is prodded by a brutal awakening of consciousness—he goes to visit his former philosophy student in his flat in Prague and gets cornered by the police, missing this frivolous football match which is the real reason for his visit—he is prodded by this brutal awakening, his new consciousness, to engage himself in a moral action: he changes the speech he was going to deliver.

STOPPARD: Yes.

GOLLOB: And if you'll allow me to expand on this, I feel there is something emblematic about this speech he has changed, from what to what, which suggests a kind of change in your writing, in that, taking another character like McKendrick with his brilliant 'Catastrophe Theory' and its mathematical, verbal beauty, this disinterested player of the mind who fundamentally is an ass and a boor is contrasted with someone like Anderson who becomes engaged in a quest for some kind of fundamental ethical basis based on something that has touched him personally ... and I think there is a movement away from this, well some people have said trivial side of your writing ... do you see what I mean?

STOPPARD: I do. However, taking your idea about Anderson's lecture and the change it goes through and about there being something emblematic in this, that's not really so clear because we don't know what his speech would have been. What we do know is derived from his conversation in the hotel corridor with the Czech boy—in other words Anderson produces his arguments about why he shouldn't act, why he shouldn't interfere in Czech politics, and then what happens is something extremely simple ... he just brushes up against the specific reality of the mother and the child, especially the child.

You can make a case for what you're saying, but wielding Occam's razor upon it, the same thing can be said in a much simpler way. What happens is that he's got a perfectly respectable philosophical thesis and he encounters a mother and a child who are victims of this society, and it cuts through all the theory. It's as though there are two moralities: one to do with systems of government and an alternative morality to do with relationships between individuals. The latter is governed by instinctive feelings about what good and bad behaviour consist of and an instant and instinctive recognition of each when they occur. The pay-off really is that when Anderson puts his friend at risk by hiding the essay which he is smuggling in his colleague's briefcase, he says something like, 'I thought you would approve'! This is the man's public stance. And of course his colleague makes the same discovery that it's all very well in the bloody textbooks, but this is *me*, I could be in jail, this is *my* briefcase, you bastard!

So it's more to do with a man being educated by experience beyond the education he's received from thinking.

GOLLOB: Good, but if you'll allow me to pursue this, because I like digging, the text of the speech Anderson substitutes bears an uncanny resemblance to an argument—if I'm not mistaken—in a Havel play...

STOPPARD: Really!

GOLLOB: I think it might be from 'Conspirators' . . . [Ed. note: In fact Gollob was referring to a letter by Havel, quoted in Tynan's article, about *Conspirators*.]

STOPPARD: Have you ever read *Conspirators?*

GOLLOB: No, I haven't.

STOPPARD: Oh, because I've never seen *Conspirators.*

GOLLOB: Maybe this is a rather curious coincidence, then?

STOPPARD: Not that curious, is it? I mean it's not that curious that somebody like Havel would have a similar argument.

GOLLOB: 'Truth is guaranteed only by the full weight of humanity behind it.' Am I quoting from you, or am I quoting from Havel?

STOPPARD: It must be Havel.

GOLLOB: Looking at *Professional Foul* from the outside, it sounds almost as if when Anderson begins speaking with a different voice, it's also Stoppard who is beginning to inflect his voice differently, taking an ethical stance with more force. I felt a remarkable sort of kinship was being illustrated here.

STOPPARD: In fact I've had a feeling of kinship with Havel for a hell of a long time. When I read *The Garden Party* about twelve years ago, I just thought he was somebody who wrote like I would like to write if I was writing on the same subject. There are playwrights one admires because one could never do what they do, and there are those one admires because one *could* do exactly what they do and would wish to. But as far as Anderson's statement being the shadow on the wall of something that has happened to me—straining the natural courtesy which makes the interviewee wish the interviewer to have got it right, I don't think you have.

The reason why Anderson talks the way he does is because people like him to talk like that. I can honestly say that I have held Anderson's final view on the subject for years and years, and years before Anderson ever existed. I think something has made you believe that the arc of my development has intersected with the arc of the fictitious character's development and they cross when he speaks.

GOLLOB: I don't. I'm just constructing a pattern. It's what critics do.

STOPPARD: I wanted to write about somebody coming from England to a totalitarian society, brushing up against it, and getting a little soiled and a little wiser. I spent a long time wondering what to do ... and I thought: a ballroom dancing team, with those wonderful ladies in tangerine tulle ... 'Come Dancing' in Prague ... but I was really interested in the moral implications, and the equation just simplified itself until the formation dancers became moral philosophers. What you've got then is a desire to write about a moral philosopher who goes to Prague. An appeal is made to him by a former student, the appeal is rejected, he gets his nose rubbed in it slightly, learns, and acts. But what he learns isn't something which the writer is simultaneously learning in the course of writing the play. On the contrary, that's the end objective of the original desire to write the play.

GOLLOB: I think you once said—and this is supposed to be a quote—'. . . . the ideas are the product . . . '

STOPPARD: *(coming to the rescue)* Yes I know what you mean, and it has the overstatement of most epigrams: 'the ideas are the end-product of the play, not the other way round'. That used to be something I said with complete sincerity because after I had written *Rosencrantz and Guildenstern* I encountered over the next few years all kinds of interpretations of the events of the play, and it seemed to me that the play had somehow created all these ideas in the mind of the watcher and so were in that sense the end-product of a play about two Elizabethan courtiers trapped by the action of *Hamlet.* I was at some pains to try and say that I didn't start off with certain abstract ideas and then look around for a vessel to contain them. And I did tend to plug that because I found—and still find—many people (I'm thinking of students and school children) who write to one with the firm conviction that there's some sort of secret code which I know and they don't and which they're supposed to work out. But of course what you were quoting stopped being applicable round about the time I started writing *Jumpers*.

There the play was the end-product of an idea as much as the converse. I wanted to write about the dispute between somebody who thinks that morality is an absolute and somebody who thinks that it's a convention which we have evolved like the rules of tennis, and which can be altered.

ROPER: Are you familiar with a recent TV play about a writer who was interested in a dissident?

STOPPARD: No, unfortunately I didn't know anything about it until I read the review of it.

ROPER: It bore curious resemblances to what you yourself have done but it made precisely the opposite point from the one you've just corrected. First one took one's dissident and then made something of it.

STOPPARD: I haven't entirely corrected it, because *Every Good Boy* is a play which does something like that. There is another sort of writing where you could write a play set in Arundel Gardens which says something about dissidents but only had us in it and never mentioned the word 'dissidents'. It could be about this piece of cake.

I think the thing which I haven't quite said is that the proposition which you began with and which has led to this entire forty minutes is fundamentally true. It's actually true that I began writing at a time when the climate was such that theatre seemed to exist for the specific purpose of commenting on our own society directly. Temperamentally this didn't suit me, because I would much rather have written *The Importance of Being Earnest* than ... than ...

GOLLOB: *(breaking in)* Than *Look Back in Anger*?

STOPPARD: Yes. Well, hang on, that's more complicated because *Look Back in Anger* is full of wonderful speeches which I would like to have been able to write. And I don't think it would be nice to name the sort of play which is engaged with society but which doesn't contain anything I admire, and there are such plays. And so, I took on a sort of 'travelling pose' which exaggerated my insecurity about not being able to fit into this scheme, and I tended to overcorrect, as though in some peculiar way *Earnest* was actually more important than a play which grappled, right? So, what you say is fundamentally true . . . I did, I had to change as time went by, and began looking for a marriage between the play of ideas and the work of wit.

ROPER: But there's a further paradox: if you start writing about society then you once again assume one of these absolute models. If you then move to writing a play about an individual are you then, in shifting away from absolute positions, writing about Man, about Society. Are you then denying yourself the possibility of appealing to a majority audience?

STOPPARD: Well, it's generally true, isn't it, that one's appeal to an audience is less to do with what one is saying than how one is saying it, and in that respect there is surprisingly little choice to be made by a writer. Whatever comes to your mill, you grind it the same. There's only one way you *can* write in the end, and that's the way you *do* write . . . the difference between *Night and Day* and *Travesties* is more to do with structure than how I write.

I find that people who saw these two plays are divided along those who congratulate me on getting past the 'hummingbird' phase and those who say 'What are you *doing*? It's all naturalistic, with a beginning, a middle, and an end!' But there's no external position where you say, 'I think that in view of what so-and-so's been writing about me I'd better get to grips with something recognisable and do it properly.' Nothing like that happens . . . and though I haven't begun a new play and have only the vaguest idea of the area I'd like to write about, it's perfectly possible that it will be a play that will disappoint people who liked *Night and Day* or *Professional Foul.*

GOLLOB: To change the subject slightly, Tom Lehrer was in town recently for the opening of a new show, *Tomfoolery,* and I overheard him say that there is no question of him going back to writing songs— that he feels this sort of humour is no longer possible. That the flippancy of tone informing these satires of literally burning human issues is *mal à propos,* as if the bottom had fallen out of the humour market.

STOPPARD: They're nostalgia.

GOLLOB: Right, and they refer us back to the period in which they were conceived, just as *Rosencrantz and Guildenstern* is doing now in London and Paris.

STOPPARD: Actually I want to go to Paris, because it sounds fascinating. They've got three actors and a lot of puppets. God knows what they're doing, I'd love to see it.

GOLLOB: I think there's been a general darkening since then, and I'm not just thinking of the platitudes to do with recession and so on, but the prevalence of such things as the 'bad' movie cult, where audiences go to laugh at and feel superior to a given art form.

STOPPARD: It's a form of decadence.

GOLLOB: Audiences so hungry for confirmation that they cannot afford imaginatively to step out to appreciate a 'new' *Rosencrantz*. I think a 'new' *Travesties* would be slammed—slammed because of a contraction of what the imagination of the theatre-going public is willing to concede.

STOPPARD: Do you really think that's true?

GOLLOB: Look at 1980, so far . . .

ROPER: Well, let's say that the seventies were filled with young writers writing socialist realism, partly because of audiences, though you can find audiences for anything, but because theatres such as the Warehouse and the Royal Court have been sponsoring that kind of thing.

STOPPARD: But, you see, Stuart Burge told me months ago that he'd love to get a play which upset that apple-cart completely, which upset one's preconceptions about what sort of play the Royal Court does. But you see, it's a vicious circle. The Royal Court does certain kinds of plays and therefore receives certain kinds of plays to do.

ROPER: Haven't you therefore categorised yourself as a non-Royal Court writer?

STOPPARD: Well, I sent them *Rosencrantz and Guildenstern* before it was ever done by anybody. But nothing happened.

GOLLOB: One of the Court's less successful efforts of the seventies—to try and hook up with what I was saying before—tried to use laughter as a double-edged weapon. I'm referring to Peter Barnes' play *Laughter*. Bernard Levin once said of you that you could write a play about Auschwitz and he would laugh.

STOPPARD: I don't think I could actually, or would wish to.

GOLLOB: In fact it's an amazing thing to say, but Barnes seems to have picked up the glove, so to speak, making a play where he goes into Auschwitz to try and point out how we use laughter as an escape, at the same time trying to make us laugh.

STOPPARD: What do you think yourself?

GOLLOB: I don't think it worked.

STOPPARD: Was it the principle at fault, or the execution?

GOLLOB: Well, let's put it this way. I think it was misconceived from the beginning. Comedy is based on incongruous juxtapositions, but this was a juxtaposition incapable of comedy.

STOPPARD: Yes, but the interesting thing about comedy is that it works in two completely different ways. It works by surprising people and by gratifying their expectations. I saw *The Hothouse* the other night and it was wonderful just to sit there and travel through the pause with the actor. There's no sense of being surprised, it's entirely to do with the inevitable gratification, when one says 'He's dead,' and you sort of wait, and wait, till the other says, 'Dead?'—it's marvellous, because there isn't any sort of wit involved in that exchange, but it's hilarious.

GOLLOB: Well isn't that 'bad'?

STOPPARD: No, no, the author is totally in control.

GOLLOB: By the time Barnes tried to make us laugh we'd already done too much of it. Something had happened to make us resistant to it, perhaps it was the jolt of '73–74 with the Yom Kippur War and the three-day week. And even though he was only trying to get us to laugh in order to force it back down our throats again, he failed because he couldn't get us motivated to do it in the first place.

STOPPARD: I'm just testing your general theory against experience. I'm not sure it holds up. It may be that people would have laughed in 1968 at *that* play, whereas they wouldn't in 1978. But people's willingness to laugh is something else ... I'm just trying to think whether I feel differently about comedy.

GOLLOB: Good—as that is what I in my prolix way am trying to find out.

STOPPARD: Well, it's hard to be sure, but I don't think so. I think like a lot of writers I've got a cheap side and an expensive side. I mean rather like a musician might stop composing for a few days to do a jingle for 'Katomeat' because he thinks it's fun. And I honestly can't believe that because of something that happened to the world or to England I'll never write a 50-minute rompy farce for Ed Berman. I think I'd do it with as much pleasure as ten years ago.

But on the other side of the coin I think that you *are* onto something, that perhaps there is something in recent history which makes me feel that a play of more substance and less frivolity is more likely than the converse. I'm expressing this so carefully and so formally in order to try and get it right for myself. But one of the artificial—I nearly said false—things about being interviewed is that one pretends to have coherent ideas about oneself in order to gratify the expectations of the interviewer. But this isn't visible at all in the practice of writing a play, which is intimate and more to do with the next ninety seconds than the last nine years.

ROPER: Assuming you'd just written this 50-minute comedy, do you feel no political or moral ineptitude?

STOPPARD: That I can categorically answer to: none whatever. If I only wrote 50-minute farces, and you were to ask did I feel any sense of failure, the answer would be yes. But I don't think that anything that has happened in the world compromises the acceptability of the entertainment.

ROPER: You choose to live and work without this focus, then.

STOPPARD: Well, not all plays are written because of a gut need to write about factor X. In common with all professional writers one is asked whether one would like to do certain things . . . the BBC asks you if you'd like to adapt *Three Men in a Boat* and you don't think, 'These are not the times.' You say, 'Yeah, it's one of my favourite books, I'd love to have a crack at that.' And you do it. When it's a thing like that you're more a craftsman than an artist. I think it's right to take pride in one's craftmanship as much as one's originality.

GOLLOB: Somebody once said—I think Griffiths in *Comedians*—that comedy is essentially conservative, even reactionary.

STOPPARD: What an extraordinary thing to say! Is it?

ROPER: I think it is. Comedy is grounded in a kind of fellow-feeling, a sharing of feeling about society that reinforces those feelings and militates against change.

STOPPARD: That's very bright.

GOLLOB: It needs to be pessimistic about the outcome of change or innovation.

ROPER: It reinforces stasis, it makes you feel secure in what you are.

STOPPARD: Well, think of Tom Lehrer, does he reinforce shared values between performer and audience?

ROPER: Well, perhaps there's . . .

GOLLOB: *(interrupting)* I think he does!

ROPER: . . . a difference between comedy and strong satire.

STOPPARD: Well, I think you've got your knife out again to cut your sausage to suit you. If I said to you (and if we hadn't had this conversation) that comedy is a radical force, it wouldn't strike you immediately as being nonsense, one could make a case for it as much as you could for its being reactionary.

ROPER: You could, but if you were trying to make a serious point, you'd embarrass your audience. You embarrass them by trying to make them laugh at Auschwitz.

GOLLOB: Which is what Barnes did.

STOPPARD: But then is it still comedy?

GOLLOB: Quite . . . but if comedy contained a kind of constitutional inertia and were in some way resistant to change, could it be said that in your comic writing you regard man as not being perfectible, and that change should be resisted?

STOPPARD: Nothing could be further from the truth. First of all ... the desire to reach perfection and the conviction that it is unattainable are compatible instincts. I think perfection is unattainable because it means different things to different people, but the need to make things better is constant and important. Otherwise you're into a sort of nihilism ... You ring a bell with me somewhere ... I think in the Tynan article. Somehow he got it wrong. Something I said made him conclude that I was somehow a writer who was not part of an effort to perfect society, some sort of striving for perfectibility. When I read it I thought, 'My God, how can he've got it so *wrong?*' Did you connect that with comedy in some way?

GOLLOB: Yes, I did. Let's look at *Night and Day* where the character Wagner comes in for a lot of sarcastic, comic roughing up. I too am a foreigner here, which perhaps made me feel sensitive or suspicious about the way this was happening. I began to identify not only with Wagner as a foreigner but also as someone associated with another kind of intrusion—the intrusion of unions into the area of 'free speech' and also as the intrusion of a man who uses language in a certain way, not to mention a man who doesn't play the game according to the rules of cricket. Contrast this with Milne, so obviously public school background, the right sort of background which leads one to have the right sort of fundamental moral assumptions, closer to your heart, I felt, than Wagner. I saw the latter as a kind of usurper.

STOPPARD: My feelings about Wagner in particular and about journalism are rather ambivalent, but I admire Wagner rather a lot as a character. I would admire him if he existed. I admire good professionals. I'm a bit of a journalism groupie anyway. I think journalism is what Milne says it is, the last line of defence in this country. And surrounding this approbation is the knowledge that a great deal of journalism is despised and rightly so. I mean there is a lot of abuse in the mouths of other characters, particularly the woman. And she speaks for me as well. Nobody can have a cut and dried good/bad attitude towards Wagner or journalism because there are things to be said on different sides. She's a prejudiced observer with her own experience.

GOLLOB: You don't feel her voice is somehow more privileged by the fact that she's given two roles in the play, the other being this internal voice which can speak 'out' from behind the social mask.

STOPPARD: I didn't intend her to be privileged because of that. In fact I would have thought that—if there is such a person—the average watcher of this play would find that Milne carries more conviction than Ruth. Ruth has got a gift for sarcastic abuse, but what Milne says is true. I mean it is true: with a free press everything is correctible, however imperfect things are they are correctible if people know they're going on. If we don't know they're going on, it's concealable: true. I believe it to be a true statement. Milne has my prejudice if you like. Somehow unconsciously, I wanted him to be known to be speaking the truth.

GOLLOB: But he gets killed, though, doesn't he.

STOPPARD: That's what happens in myth. That in a sense confirms—not directly, but in some psychological way—the truth which he becomes a martyr to.

GOLLOB: But no I mean, it depends on the treatment. Take a Christian sort of truth, like the kind you are taking, which is true in a sense essentially *because* it cannot survive—

STOPPARD: *(interrupting)* The play won't bear that sort of profundity, you see . . . you can follow that line of thought and it would be there in parallel with *Night and Day* and my experience of writing it, but because the play didn't spring from that kind of profound thought it's not that relevant to it. The press is a *real thing*, you know, papers are *real things* which you can *read*. And you like some of it and think it's important, and some of it you think is despicable. What one is trying to say is that a lot of it is hardly defensible but it's the price you pay for the part that matters. And that's all there is to it . . . Though there are other matters, as I said, I admire Wagner as a person because he takes his job seriously and is good at it and isn't a hack.

GOLLOB: I think there is a certain kind of typification going on in the way he is contrasted with Milne.

STOPPARD: Indeed, yes.

GOLLOB: Milne is a greenhorn, wet behind the ears, because he *believes* in his truth, and one isn't supposed to believe in things nowadays. We may admire him for having the courage of his convictions, but we ourselves tend to Wagner's more sceptical distance, tempered by experience. It seems to me that there is a kind of contrast going on between the ideal and the real, between innocence and experience. Ruth and Wagner are the critique revolving around this idealistic nucleus, as if in your thinking the very notion of freedom had an idealistic, even Kantian core.

STOPPARD: Yes, that's true.

GOLLOB: Hasn't it? I mean this notion one encounters in *Profes-*

sional Foul about human truths being self-evident things, *a priori* data one reflexively assumes to exist.

STOPPARD: Yes, yes.

GOLLOB: Now what I find so baffling is this: How does one reconcile this . . . this *idealism* with an opposite but more characteristic feature of your writing, which is the *relativism* of everything . . .

ROPER: *(interrupting)* I would've jumped back to the previous question where you said you felt that everything was going to be a striving for the better. As a philosophical construct, yes, but you have to accept that everything is polarized: Margaret Thatcher's better isn't Jim Callaghan's better. Isn't it your responsibility—if one is a writer—to acknowledge that?

STOPPARD: It's not, you see. It's not my responsibility as a writer. What I am interested in (you were talking about Kantian ideals and so on) is in what Margaret Thatcher and Jim Callaghan have *in common* which is not shared by . . . Hitler or Attila the Hun. At the ideal centre there is a way of behaving towards people which is good and a way which is bad . . . and alongside that different theories about attaining the common good—in other words, Callaghan and Thatcher each have different economic theories each designed literally to achieve the maximum general good for everybody. In other words, what you are talking about is merely a disagreement about tactic. But a play like *Professional Foul* is nothing to do with that, it's nothing to do with that at all. It's to do with the morality between individuals. I'm finding it hard to keep little boys out of my plays—my four sons aged between 5 and 14 may or may not be relevant—but something which has preoccupied me for a long time is the desire to simplify questions and take the sophistication out. A fairly simple question about morality, if debated by highly sophisticated people, can lead to almost any conclusion.

GOLLOB: Can you expand on that?

STOPPARD: Let me try. If somebody came out of East Germany through the gate in the wall and wished to communicate the idea that life inside this wall was admirable or indeed platonically good, he'd have a reasonable chance of succeeding in this if he were addressing himself to a sophisticated person. But if you tried to do this to a child, he'd blow it to smithereens. A child would say, 'But the wall is there to keep people *in,* so there must be some reason why people want to get out.'

There's a childlike truth about it. If it was good, people wouldn't want to leave. If people didn't want to leave, you wouldn't need to build a wall to keep them in. 'There's something wrong with what you are saying Professor!'

GOLLOB: I hope this doesn't make you feel I'm sophisticated but a child's logic cuts two ways. Throughout thousands of years we have been telling children on one hand that they are only children and so 'what do you know?' while on the other hand we have celebrated some kind of superhuman capacity to perceive *a priori* truths, untainted by tempering experience.

ROPER: And surely the position of the writer is *on* the wall, looking at both sides.

STOPPARD: Looping back over three sides of tape I can say that in the last few years I haven't been writing about questions whose answers I believe to be ambivalent. In *Every Good Boy* and *Professional Foul*, the author's position isn't ambiguous. Where the double-act comes into its own is in the tactical dispute between Margaret Thatcher and Jim Callaghan.

GOLLOB: Not Joseph and Benn?

STOPPARD: All I know is that I want to live in a country where that dispute can take place, and not where it's forbidden.

GOLLOB: Good, well, just to start rounding things up, is there anything you can tell us about new writing, about where you're moving to, or even where we're moving to?

STOPPARD: Well, the latter I wouldn't wish to, because I'd be busking. I don't see enough or read enough to have a proper acquaintance with what's happening or with what might happen next. As for myself, in the last three years I've written too much—more than I would comfortably wish to write . . . the only thing which I am presently committed to doing and which I am looking forward to doing is an adaptation from an Austrian play by Nestroy. Nestroy believe it or not is the man who wrote the original play which ended up as *Hello Dolly!* via Thornton Wilder.

ROPER: And do you refer to that as an adaptation or a version?

STOPPARD: It'll be much more a version than the Schnitzler *[Undiscovered Country]*.

GOLLOB: We often talk about waves and generations on the British drama scene. With whom, or on which would you like best to be seen surfing?

STOPPARD: I just think of myself as one of the people who came after the beginning. I mean, when I was on a newspaper in Bristol and

Tynan was on the *Observer,* Osborne and Arden and Wesker and Pinter were I suppose the four best-known English playwrights, other than the pre-war generation. I just think of myself as one of the people who followed after that...

Tom Stoppard: Kind Heart and Prickly Mind

Joan Juliet Buck

If the plays of the late 1970s were seen as harbingers of a new political Stoppard, the opening of *The Real Thing* in November 1982 prompted headlines such as "Stoppard as We Never Knew He Could Be" with the discovery that Stoppard could write, movingly, about love. With the London production in its second cast (of an eventual four), *The Real Thing* opened on Broadway in January 1984 to greater acclaim than any of his plays since *Rosencrantz and Guildenstern Are Dead.* Three days before the New York premiere, Stoppard encountered an interviewer who wanted to "ask him how one writes about love." After a summary of earlier plays and biographical information (omitted here), the interviewer summoned the courage to ask her question and was rewarded with one of the clearest statements Stoppard has made about how he sees the relationship of Henry and Annie in the play.

AMANDA: Have you known her long?
ELYOT: About four months, we met at a house party in Norfolk.
AMANDA: Very flat, Norfolk.
—Noel Coward, *Private Lives,* act I

HENRY: You have a cottage in . . . ?
ANNIE: Norfolk.
HENRY: Norfolk! What, up in the hills there?
ANNIE: What hills? Norfolk is absolutely—
CHARLOTTE: Oh, very funny. Stop it, Henry.
—Tom Stoppard, *The Real Thing,* act I

From [American] *Vogue,* 174 (March 1984).

The subtext of Tom Stoppard's plays used to be hunt-the-allusion. While his plays unfolded like Bach fugues or palindromes—symmetrical, precise, elaborately patterned repeating sets of events—the audience could further divert itself within the texture of that dialogue by picking out references. Tom Stoppard says it's not that different from a movie audience's getting off on references to, say, Sandra Dee in, say, a 'fifties pastiche beach movie; but of course his frames of reference seem to be somewhat larger than the high-school memories that animate popular American culture. Up until *The Real Thing*, which is playing on Broadway now to rapturous acclaim, Tom Stoppard's plays provided a glassy surface of erudition that reflected the audience's education back at them, magnified, and sent them out whistling the puns.

. . . .

In *The Real Thing*, Stoppard writing about love is Stoppard trying to find out how to be potent without being cheap. And the compromise his hero forces upon himself involves abandoning all his intellectual and moral superiority, living through the unattractively universal pain of jealousy, standing by through his wife's infidelity—suffering for love, without once falling into melodrama or cliché. He goes through the agony of romantic love, but it's to save his marriage. Until *The Real Thing*, there was little indication in his work of the grace, the kindness, the enormous generosity of the man. The walls of *Flashdance* words were hiding an open heart. Daunted by the plays I'd studied in college, I would never have approached him. With this play, I saw a breach. Good, I thought, I'll ask him how one writes about love.

. . . .

His suite at the hotel is all blue; he takes care of the coffee, notices that it's getting cold, places the club sandwiches on the table, is hospitable and worried that he's already told *The New York Times* everything there is to know. He's got on an oversized shirt, the kind heroes wear for duels in pirate movies, beige trousers, black leather slippers. Smokes Silk Cut cigarettes, English low tar, one after the other. We have friends in common, people from the past. It would be far nicer to gossip than to ask personal questions.

. . . .

The kindness is overwhelming, and it works as a good defense; the coarser questions, such as "how did you write this play about love in this way," keep getting blown away by his attention to my general condition. Still, I try:

What brought you to write this play?

He gives different reasons, so plentiful that they begin to resemble excuses. "One has to write plays if one is a playwright." He doesn't write often, only every three or four years; he'd written a bit about love and sexual attraction in *Night and Day,* but that was a minor strand, this is a play to finish writing about the subject; he'd had an idea about a play where the same situation is repeated twice, three times, and each time the reaction is different; he wanted to do a play where the first scene is the work of the person in the second scene, which means the hero has to be a playwright; he wanted to explore "public postures having the configuration of private derangement."

"One of the things about *The Real Thing* is that it's a play about a playwright despite itself, because I'm not comfortable with the idea of having a playwright protagonist. It's not central to what I'm trying to write about, I'm stuck with it."

Because of the biographical implication?

"Exactly. To me it suggested that I was at the end of the rope, because you start writing about a guy trying to write a play, where have you got to go after that?"

"It's not *only* true," he goes on, "that plays are the end product of certain ideas. It's also true that certain ideas are the end product of the play."

So, I ask, you write to find out?

"Not even that. You have certain things to start with, and you start writing a play. And then you get lost in the play a bit, and the play starts doing things which means you're finding things out, but you don't know whether that's the purpose of the play. It's just the play is difficult to write, and some of the solutions to some of the problems take the play in directions which you couldn't have written down on a note pad before you started because they just weren't there to write down. When you're writing, the problem is the next line."

I wanted, I say, to ask what you found out about love in writing this play.

"I don't know that I have found out anything about love. I haven't. I mean I don't think so. To be fair, one does feel quite emotional in getting those pages right. Because if you don't get emotional, you don't know if they are right; writing a play in one sense consists in hearing the noise the play makes. So you can't be detached from it. But you know, like all these things it's an exercise of the imagination. If the story you've written has got you correctly to that point, it shouldn't be too hard to speak for the character at that moment. I wasn't conscious of learning anything. It was kind of using what you knew or thought you knew."

He's at the desk now, phoning to find out where the milk is that we've been waiting for for two hours. I still want my answer.

"There's something wrong with the question," he says. "I don't mean that rudely; but there must be some false premise in it, and it's probably to do with your underestimating the mechanical level of writing a play. Do you mean how autobiographical is it?"

Well, yes.

"It's a kind of game. You write about a parallel world. You write truthfully about a parallel possibility. That's the game: This is how it might be if it would be."

In the New York production, Jeremy Irons and Glenn Close seem, thoughout the second act, to be at the very edge of splitting apart. Is the fragility of the relationship deliberate, I ask?

"No, that's subjective. Some people think that their relationship suggests that fundamentally everything is okay. That the right two people found each other and will sort of survive."

What do you think?

"The latter."

Fated love, destiny?

"It's not that I believe in it as an idea, it's just that in the case of the two characters in the play, it's possibly true. There's always a precipice, but some couples know it's there. It's just what keeps them together is stronger than what tends to separate them."

What keeps them together?

"Love. They're right for each other. They love each other."

Then did he make the first wife very witty and sharp to show that it isn't intellectual understanding that keeps a couple together?

"There isn't that much calculation in these things. Schematically, he leaves a woman who is pretty much his equal at the stuff which doesn't matter. The second wife, Annie, doesn't have the smart remarks. She's actually wiser than he is. He's cleverer, but she's wiser.

"But," he adds, patting my back because all this talk about love has brought on a coughing fit, "there's no superior truth in my description of the play."

"The main trouble with the premise," he says, "is that none of these thoughts is a consideration while writing a play. It's all kind of fake, and the interview makes you fake by allowing retrospective ideas to masquerade as some form of intention. One of the problems is that writers, as a whole, don't think about their work in that external way."

The play opened three days later. The reviews were raves, such raves that the audience, which had delighted in every nuance during previews, became shy in the presence of such a certified hit and was afraid to laugh at the jokes. Frank Rich in *The New York Times* was incoherent with approval; Clive Barnes in the *New York Post* pointed out that one doesn't make a buck's fizz with Dom Perignon, and the *Daily News*'s Douglas Watt called Jeremy Irons "a new matinee idol— the real thing." All responses are subjective in real life: It takes a great playwright to keep them so onstage.

Two Men on an Ocean Wave

Garry O'Connor

In his 1977 *New Yorker* profile of Stoppard, Kenneth Tynan claimed that "ten days before the première" of *Jumpers*, "the play was still running close to four hours." Tynan described the "unilateral action" he took to shorten the play: "I nipped into the rehearsal room ahead of the director and dictated to the cast a series of cuts and transpositions which reduced the text to what I considered manageable length." Seven years later that version of events was disputed in a joint interview with Tom Stoppard and Peter Wood. In conversation at the National Theatre, where they were rehearsing their latest adaptation, *Rough Crossing*, Wood and Stoppard discussed their collaboration—with each other and with André Previn who provided the music for songs in the play. The interview appeared with a large photograph showing Wood and Stoppard looming in front of an ocean liner's decks—the set of *Rough Crossing*—as if conversation between these "two men on an ocean wave" was itself a performance. Writing up the exchange, the interviewer cast himself in the role of playwright, interpolating his italicized remarks as stage directions. In fact, the *Sunday Times* published the interview with the subhead "A comic dialogue between Tom Stoppard and Peter Wood, dramatised by Garry O'Connor." Less than six months later Wood and Stoppard would be working together again, on a West End revival of *Jumpers* that restored a number of cuts made prior to that play's 1972 premiere—including, for the first time on any *Jumpers* stage, the character of Tarzan. But what Stoppard refers to as the "myth" of Tynan's cuts to

From the *Sunday Times*, 21 October 1984.

Jumpers had acquired a life of its own. When the Tynan story cropped up yet again in a review of *Arcadia*, Stoppard finally took pen in hand (in a 22 April 1993 letter to the editor of the *Financial Times*) to declare that "it is quite untrue" that Tynan "cut the play by an hour during rehearsal, unilaterally or otherwise, or needed to." Stoppard added that "the main casualty" when he himself shortened the *Jumpers* "Coda" by about ten minutes "was Tarzan, played by Alan Mitchell, who is Jellaby in *Arcadia*."

Stoppard's new play, "Rough Crossing," adapted from Ferenc Molnár, the very successful Hungarian boulevard playwright who died in 1952, has music. Stoppard went to see André Previn.

STOPPARD: Five songs have had to be written. I had to buy a Walker's rhyming dictionary—with supplement. It didn't help a lot. I'd work a couple of days and arrive at André's home panting with ten rhymed lines. He'd sit down at the piano and, in about ten minutes, say "How about this?" It seemed wonderful to me. "Oh no," he'd say, "it's only a sketch."

Peter Wood, the director of "Rough Crossing," and Stoppard's collaborator for twelve years, interrupts.

WOOD: André's been doing it since he was seventeen.

An energetic and attractive personality some ten years older than Stoppard, Wood pours wine for everyone and quickly munches a sandwich between rehearsals.

STOPPARD: After a while I'd start hearing tunes as I wrote. "I have a tune," I'd say to André, and I'd sing it in my awful way. It would turn out that I'd re-invented one of his. He's extremely tolerant. I live in Iver. He calls me Iver Novello.

The literal translation of the title of Molnár's play, written in 1924, is "Play at the Castle." It is a situation comedy about two co-authors, an actor and an actress, and a composer. In the Molnár they are rehearsing a two-hander for the boulevard, in the Stoppard a musical comedy for Broadway. The time has been updated to the art-deco Thirties, before the real rise of Nazism. Stoppard has transposed the setting from a feudal castle to on board an Atlantic liner. An elderly house servant becomes a steward. And so on.

STOPPARD: I've only travelled once on an ocean liner. I went on the Queen Mary in 1967 to New York. I didn't travel first class and I had a little prowl to see what it was like. I got to a window and like an urchin in a storm looked through at the rich folks within and saw this vast, ostentatious ballroom type of place where twelve people, rather well-dressed, were playing bingo. I went back to tourist quarters feeling quite reassured.

Stoppard was born in Zlin, Czechoslovakia in 1937, and has a trace of accent although he denies an East-European influence on his thought. He is detached, enigmatic, with a solid, dark-haired presence. An engineer with words, a calculator of stress and flow of pitfalls and mnemonics.

STOPPARD: Broadly speaking, we've left Molnár's characters as Hungarian, though the male lead is English, and the composer French. They aren't, as it were, being translated for our benefit.

WOOD: That kind of amalgam was a famous thing in the 1930s. There was an enormous traffic of people across the Atlantic like William Wyler, Ernst Lubitsch, and of course the Kordas.

STOPPARD: The Korda context is roughly right. The point about *Rough Crossing* is that they are speaking and working in English.

WOOD: It was very much the age of the foreign European star who prided him or herself on bi-linguality. The Dietrichs, the Garbos, were the real thing. People like Theda Bara were actually created to seem foreign . . .

STOPPARD: Sorry to interrupt. The short answer is that they're still Hungarians. They're uprooted Hungarians, whereas in the Molnár they're, as it were, *rooted* Hungarians.

This is the third adaptation Wood and Stoppard have worked on together, the others being "Undiscovered Country" by Schnitzler and "On the Razzle" by Nestroy. The NT provided a literal translation.

STOPPARD: It's liberating to be given the plot and characters, because the bit I like doing best is then there to be done. Molnár wasn't interested in repartee, or even wit really. My particular twitch is to try to make the lines funny. *Stoppard is noted for his sometimes abstruse puns. He turns to Wood.* It's not a very punny play is it? I can't remember.

WOOD: It's extremely well-behaved. "Pre-madonna" has been cut.

STOPPARD: I hope to get that back before we open.

WOOD: Get it back, and then you'll say, "What are they groaning at?" The moment they groan it has to come out.

STOPPARD: My family groan. My sons are like litmus paper.

Wood and Stoppard's collaboration began when Wood was called in by Laurence Olivier, who was then running the NT at the Old Vic, to direct "Jumpers."

WOOD: Sir Laurence said, "You've got a very tricky bill of goods here with that boy." I was kid-glovey at first. *(To Stoppard.)* And you crouched over the text very defensively.

Although he did not receive satisfactory replies as to what the play was about—Stoppard told him that it was about a man writing a speech—Wood loved "Jumpers" because it raised the whole question of the nature of belief. When Wood boldly reversed the two halves of the first act, it built trust between the pair. The claim by Kenneth Tynan, then literary manager of the NT, that he drastically cut the text of "Jumpers" just before it opened was dismissed by Wood as totally unfair.

WOOD: It was the opening night, and all of a sudden you produced a piece of paper with that tiny elegant writing with about twenty notes for the actors and you thought I was going to go round the dressing room with these notes, and I just looked at you with my eyes falling out of my head, and you said, "Oh, it will do tomorrow if you like."

Wood went on to direct "Travesties," "Night and Day" and "The Real Thing."

WOOD: What Tom's done for me is to make me work much harder. I used to assume that directing a play meant assembling a text and a group of players and giving it a little flick of the paddle now and again to make it happily float downstream. A lot of directors might resent having the author at rehearsals. I resent *not* having him there.

His restraint still amazes me. I don't know how he has the patience to put up with something sounding radically wrong in his ear, but he does again and again, and that is marvellous because, curiously enough, the performance lies somewhere suspended like a hammock between the play he writes and what could be called the production.

Of course we have our differences and there's a great deal of shouting as we thrash them out over a weekend at Iver—in *The Real Thing,* with Miriam [Stoppard] blowing the whistle. But there is never an impasse.

STOPPARD: *(with a laugh)* I think you could say that the rehearsal and preview period gives me an opportunity to write the play you are willing to direct.

WOOD: But there is another play created apart from the amalgam of the talents of author, actors, and directors, a fourth force at work greater than the sum of all these—the audience.

Both pause. The audience . . . .

STOPPARD: I hate first nights for reasons to do with mechanics. I sit there desperate about the sound cues, things revolving, doors opening—once we had a door come off its hinges at the first night.

WOOD: The entire architrave came away.

STOPPARD: But there is something else, more subtle and nightmarish than that. Trying to write comedy makes you acutely aware of it. A funny line at which nobody laughs is a very interesting internal contradiction. In what sense can you say that it is still funny?

Tom Stoppard: The Art of Theater VII

Shusha Guppy

Although the London opening of *The Real Thing* in November 1982 was followed just three weeks later by a new radio play (*The Dog It Was That Died*), Stoppard would not have another original stage play on the boards until 1988. In the interim, Stoppard revised the text of plays in production, translated and adapted plays by others, wrote *Squaring the Circle* for television, and worked on screenplays. By the time *The Real Thing* opened in New York in January 1984, Stoppard had reworked it into a version that the newly established American branch of Faber and Faber published as the "Broadway Edition" of the play. Meanwhile in London, Roger Rees and Felicity Kendal—who created the roles of Henry and Annie—had been replaced in August 1983 by a second cast at the Strand Theatre. A third cast took over in May 1984, and a fourth cast, headed by Michael Pennington and Lucy Gutteridge, appeared from November 1984 until *The Real Thing* finally closed at the Strand Theatre in March 1985. Stoppard not only was involved in rehearsing all four London casts but also continued to revise the script as each new cast took over the play. During rehearsals for the West End revival of *Jumpers* that opened next door at the Aldwych Theatre on 1 April 1985 with Felicity Kendal as Dotty, Stoppard made even more extensive changes, restoring Scott, who had been cut from the *Jumpers* "Coda" in 1973, and even bringing back Tarzan, who had not survived previews prior

From *The Paris Review*, 109 (Winter 1988).

to the play's 1972 National Theatre premiere. A script for Stoppard's next play, his first original stage play since 1982, was ready in early 1987, and the original plans were for a production that summer. However, Stoppard wanted the title role of *Hapgood* to be played by Felicity Kendal, and the production was delayed by six months until she was available following the birth of her baby. Stoppard's participation in the distinguished *Paris Review* series of interviews came near the end of rehearsals for *Hapgood*. Talking in some detail about last-minute changes he was making in preparation for the play's London opening on 8 March 1988, Stoppard discusses the way his plays evolve and change.

GUPPY: How are the rehearsals going?

STOPPARD: So far they are conforming to pattern, alas! I mean I am suffering from the usual delusion that the play was ready before we went into production. It happens every time. I give my publisher the finished text of the play so that it can be published not too long after the opening in London, but by the time the galleys arrive they're hopelessly out of date because of all the changes I've made during rehearsals. This time I gave them *Hapgood* and told them that it was folly to pretend it would be unaltered, but I added, "I think it won't be as bad as the others." It turned out to be worse. Yesterday I realized that a chunk of information in the third scene ought to be in the second scene, and it's like pulling out entrails: as in any surgery there's blood. As I was doing it I watched a documentary about Crick and Watson's discovery of the structure of DNA—the double helix. There was only one way all the information they had could fit but they couldn't figure out what it was. I felt the same. So the answer to your question is that the rehearsals are going well and enjoyably, but that I'm very busy with my pencil.

GUPPY: What provokes the changes? Does the transfer from your imagination to the stage alter your perception? Or do the director and the actors make suggestions?

STOPPARD: They make a few suggestions which I am often happy to act upon. In the theater there is often a tension, almost a contradiction, between the way real people would think and behave, and a kind of imposed dramaticness. I like dialogue which is slightly more brittle than life. I have always admired and wished to write one of those 1940s film scripts where every line is written with a sharpness and economy which is frankly artificial. Peter Wood, the director with whom I've worked for sixteen years, sometimes feels obliged to find a humanity, perhaps a romantic ambiguity, in scenes which are not written like that but which, I hope, contain the possibility. I like surface gloss, but it's all too easy to get that right for the first night only to find that *that* was the best performance of the play; from then on the gloss starts cracking apart. The ideal is to make the groundwork so deep and solid that the actors are continually discovering new possibilities under the surface, so that the best performance turns out to be the last one. In my plays there are usually a few lines which Peter loathes, for their slickness or coldness, and we have a lot of fairly enjoyable squabbles which entail some messing about with the text as we rehearse. In the case of *Hapgood* there is a further problem which has to do with the narrative mechanics, because it's a plotty play, and I can't do plots and have no interest in plots.

GUPPY: Yet you have produced some complex and plausible plots. So why the aversion?

STOPPARD: The subject matter of the play exists before the story and it is always something abstract. I get interested by a notion of some kind and see that it has dramatic possibilities. Gradually I see how a pure idea can be married with a dramatic event. But it is still not a play until you invent a plausible narrative. Sometimes this is not too hard—*The Real Thing* was fairly straightforward. For *Hapgood*, the thing that I wanted to write about seemed to suit the form of an espionage thriller. It's not the sort of thing I read or write.

GUPPY: What was the original idea that made you think of an espionage thriller?

STOPPARD: It had to do with mathematics. I am not a mathematician but I was aware that for centuries mathematics was considered the queen of the sciences because it claimed certainty. It was grounded on some fundamental certainties—axioms—which led to others. But then, in a sense, it all started going wrong, with concepts like non-euclidean geometry—I mean, looking at it from Euclid's point of view. The mathematics of physics turned out to be grounded on *un*certainties, on probability and chance. And if you're me, you think—there's a play in that. Finding an idea for a play is like picking up a shell on a beach. I started reading about mathematics without finding what I was looking for. In the end I realized that what I was after was something which any first-year physics student is familiar with, namely quantum mechanics. So I started reading about that.

GUPPY: It is said that you research your plays thoroughly.

STOPPARD: I don't think of it as research. I read for interest and enjoyment, and when I cease to enjoy it I stop. I didn't research quantum mechanics but I was fascinated by the mystery which lies in the foundation of the observable world, of which the most familiar example is the wave/particle duality of light. I thought it was a good metaphor for human personality. The language of espionage lends itself to this duality—think of the double agent.

GUPPY: You seem to think the success of the play has so much to do with its production. Do you, therefore, get involved with the lighting, costumes, etc.? Please give examples, anecdotes.

STOPPARD: It is obvious that a given text (think of any classic) can give rise to a satisfying event or an unsatisfying one. These are the only relative values which end up mattering in the theater. A great production of a *Black Comedy* is better than a mediocre production of a *Comedy of Errors*. When the writing is over, the event is the thing. I attend the first rehearsal of a new play and every rehearsal after that, as well as discussions with designers, lighting designers, costume designers...I like to be there, even though I'm doing more listening than talking. When *Hapgood* was being designed, I kept insisting that the shower in the first scene wouldn't work unless it was in the middle of the upper stage, so that Hapgood could approach us facing down the middle. Peter and Carl insisted that the scene wouldn't work unless the main entrance doors were facing the audience. They were quite right, but so was I. We opened out of town with the shower in the wings, and it didn't work at all, so we ended up having to find a way to have both the doors and the shower in view of the audience. The look of the thing is one thing. The sound of it is more important. David Lean was quoted as saying somewhere that the hardest part of making films is knowing how fast or slow to make the actors speak. I suddenly saw how *horribly* difficult that made it to make a film. Because you can't change your mind. When you write a play, it makes a certain kind of noise in your head, and for me rehearsals are largely a process of trying to reproduce that noise. It is not always wise to reproduce it in every instance, but that's another question. The first time I met Laurence Olivier, we were casting *Rosencrantz and Guildenstern*. He asked me about the Player. I said the Player should be a sneaky, snake-like sort of person. Olivier looked dubious. The part was given, thank God, or Olivier, to Graham Crowden who is about six-foot four and roars like a lion. Olivier came to rehearsal one day. He watched for about fifteen minutes, and then, leaving, made one suggestion. I forget what it was. At the door he turned, twinkled at us all and said, "Just the odd pearl," and left.

GUPPY: Is it a very anxious moment for you, working up to the first night?

STOPPARD: Yes. You are trying to imagine the effect on people who know nothing about what is going on and whom you are taking through the story. In a normal spy thriller you contrive to delude the reader until all is revealed in the dénouement. This is the exact opposite of a scientific paper in which the dénouement—the discovery—is announced at the beginning. *Hapgood* to some extent follows this latter procedure. It is not a whodunnit because we are told who has done it near the beginning of the first act, so the story becomes *how* he did it.

GUPPY: Did you draw on some famous spies, like Philby or Blunt, for your characters?

STOPPARD: Not at all. I wasn't really interested in authenticity. John le Carré's *A Perfect Spy* uses the word "joe" for an agent who is being run by somebody, and I picked it up. I have no idea whether it is authentic or invented by le Carré.

GUPPY: What happens on the first night? Do you sit among the audience or in a concealed place at the back? And what do you do afterwards?

STOPPARD: The first *audience* is more interesting than the first night. We now have previews, which makes a difference. Actually, my play *The Real Inspector Hound* was the first to have previews in London, in 1968. Previews are essential. The idea of going straight from a dress-rehearsal to a first night is frightening. It happened with *Rosencrantz and Guildenstern* and we got away with it, but for *Jumpers* we had several previews by the end of which I had taken fifteen minutes out of the play. I hate first nights. I attend out of courtesy for the actors and afterwards we all have a drink and go home.

GUPPY: How does the London theater world differ from New York?

STOPPARD: Theater in New York is nearer to the street. In London you have to go deep into the building, usually, to reach the place where theater happens. On Broadway, only the fire doors separate you from the sidewalk and you're lucky if the sound of a police car doesn't rip the envelope twice a night. This difference means something, I'm not quite sure what. Well, as Peter Brook will tell you, the theater has its roots in something holy, and perhaps we in London are still a little holier than thou. The potential rewards of theater in New York are really too great for its own good. One bull's-eye and you're rich and famous. The rich get more famous and the famous get richer. You're the talk of the town. The taxi drivers have read about you and they remember you for a fortnight. You get to be photographed for *Vogue* with new clothes and Vuitton luggage, if that's your bag. If it's a new play, everyone owes the writer, they celebrate him—the theater owners, the producers, the actors. Even the stage doorman is somehow touched by the wand. The sense of so much depending on success is very hard to ignore, perhaps impossible. It leads to disproportionate anxiety and disproportionate relief or disappointment. The British are more phlegmatic about these things. You know about British phlegm. The audiences, respectively, are included in this. In New York, expressions of appreciation have succumbed to galloping inflation—in London only the Americans stand up to applaud the actors, and only American audiences emit those high-pitched barks which signify the highest form of approval. But if you mean the difference between what happens on stage in London and New York, there isn't much, and there's no difference between the best. Cross-fertilization has evened out what I believe used to be quite a sharp difference between styles of American and British acting, although it is probably still a little harder to find American actors with an easy command of rhetoric, and British actors who can produce that controlled untidiness which, when we encountered it a generation ago, seemed to make acting life-like for the first time.

GUPPY: I have heard that in New York people sit up and wait for the *New York Times* review, which makes or breaks a show. It is not like that in London, but do you worry all night until the reviews come out the next day?

STOPPARD: Certainly I'm anxious. One is implicated in other people's fortunes—producers, directors, actors—and one wants the play to succeed for their sake as much as for one's own. If there is a favorable consensus among the reviewers, you accept it as a reasonable judgment. If you get mixed reviews, you are heartened by those who enjoyed it and depressed by the rejections. What one is anxious about is the judgment on the event rather than the play. None of us would have worked so hard if we didn't believe in the play, and so we don't need a critic to tell us whether we liked it, but whether we succeeded in putting it across. For the text is only one aspect of an evening at the theater; often the most memorable moments have little to do with the words uttered. It is the totality—to use the jargon—which is being judged. A favorable judgment means that on that occasion the play has worked, which does not mean that it always will.

GUPPY: Do critics matter as much?

STOPPARD: In the long term, not at all. In the short term they give an extra push, or conversely give you more to push against; but favorable reviews won't save a play for long if the audiences don't like it, and vice versa. The play has to *work*.

GUPPY: I would like to know what you mean by "work."

STOPPARD: It has to be truthful. The audience must believe. But the play is also a physical mechanism. Getting that mechanism to work takes an awful lot of time and preoccupation. The way music comes in and out, lights vary, etc. When you've got all that right you can get back to the text. Otherwise, the fact that it seems right on paper won't help you.

GUPPY: Do you change things according to what the reviews say?

STOPPARD: No. But I change things according to what happens to the play, and what I think of it. Sometimes one is involved in a revival and one wants to change things because one has changed oneself, and what used to seem intriguing or amusing might now strike one as banal. Any revival in which I am involved is liable to change.

GUPPY: It has been said that Kenneth Tynan was the last critic who had a definite point of view and was bold enough to express it, thereby influencing the direction of the theater. So perhaps critics do make a difference.

STOPPARD: Ken had enthusiasms. Some lasted longer than others and while he had them he pushed them. But you have to read critics critically and make the necessary adjustment according to what you know about them. When I was a critic—on my local paper in Bristol and later for a magazine in London—I floundered between pronouncing what I hoped were magisterial judgments and merely declaring my own taste. If I might quote myself from a previous interview—"I was not a good critic because I never had the moral character to pan a friend. I'll rephrase that—I had the moral character never to pan a friend."

GUPPY: But Tynan introduced into England what one associates with French intellectual life—a kind of intellectual terrorism, when suddenly one author or school is "in" and another "out," and woe betide he who disagrees! He destroyed people like Terence Rattigan and Christopher Fry and all those he called "bourgeois" playwrights, and you had to love Osborne and Brecht or else! But I recently saw Rattigan's *Separate Tables* and thought it very good indeed, infinitely better than some of the plays Ken had praised and made fashionable.

STOPPARD: Which shows that he didn't destroy them. However, I know what you mean, and one or two of my close friends thoroughly disapproved of Ken. But I hope they know what I mean when I stick up for him. The first time I met Ken was when I was summoned to his tiny office when the National Theatre offices consisted of a wooden hut on waste ground, and I was so awed by being in a small room with him that I began to stutter. Ken stuttered, as you know. So we sat stuttering at each other, mainly about his shirt which was pale lemon and came from Turnbull and Asser in Jermyn Street. This was in the late summer of 1966 when we wore roll-neck shirts.

GUPPY: You have been praised for your eloquence, your use of language—your aphorisms, puns, epigrams—as if you invented them, wrote them down and put them into your characters' mouths. Do you?

STOPPARD: No. They tend to show up when I need them. But perhaps it is significant that very often a particular line is more or less arbitrarily attached to a particular character. I can take a line from one character and give it to another. As I just told you, there was something in the third scene of *Hapgood* which I had to put in the second scene. But the dialogue was not between the same two people—only one of them was the same. So the lines of a female character became those of a male, and it made no difference. In *Night and Day* I had to invent an African dictator, but there was no way I could do it unless he was the only African dictator who had been to the London School of Economics. You don't have to be African or a dictator to make those observations about the British press. I rely heavily on an actor's performance to help individualize a character.

GUPPY: Do you act out all the characters as you write?

STOPPARD: Sometimes. I walk around the room speaking the dialogue.

GUPPY: Once you've got the idea and devised the narrative, do you take notes while you're reading up on the subject?

STOPPARD: Not really. Sometimes, over the course of several months, I might cover a page with odds and ends, many of which might find their way into the play. But I don't write down in notebooks, nor jot down what I overhear—nothing like that.

GUPPY: In the course of writing the play, do you get surprises, because for example, you don't know what a character is going to do next, or how the story will end?

STOPPARD: Absolutely.

GUPPY: What about the order of the play, the number of acts and scenes?

STOPPARD: I don't work out the whole plot before I begin, just the general outline. The play alters as you write it. For example, in *Jumpers* the end of the first act in my scheme turned out to be the end of the second act, followed by only an epilogue. *Hapgood* was in three acts and is now in two. The reason for the change is partly intrinsic and partly circumstantial. Managements prefer two-act plays because they think that audiences like only one interval, and Peter thought it would be better for the play. It shows how pragmatic the theater is, perhaps the most pragmatic art form, apart from advertising. For example, the male secretary, Maggs, used to be Madge, a woman. But when we came to choose the understudies we realized that if the secretary were male he could understudy so-and-so. It turned out to be better for the play also, because then Hapgood is the only woman surrounded by all these men. But at first it was a question of casting.

GUPPY: Having got your outline, do you proceed from the beginning to the end chronologically?

STOPPARD: Yes I do. I write plays from beginning to end, without making stabs at intermediate scenes, so the first thing I write is the first line of the play. By that time I have formed some idea of the set but I don't write that down. I don't write down anything which I can keep in my head—stage directions and so on. When I have got to the end of the play—which I write with a fountain pen; you can't scribble with a typewriter—there is almost nothing on the page except what people say. Then I dictate the play, ad-libbing all the stage directions into a tape machine from which my secretary transcribes the first script.

GUPPY: What are the pitfalls on the way? Things that might get you stuck?

STOPPARD: It is not like playing the violin—not difficult in that way. The difficulties vary at different stages. The first is that you haven't got anything you wish to write a play about. Then you get an idea, but it might be several ideas that could belong to two or three plays. Finally, if you are lucky, they may fit into the same play. The next difficulty, as I said before, is to translate these abstract ideas into concrete situations. That is a very long and elaborate period. Another difficulty is knowing when to start; it's chicken-and-egg—you don't know what you're going to write until you start, and you can't start until you know. Finally, in some strange, quantum mechanical way, the two trains arrive on the same line without colliding, and you can begin. The following stage is not exactly pleasant but exciting and absorbing—you live with the fear that "it" may go away. There is a three-month period when I don't want to say good morning to anyone lest I miss the thought that would make all the difference.

GUPPY: Once the play begins to take shape, what do you feel?

STOPPARD: Tremendous joy. Because whenever I finish a play I have no feeling that I would ever have another one to write.

GUPPY: Do you disappear from home to write?

STOPPARD: I disappear into myself. Sometimes I go away for a short period, say a week, to think and concentrate, then I come back home to carry on.

GUPPY: Where do you work and when?

STOPPARD: I have a very nice long room, which used to be the stable. It has a desk and lots of paper, etc. But most of my plays are written on the kitchen table at night, when everybody has gone to bed and I feel completely at peace. During the day, somehow I don't get much done; although I have a secretary who answers the phone, I always want to know who it is, and I generally get distracted.

GUPPY: Do you have an ideal spectator in mind when you write?

STOPPARD: Perhaps I do. Peter Wood has quite a different spectator in mind, one who is a cross between Rupert Bear and Winnie the Pooh. He assumes bafflement in order to force me to explain on a level of banality. If I had an ideal spectator it would be someone more sharp-witted and attentive than the average theatergoer whom Peter thinks of. A lot of changes in rehearsals have to do with reconciling his spectator with mine.

GUPPY: You have said that all the characters talk like you. Does that mean that you have trouble creating female characters? You once said, "There is an area of mystery about women which I find difficult to penetrate." Yet the eponymous character of your new play, *Hapgood*, is a woman.

STOPPARD: I wonder when I said that! It is not what I feel now. When I said I wasn't interested by plot or character I meant that they are not the point for me. Before writing *Night and Day* I thought, I'm sick of people saying there are no good parts for women in my plays, so I'll do one. It turned out not to be just about a woman, and I thought, well, one day I'll do a Joan of Arc. But I never think, "I'm writing for a woman so it had better be different."

GUPPY: How important are curtain lines?

STOPPARD: Very important, because they define the play's shape, like the spans of a bridge. It's like architecture—there is a structure and a conscious architect at work. Otherwise you could decide to have an interval at 8:30, and whatever was being said at that moment would be your curtain line. It wouldn't do.

GUPPY: You said that you have worked with Peter Wood for sixteen years, but are you always closely involved with your plays' productions?

STOPPARD: In this country, yes. In America I was involved with the production of *The Real Thing*, which was directed by Mike Nichols. But who knows what's going on elsewhere? You are pleased the plays are being done and hope for the best.

GUPPY: You have been accused of superficiality; some people say that your plays are all linguistic pyrotechnics, dazzling wordplay, intelligent punning, but that they don't have much substance. How do you react to that charge?

STOPPARD: I suppose there is a certain justice in it, insofar as if I were to write an essay instead of a play about any of these subjects it wouldn't be a profound essay.

GUPPY: Nowadays fame has become a thing in itself. In French the word is "gloire," which is nicer because it denotes achievement; it has connotations of glory. But fame doesn't: you can be famous just for being famous. Now that you are, do you still feel excited by it, or do you think it isn't that important?

STOPPARD: Oh, I like it. The benefits are psychological, social and material. The first because I don't have to worry about who I am—I am the man who has written these plays. The social advantages appeal to half of me because there are two of me: the recluse and the fan. And the fan in me is still thrilled to meet people I admire. As for the material side, I like having some money. The best way to gauge wealth is to consider the amount of money which you can spend *thoughtlessly*—a casual purchase which simply doesn't register. The really rich can do it in Cartier's; I'm quite happy if I can do it in a good bookshop or a good restaurant.

GUPPY: What about the company of your peers. Harold Pinter?

STOPPARD: The first time I met Harold Pinter was when I was a journalist in Bristol and he came down to see a student production of *The Birthday Party*. I realized he was sitting in the seat in front of me. I was tremendously intimidated and spent a good long time working out how to engage him in conversation. Finally, I tapped him on the shoulder and said, "Are you Harold Pinter or do you just look like him?" He said, "What?" So that was the end of that.

GUPPY: Going back to your work, *Jumpers* was about moral philosophy, and in it you attacked logical positivism and its denial that metaphysical questions are valid . . .

STOPPARD: Ah, but remember that I was attacking a dodo—logical positivism was over by the time I wrote the play. I was amused to see Freddy [Sir Alfred] Ayer being interviewed on television. The interviewer asked him what were the defects of logical positivism, and Freddy answered, "I suppose its main defect was that it wasn't true." The play addressed itself to a set of attitudes which people didn't think of as philosophical but which in fact were. At the same time, it tried to be a moral play, because while George has the right ideas, he is also a culpable person; while he is defending his ideas and attacking the opposition, he is also neglecting everyone around him and shutting out his wife who is in need, not to mention shooting his hare and stepping on his tortoise.

GUPPY: In the play you say that the Ten Commandments, unlike tennis rules, can't be changed, implying that there are fundamental moral principles which are eternally valid because of their transcendental provenance—their foundation in religion. Do you believe that?

STOPPARD: Yes, I do.

GUPPY: Are you religious?

STOPPARD: Well, I keep looking over my shoulder. When I am asked whether I believe in God, my answer is that I don't know what the question means. I approve of belief in God and I try to behave as if there is one, but that hardly amounts to faith. I don't know what religious certainty would consist of, though many apparently have it. I am uneasy with religious ceremonials, because I think intellectually, and the case for God is not an intellectual one. However, militant humanism grates on me much more than evangelism.

GUPPY: I would like to ask you about your early influences. What about the angry young men and the kitchen-sink school of the fifties, or Beckett, whom you are quoted as saying had the greatest impact on you?

STOPPARD: There were good plays and not-so-good plays. I was moved and interested by John Osborne's *Look Back in Anger,* Beckett's *Waiting for Godot, The Birthday Party* by Pinter, *Next Time I'll Sing To You*... I mean when I was starting to write plays. I'd be wary of calling them influences. I don't write the way I write because I liked them, I liked them because of the way I write, or despite it.

GUPPY: So if we forget about "influence," who are the writers you admire and go back to?

STOPPARD: I had a passion for Hemingway and Evelyn Waugh, and I think I will always return to them, apart from anyone else.

GUPPY: Does it annoy you that people compare you to George Bernard Shaw?

STOPPARD: I don't think they do very much. I find the comparison embarrassing, by which I mean flattering. Shaw raises conversation to the power of drama, and he does it for three acts. I sometimes do it for three pages, though the tone is very different; but my theatrical impulses are flashier. The result can be exhilarating when things go right, and pathetic when things go wrong. Anyway, one's admirations don't have much to do with the way one likes to write. I've been going around for years saying that Alan Bennett is one of the best playwrights we've had this century, and he does exactly what I don't do and can't do; he makes drama out of character study. The fact that his jokes are very good helps but he's really a social anthropologist who prefers to report in the form of plays. Incidentally, I think Bennett's comparative lack of recognition among the academically-minded has most to do with a snobbishness about television—where much of his best work appears. David Mamet is another great enthusiasm of mine, and another writer who has almost nothing in common with me.

GUPPY: What actually led you to write plays? Could you describe the genesis of your plays other than *Hapgood* and *Jumpers*?

STOPPARD: I started writing plays because everybody else was doing it at the time. As for the genesis of plays, it is never the story. The story comes just about last. I'm not sure I can generalize. The genesis of *Travesties* was simply the information that James Joyce, Tristan Tzara and Lenin were all in Zurich at the same time. Anybody can see that there was some kind of play in that. But what play? I started to read Richard Ellmann's biography of Joyce, and came across Henry Carr, and so on and so on. In the case of *Night and Day*, it was merely that I had been a reporter, that I knew quite a lot about journalism, and that I should have been writing another play about *something* and that therefore it was probably a good idea to write a play about journalists. After that, it was just a case of shuffling around my bits of knowledge and my prejudices until they began to suggest some kind of story. I was also shuffling a separate pack of cards which had to do with sexual attractions. Quite soon I started trying to integrate the two packs. And so on.

GUPPY: There's another aspect of your work which I would like to talk about, that is adaptations of other playwrights' plays. Are the two activities very different?

STOPPARD: Yes, they are. I don't do adaptations because I have a thing about them, but to keep busy. I write a play every three or four years and they don't take that long—perhaps a year each.

GUPPY: Does someone do the literal translation for you from the original language first?

STOPPARD: Yes, since I don't read any other languages. I have done two plays by Arthur Schnitzler, *Dalliance* and *Undiscovered Country,* one by Molnár, *Rough Crossing,* and a play by Johann Nestroy which became *On The Razzle.*

GUPPY: Do you tinker with the original text?

STOPPARD: There is no general rule. *Undiscovered Country* was pretty faithful. I thought of Schnitzler as a modern classic, not to be monkeyed about with. But you're not doing an author a favor if the adaptation is not vibrant. So in the end I started "helping," not because Schnitzler was defective but because he was writing in 1905 in Vienna. When you are writing a play you use cultural references by the thousands, and they all interconnect like a nervous system. In the case of *Dalliance*, Peter Wood started with the idea that the third act should be transferred to the wings of the opera. He did it beautifully and it worked very well. The number of critics who suddenly turned out to be Schnitzler purists was quite surprising. As for *On The Razzle*, that had a wonderful plot—which wasn't Nestroy's own anyway—and I invented most of the dialogue. The Molnár play was set in an Italian castle and I put it on an ocean liner called "The Italian Castle." And I also made up nearly all the dialogue. So you can see there's a difference between "translation" and "adaptation."

GUPPY: So far your adaptations have been of plays. Have you ever thought of adapting a novel, or a book of testimony, into a play or a series of plays? For example, Primo Levi's *If This Is a Man,* or Nadezhda Mandelstam's *Hope Against Hope?* I mention these because I know you admire them as much as I do.

STOPPARD: I think Nadezhda Mandelstam's books are two of the greatest books written in this century. But what would be the point of turning them into plays?

GUPPY: To make them accessible to a larger audience, the way Olivia Manning's *The Balkan Trilogy* was resurrected and became a bestseller after it was shown on television as a six-part series.

STOPPARD: It would be admirable if it made people turn to the Mandelstam books. I quite agree that television would be the way to do it.

GUPPY: Let's talk about another of your activities—writing filmscripts. You have never written an original one. Why not?

STOPPARD: Because I don't have any original ideas to spare.

GUPPY: What if someone gave you the idea?

STOPPARD: That is possible, but it would be pure accident if you gave me the right one. The reason is that all you know about me is what I have written so far; it has nothing to do with what I want to do next because I don't know, either.

GUPPY: What is the difference between writing a play and writing a filmscript?

STOPPARD: The main difference is that in films the writer serves the director, and in the theater the director serves the writer—broadly speaking.

GUPPY: Now for the first time you are going to direct your own film version of *Rosencrantz and Guildenstern.* Are you looking forward to it?

STOPPARD: The reason why I agreed to do it myself was that the producers gave me a list of twenty possible directors and I couldn't see why any of them should or should not do it, since I had no idea what each would wish to do. So I suggested myself, because it was the line of least resistance, and also because I am the only director willing to commit the necessary violence to the play—I've thrown masses of it out, and I've added things.

GUPPY: You are friendly with Czech playwrights, like Václav Havel and others. Do you feel any special affinity with them as a result of your own Czech origin?

STOPPARD: This whole Czech thing about me has got wildly out of hand. I wasn't two years old when I left the country and I was back one week in 1977. I went to an English school and was brought up in English. So I don't feel Czech. I like what Havel writes. When I first came across his work, I thought *The Memorandum* was a play I'd have liked to have written, and you don't think that of many plays. And when I met him I loved him as a person. I met other writers there I liked and admired, and I felt their situation keenly. But I could have got onto the wrong plane and landed in Poland or Paraguay and felt the same about writers' situations there.

GUPPY: I wanted to ask you about radio plays, because you started out writing some, and before *Rosencrantz* had a number of them produced on the radio. It is always astonishing that despite television, radio is still so popular, especially for plays. What are your feelings about radio—its technique, possibilities, and differences from other dramatic forms?

STOPPARD: Radio plays are neither easier nor harder. I'm supposed to be writing one now,* and the hard part is simply finding a play to write. The pleasant part will be writing it. There is nothing much to be said about radio technique except what is obvious—scene setting through dialogue and sound effects. I'd like to write a radio play which consisted entirely of sound effects but I suppose it would be rather a short one.

---

*In the Native State

GUPPY: After you have seen *Hapgood* through, what are you going to do?

STOPPARD: I would like to write a very simple play, perhaps with two or three people in one setting. A literature play rather than an event play. Getting *Hapgood* ready was exhausting and frustrating—it has as many scene changes, light cues, sound cues, etc., as a musical. I'd like to write a play where all the time and the energy can be devoted to language, thought process and emotion.

GUPPY: It is often said that a writer's output is the product of a psychosis, of self-examination. Is there any indication of this in your case?

STOPPARD: You tell me!

GUPPY: What is the most difficult aspect of playwriting?

STOPPARD: Structure.

GUPPY: And the easiest?

STOPPARD: Dialogue.

GUPPY: What about the curtain lines? Do they come first and then you work your way towards them, or do they arrive in the natural progression of writing the dialogue?

STOPPARD: Curtain lines tend to be produced under the pressure of the preceding two or three acts, and usually they seem so dead right, to me anyway, that it really is as if they were in the DNA, unique and inevitable.

GUPPY: What are some of your favorite curtain lines—and not necessarily those in your own plays?

STOPPARD: "The son of a bitch stole my watch" [from *The Front Page*]—I quote from memory—and "You that way; we this way" [from *Love's Labour's Lost*].

GUPPY: Not to put you to the test, but can you provide a curtain line for this interview?

STOPPARD: "That's all, folks."

Stoppard's Secret Agent

Michael Billington

Although *Hapgood* opened on 8 March 1988 "to mingled cries of delight and disbelief" (as an editorial in *The Guardian* put it), the overnight reviewers found the "convoluted" play's "passionless permutations" so "thoroughly incomprehensible" that "it would need a seeing eye dog with A-level physics to guide most of us through what was going on." The play was so "user-hostile," said one reviewer, "it seems to me that, with *Hapgood,* Mr. Stoppard is signalling his intention to give up any pretence of being a serious playwright." Michael Billington's carefully balanced observation that he "found it as fascinating as it was perplexing" was about as close as any reviewer came to a cry of delight. Billington caught up with a chastened but still combative Stoppard the morning after reviews had panned Stoppard's first major stage play in six years. Smarting from the worst reviews he had ever received, Stoppard was at pains both to defend the response *Hapgood* was accorded by "your ordinary punter" and to spell out the "central idea" of the play. Despite his image of being cool and dispassionate, Stoppard describes himself as "a very emotional person" and discusses the emotional resonances of *Jumpers* and *Professional Foul.*

Tom Stoppard recalls that during the run of *Rosencrantz and Guildenstern Are Dead* on Broadway a woman rushed up to him outside the theatre and asked if he was the author of the play. With becoming modesty, he said Yes. "Well," she said, "I want you to know that it's the worst play I ever saw in my life."

From *The Guardian,* 18 March 1988.

Nothing like that has happened to Stoppard outside the Aldwych since the opening of *Hapgood*. All the same Stoppard, 36 hours after the first night, seems ruefully pensive. He envies the breezy elan of Cole Porter who, just before his own Broadway premieres, used to set off on a world cruise. In contrast, Stoppard is still fine-tuning the text of *Hapgood* and seems less than gruntled at the tone of some of the reviews.

"The play," he says, "has been written about as though it were incomprehensibly baffling. It doesn't seem to me to be borne out by experience. After all these years one thing you learn is what's going on in an audience and by God you know when you're losing them. It's like getting a temperature: you can't miss it. My impression is that your ordinary punter has less trouble with it than some of our critics.

"But critical response is like a branch of natural history. It's a cycle as inevitable as that of the sea anemone. It's nice to be discovered as a bright young man but then the playwright gets older and the critic becomes the bright young man who's not going to be taken in. It's nothing to complain about. But the truth is you get overpraised when you're young and sandbagged a bit when you're older."

Hapgood, on reflection, strikes me as taxing but penetrable: an engrossing theatrical equivalent of David Mamet's *House of Games.* The problem is we are so used to up-front, single-issue plays we tend to get thrown by a multi-layered, hydra-headed animal like *Hapgood.* I counted half a dozen issues whirling through it. Was it finally saying that if the laws of quantum physics are not susceptible of proof, then everything else is treacherously uncertain?

"No," says Stoppard. "That's too sweeping. If there's a central idea it is the proposition that in each of our characters—yours and mine are doubtless exceptions—the person who gets up in the morning and puts on the clothes is the working majority of a dual personality, part of which is always there in a submerged state. That doesn't seem to me a profound or original idea but I still find it interesting.

"The play is specifically about a woman—Hapgood—who is one person in the morning but who finds that, under certain pressures, there is a little anarchist upsetting the apple-cart. The central idea is that inside Hapgood One there is a Hapgood Two sharing the same body; and that goes for most of us."

In that case who is Stoppard Two? Who is the sleeper lurking inside the genial, ironic, surprisingly boyish 51-year-old playwright, expensively accoutred in a brown-suede overcoat and, give or take the overnight reviews, pretty much at ease with the world?

A pause.

"I haven't considered revealing my other side to more than one person at a time. But I suspect the genial interviewee is a sort of cover. I do have periods when I'm extremely cross with life and I try to behave well. My metabolism is much higher than it ought to be for a professional playwright and, as I get close to a first night, I try to do eighteen things an hour: if you go on like that, you blow the circuits. I am a very emotional person. People wish to perceive me as someone who works out ideas in a cool, dispassionate way but I don't think that's my personality at all."

Stoppard's double identity, even as a playwright, is territory that has been too little explored. His plays, from *Rosencrantz and Guildenstern* to *Hapgood*, have been analysed as if they were intellectual conceits: I suspect they only work because of their emotional ground-base.

That first play is anchored in what John Wood once called the 'bravery' of those two attendant lords whistling in the Elsinore dark. In *Jumpers*—more in the Aldwych revival than the original Old Vic production—you felt the pain of a marriage audibly splintering. In *The Real Thing*—more in the New York than the London version—you were aware of the torturing self-abasement that stems from the knowledge of infidelity. Stoppard reveals that his regular director, Peter Wood, is always on at him to up the emotional ante.

"Imagine," says Stoppard, "I write a play about astronomy because I've got all these fascinating things to say about Neptune and Ursa Major and that I also feature a married couple. Peter will say these people are married and can we take their relationship out of the fridge. He always bullies me and says I am stingy about this side of things.

"For instance, there's a scene in *Jumpers* where George recalls the first day Dotty walked into his class and, because her hair was wet, he called her 'the hyacinth girl.' These lines give the play emotional leverage and make it a play about marriage rather than moral philosophy.

"Peter tries to get me to put a hyacinth girl into every play including *Hapgood*. I always think I've done it and he says I haven't. Peter is an advocate for the audience and tries to make the plays work for an imaginary spectator called Rupert who he believes was the bear of little brain. It's no good my telling him that was actually Pooh."

Stoppard, I would claim, has a dual political as well as emotional identity. On the one hand there is the Stoppard who regretfully says, "We live in an age where the leper is the don't-know." On the other hand, there is the Stoppard of *Professional Foul* and *Every Good Boy Deserves Favour* who has taken a clear stand on the question of human rights in the Eastern bloc. But even now Stoppard is wary of being dubbed a committed playwright.

"With Eastern Europe I don't feel I am carrying some kind of torch for the causes that might crop up in this or that play. Because what I do—which is write plays—is something whose problems are empirical. With *Professional Foul,* I didn't sit down to sound off about human rights. It happened to be Prisoner of Conscience Year in 1977 and Amnesty asked if I could write a play to mark the event. Well I obviously couldn't do a play about a couple who go *Come Dancing* in Prague. What happens is you sit down in a practical, level-headed way and you end up with *Professional Foul.*

"If you're writing plays or painting pictures, whatever your public postures, what you're trying to do is write a good play or paint a good picture. I still believe that if your aim is to change the world, journalism is a more immediate, short-term weapon. But art is important in the long-term in that it lays down some kind of matrix of moral responsibility. It's on that one pins one's hopes of the thing lasting. I mean can you think of a play that has helped to change anything?"

I suggest that *The Normal Heart* did an effective job of raising consciousness about Aids.

"Fair enough. But will it last as long as *Ghosts* which hardly even mentions directly the subject of a transmitted sexual disease? My point is that plays work through metaphor. In the end the best play about Vietnam will probably turn out to have been written by Sophocles."

If there is a moral touchstone in Stoppard's work it is probably to be found in children: the boy Sacha in *Professional Foul,* the son in *Hapgood,* and now the 11-year-old hero of the film, *Empire of the Sun,* directed by Steven Spielberg, which Stoppard has adapted from the J. G. Ballard novel about a boy surviving the 1941 Japanese invasion of Shanghai. Why this enduring faith in children?

"It's to do with their innocence which isn't something they acquire but which is something they haven't lost. I do have an idea which crops up all the time which is that children are very wise because they don't know how to be taken in. You can fool people if they are very clever but it's quite hard to fool a child. I think children start off with a sense of natural justice which is obscured through a process of corrupting sophistication."

But although *Empire of the Sun* endorses the idea of the moral wisdom and survival-capacity of children, Stoppard does not see it as essentially a writer's film.

"It was a happy experience but on a film like that the writer is there to serve the director who himself is serving the narrative. It's nothing like the theatre which is the other way round. I didn't write *Empire of the Sun*. J. G. Ballard did. It's not supposed to be Stoppardian. But the cinema is a wonderfully madcap world in that you're writing 18 months before a camera turns and so the whole thing is quite leisurely. Then when they are shooting you get a phone-call from Seville at eight in the evening asking for a new speech to be shot at seven the following morning.

"What I actually wrote was more modest than the film turns out to be. When I started, it wasn't a Spielberg film and I was a little wary of putting in World War Two aeroplanes flying about and shooting at each other. In the event there were Mustangs and Zeros flying around the south of Seville and it was highly exciting. But writing for the movies is a technical challenge. If I had tried to express my personality and favourite leanings it is doubtful if Steven would have shot it or that it would have been in the finished film."

Stoppard actually seems to enjoy the nuts-and-bolts side of writing as much as the high-flying ideas. This week, for instance, he has inserted four speeches running to about eight lines into *Hapgood* because he knew something was missing: the precise point at which the heroine moves from entrapment to warning and realises that the technical traitor is also the person most anxious to help her son. Stoppard the brain-box is also the practical mechanic.

But that is just another symptom of Stoppard's double identity. He is the intellectual firecracker who writes about emotional havoc. The apostle of non-commitment whose stand on human rights is unequivocal. The thriving playwright (and ex-hack) still gnawed by thoughts of the public prints. The wordsmith who admires Ayckbourn because "I have a predilection for plays that don't depend on lines you can quote."

If he were not Tom Stoppard, who would he like to be? "Someone who sings or plays a musical instrument well. It causes me intense grief that I can't do it or even tell good from bad. I'm not talking about being Placido Domingo. I'd just be happy to be someone who plays piano in a pub."

As we finish talking we make our way down Carnaby Street with its extraordinary hungover Sixties aroma. "I feel it should be in the V and A rather than out here," says Stoppard. As he sets off in a taxi to do a television interview, his parting shot is that he can't wait to get the Sunday reviews over and done with as if he were a tyro-playwright undergoing ordeal by criticism. I feel as if I've had a sudden, touching glimpse of Stoppard Two: the anxious self-doubting Thomas that still lurks under the poised, equable figure of the success-wreathed, acclaimed public playwright.

The Event and the Text

Tom Stoppard

In November 1981 Stoppard spent two weeks as artist-in-residence at San Diego State University, participated in revising and rehearsing a play billed as *Mackoon's Hamlet, Cahoot's Macbeth* (complete with numerous San Diego references) for the SDSU stage, and gave a public lecture on the topic "The Event and the Text." Invited as featured speaker at the Third International Conference on the Fantastic in Boca Raton, Florida, in March 1982, Stoppard gave a keynote address entitled "The Event and the Text." Giving The Whidden Lectures at McMaster University in Hamilton, Ontario, in October 1988, Stoppard chose as his title "The Event and the Text." Despite sharing the same title, these free-associative, informal talks differ in content. In San Diego Stoppard read out multiple versions of the telegram in *Night and Day* as he had successively revised it for an American audience. In Florida he announced that he had "just finished a play which is about a playwright" and read several speeches from an as-yet-unperformed script of *The Real Thing*. In Ontario he admiringly describes moments from Shakespeare productions that were not in Shakespeare's text. But in all of his talks he offers an engaging, conversational, but finally impassioned affirmation of what he described in San Diego as his "theme for *life*," the claim that a play is not a text but an event, that a playwright does not write literature to be studied but crafts theatrical events to be performed.

The Whidden Lectures, McMaster University, Hamilton, Ontario, 24 October 1988. Transcribed and edited by Doreen DelVecchio for *Ta Panta* (McMaster University Faculty Association), 6, no. 1 (1988).

I'm going to begin with a description of part of a production which I never saw myself. When I started out trying to write plays there was a celebrated production of *The Tempest* at one of the Oxford colleges and later on I got to work with some people who had been to see this. Surprisingly often, over the years, the memory of this production would come up. The director I worked with, the designer I worked with—it was something which had stayed in their memory. This was now 30 years ago, and it's still a vignette which comes up in conversation occasionally among people I work with. This production of *The Tempest* took place in the open air in the early evening, and when it became time for Ariel to leave the action of the play he turned and he ran up the stage, away from the audience. Now the stage was a lawn, and the lawn backed on to a lake. He ran across the grass and got to the edge of the lake, and he just kept running, because the director had had the foresight to put a plank walkway just underneath the surface of the water. So you have to imagine: it's become dusk, and quite a lot of the artificial lighting has come on, and back there in the gloom is this lake. And Ariel says his last words and he turns and he runs and he gets to the water and he runs and he goes splish splash, splish splash, right across the lake and into the enfolding dark, until one can only just hear his footsteps making these little splashes, and then ultimately his little figure disappeared from view. And at that moment, from the further shore, a firework rocket was ignited and just went whoosh into the sky and burst into lots of sparks. All the sparks went out one by one and Ariel had gone. This is the thing: you can't write anything as good as that. If you look it up, it says, "Exit Ariel."

Now the thing you look it up in appears to be a book. It is a book. It appears to be the same kind of "thing" that you hold in your hand when you're looking something up in *David Copperfield* or *The Golden Bowl* or whatever. It seems to be a piece of literature—this book thing. This is a coincidence. Really, the point of the distinction which this lecture is going to be making would be made much more quickly, indeed instantly, if there had been an alternative convention for the dissemination of plays. Suppose we just did scrolls, or it all came out on disk, and nobody ever thought of making it look like *David Copperfield* or *For Whom the Bell Tolls* or *Brighton Rock,* or whatever. But they keep looking as though they are the same sort of thing. If you work in the theatre, I think probably especially if you work in the theatre as a writer, you understand very early that they are not the same sort of thing.

I think that you are probably aware of the truism, that poems never get finished; they merely get abandoned. I think that plays never quite get finished either; they get interrupted by rehearsal. The production impedes a process which then very often continues after that first performance has evolved and gone its way and finished and so on. Not all playwrights would stand beside me here and say this. I think that there are a number of writers, perhaps for all I know the majority, who see what they do as nearer a piece of literature than I do: what gets handed in on the first day of rehearsal—I mean that is it—you don't mess about, you don't come back and rewrite it or ask the actors if they have a better idea.

I like a kind of rough theatre where everything goes into the melting pot. I'm extremely jealous of my frontiers, in the sense that I wish to be the only person who can move them, but I consider them to be moveable. When you write a play it makes a certain kind of noise in your head, and the rehearsal and staging is an attempt to persuade the actors to reproduce this noise. Sometimes the actors have a better noise to offer. You know what I'm saying, don't you, about this noise? "She shouts," "she whispers," "she goes on her knees and pleads," "she whines," or "she laughs" . . . there's a cadence and a rhythm, and of course, it's expressed in language. But theatre is a curious equation in which language is merely one of the components. The point about this equation is that it has to come out nicely. In other words, you can't mess about with one side of the equals sign without doing some compensating act on the other side. It has to still work as a piece of algebra, if you like. But time and again one discovers that if one walks into the process of staging a play with an algebraic equation in mind, and everybody has to do exactly $4y$ and you do $3x$ and you do something cubed: what you get is a sort of very rigid structure which is never going to be as good again as it is on the night you open.

In the best possible world the best show you give is the last one because really you ought to come in with something which remains organic. This, of course, is sometimes a disadvantage as well because plays can go off, like fruit; and of course the soft part goes first, as in fruit. But nevertheless I think if you have the alternative idea that a play is something like this ashtray—here it is and you put it down and you come back in three weeks and there it is again; it hasn't moved, it hasn't changed: then I think what actually happens is that they break. The noise of a play breaking is something which keeps playwrights awake: once they hear it they never forget that noise.

The equation I'm talking about contains, among its elements, not merely the obvious things like the physical limitations: it contains the music of a play, it contains the lighting of a play. I don't know whether this sounds like a truism or something which is faintly surprising, but the length or even the necessary presence of a speech may be altered, one's sense of it, of its necessity, or one's sense of its being too long or not long enough—that can actually be altered by a light. This is why I'm trying to say that what we don't do is what people do when they write *David Copperfield*. We're doing something else. Of course this thing which contains the play, this book—I'm not saying that it doesn't contain bits of literature; very often it may well do; in the case of *The Tempest*, obviously it does. Let's be clear about that: of course there's literature in it. But the expression of it is slightly different. (All these things are my prejudices; don't buy everything!)

To me what is in this book is two things: the one turns into the other. The first thing is an attempt to describe an event which you wish to take place one day; you write this play and you're trying to describe what you want to happen here. The other thing is it's a record of some mythical production which has taken place. It becomes a description retroactively, not of a particular production but a description of an event which may take place again in one form or another—an event which has taken place. I make this distinction because there's a kind of pivot point; it's when the author dies. When you're dead you've had your chance and now it's somebody else's turn. The truism which I want to offer to you, and I think it is one, is that a given text, irrespective of its literary aspirations, or the degree to which it succeeds in realising these aspirations—a given text can give rise to an extraordinarily satisfying and a deeply satisfactory experience, or a lousy one. Otherwise there wouldn't be any bad productions of Shakespeare. Why would there be?

What in fact happens is that the manipulation of the elements tries to achieve some kind of balance with the utterance, the psychological relationships, and the movement of the narrative. I think I could actually now deliver this to you as a question, which you don't have to take as rhetorical, though you don't have to answer out loud either. The first time I ever lectured like this was eighteen years ago—I haven't done it much since—but eighteen years ago when I was a "promising young playwright" I did this very thing at an American university, just like this, on a campus in the Midwest; I was very innocent in those days and without intending any kind of malice I remarked at one point that I'd never written anything for "study." A ripple of consternation went over the auditorium. That was what they

202

did with plays: plays were what you "studied." It was a new idea to me that one studies plays. It was a new idea to my audience that one did anything else with plays. But when you look back, those of you who actually go to the theatre, when you look back on things that you've seen, when you remember things which happened to you in a theatre, very often, surprisingly often, what you remember is not actually to do with what anybody wrote—remember Ariel.

I find that that's true of me with my own plays. I'll probably refer to things I wrote myself now and again: this is not an incipient megalomania; it's because it's the only experience I have: I don't go to other people's rehearsals. I did an adaptation of a play by Schnitzler; it's called *Das weite Land* (we called it *Undiscovered Country*). It's a big play, and Schnitzler wanted it done in three acts, with two intermissions. This was at the National Theatre in London, and the director, Peter Wood, was insistent that he wanted to do it with one intermission. And this meant that we did the play right through Act One and half-way through Act Two; we had an intermission and then we did the second half of Act Two and Act Three. Now Act One of this play took place in the garden and conservatory of the house of a rich Viennese industrialist. Act Two took place in the lobby of a chic mountaineering hotel in the Dolomites—in this case it even had a working elevator. The idea was that without anybody going out and having a drink you would go from this garden and conservatory and then you'd be in this hotel lobby in the Dolomites, and you'd still be there, thinking this is great.

Come the technical rehearsal, we got to the end of Act One (because it was a translation/adaption I hadn't been quite as present during rehearsals as I normally am with my own plays) and they were about to embark on this transition. I sat at the back and what was on that stage was just too alarming and depressing for words. There were people wandering around trailing cables and there were greenhouses falling about and hotel lobbies falling in and everything had stopped and it just looked dreadful! The director (I'd known him for ten years by then, we'd done a lot of work together) was his usual insouciant self. I thought this time he really has pushed it and blown it. But that was a dry run, and I'll describe what happened ultimately when he got what he wanted. As we got to the end of Act One and time to do the scene change, a lot of dry ice began to be pumped from all around. After a very short time the stage was up to about shoulder height in this white fog. This gave a certain coherence to the chaos; it certainly improved matters. I was still reserving my judgement at that point. The next thing that happened was that in the middle of the stage—out of this fog—a fist holding an ice-axe went straight up and was followed by a shoulder with a coil of rope, and then a little woolly hat, and then a mountaineer was standing there; he started pulling on his rope, and pulled another mountaineer up out of this fog (there was no trapdoor; he crawled through the fog from the wings). Then these two guys started pulling on the rope, and a third person with woolly hat and ice-axe and whatever came through. It was very interesting. They all stood there and clapped each other on the back and congratulated each other, and looked around and all that and then by this time the fog was beginning to disperse because the dry ice just—whatever dry ice does—you chemistry people will tell me later. These three mountaineering guys were then just standing in this hotel lobby with the lift going up and down. For years afterwards, even occasionally now, somebody says, "*Undiscovered Country*, you . . . you did . . . you wrote that? That was wonderful, when that fog came in and the mountaineers . . ." I say, "Yeah, I wrote that."

The moment at which you give the audience "the information" is something which can be under the control of the writer. This is the conventional view. As a matter of fact it was my view: you wrote a play and theatre was what happened to it. You gave it to them and they gratefully took it and then they did your play. The way this thing drip-fed from here to there was what you'd written and it drip-fed at the rate you wrote it and in the order in which you wrote it. This is nonsense. There was a production of *Comedy of Errors* Trevor Nunn did in London about fifteen years ago. It was a modern dress thing. Now *Comedy of Errors*—I know you know but I'll bore you anyway: it begins in Ephesus. The situation is that Ephesus is at war with Syracuse. The play begins with this old guy who is this sort of chief fellow in Ephesus, and what he's saying is that we have this hostile situation with Syracuse and anybody from Syracuse caught here in Ephesus will be put to death. At which point one of the people who has been listening to this long speech turns around, and he's got this sort of wary, terrified smile on his face—he's wearing a Syracuse T-shirt. Now, Shakespeare didn't know that he would do this. And then there is some language which tells us what we've just been told. I'm not criticizing, I'm just pointing this out. This production was absolutely wonderful; I say I absolutely adored it, to make the point that in fact it went just slightly soft at that point because the writer was dead and he wasn't there to take it out. They might have done it for him.

Shakespeare theatre-going, Shakespeare-watching and so on, is ac-Otually in itself as you can imagine, a rich enough field to explicate any point that I might make and more beyond. I hardly know where to stop. It does encourage what I suppose many people here might consider to be liberties, the taking of liberties, some of them quite notorious if that's the word. Some of you may know of a very famous production of *King Lear* by Peter Brook which Paul Scofield did I suppose twenty years ago. In *King Lear* there's a scene where Gloucester is blinded. They carried the play right through until Gloucester's blinding and then they had an intermission. So we had blind Gloucester staggering about, with blood pouring down from his eyes looking really horribly wounded; it was quite grisly. What made it worse was that the servants who were moving the furniture away and generally tidying up were jostling him and adding to his injury and being extremely callous towards him. As all this was going on, Brook brought up the house lights and—it was really extraordinarily effective—you were in the same world as it. In a strange kind of way you were implicated because the lights were just leveled off until it looked the same there as it was here. Gloucester was staggering about and then he'd gone. Then you had to kind of pull yourself together and look around and say, "Well actually I didn't do anything," and go and have a drink. It was very good theatre. The only thing is it wasn't what Shakespeare actually wrote: he didn't write these servants jostling him and ignoring him. They were actually running around offering him whites of egg and trying to make his eyes better and comforting him. Brook cut all that.

I do want you to ask yourselves where you stand on this point. And I'm not going to belabour it. It's just that we need to be reminded what happens in theatre, what the people who practise theatre feel they can do. I'm not in any sense standing here rebuking, "j'accuse" stuff—not at all—it interests me too. It's going to interest me even more when I'm dead. Harold Pinter, you know, once flew to Rome with a lawyer because they were doing, I think, *Betrayal,* in a boxing-ring. I don't mean that they decided oh well, we'll do the play right here. What I mean is that the set was a boxing ring and then they had two ladies making love in a bathtub. He never wrote that, and he moved in with his lawyer and stopped it. At the time I thought, "Oh Harold, for God's sake. Somebody else will do it right later, don't worry." But in the end my sympathies came round towards him. Principally because it was the first time the thing had been done in Italy; I feel—this is just pragmatic—I do feel different about the first time a play is done.

I saw a *Rosencrantz* in Italy where Rosencrantz was a woman. She didn't play it as a woman—she was the director's mistress, she always had a good role, and in this case she was wonderful, I loved the production. It also took place in a series of perspex boxes, which I also loved. The only thing which depresses a writer as a matter of fact, if he chances upon a play of his own years later, is to see a production which tries to mimic the original. That's not terribly interesting, and so I was quite pleased. If they'd done it in a boxing ring I might have felt slightly different.

All right, this equation. I'll tell you an anecdote about something which happened to a play of mine when it was done in France, and you'll see exactly what I mean by this algebraic equation. The second half of *Travesties* begins—well it began, with about twelve minutes of a young woman recounting a sort of potted history of how Lenin got from Zurich to the Finland Station in St. Petersburg. In fact, the speech began with the publication of *Das Kapital* and it went on for about five pages. And I remember thinking I might be pushing my luck here. What I was counting on was that it was the first thing which happened after the interval, so people would come back and feel it's OK; secondly it was a relatively new character, an attractive young librarian lady called Cecily, and we hadn't seen much of her before in the play. I was tempted to try this thing partly because there was a slight sense of sadism I suppose towards the audience because the first act was jolly and full of jokes and people generally sat about laughing; I thought it would be quite nice if they all went out thinking "oh this is fun isn't it," came back, and just hit them with this boring thing, as though they'd come back into the wrong theatre. So, she learned it, then we did previews and from the first moment it was clear that I'd overplayed my hand here, so I started cutting from the top and in the end (I'm very pragmatic about these things) she did the last paragraph. I mean the train was practically entering the station by the time she . . .

The play was going to be done in Paris and the director gets in touch with me and he says this and that, and any thoughts, notes, and I said, "No, that's fine—oh one thing, Cecily's speech, top of Act Two, don't feel you have to do it all." And he said, "Mais pourquoi pas? C'est magnifique." "No, no, listen, I've been there, I promise you, I thought it was a good idea but I promise you—listen, in London we actually cut it down to one paragraph." And he said, "But you know, you're crazy." He wanted to do it all. So I said "OK, I mean you do it," and so on, "sur votre tête be it"; back he went to Paris. I carried on with my work and they did the play. I heard it went pretty well, and the chap phoned up and he said everything was fine, and I said, "How was Cecily's speech at the top of Act Two?" And he said, "Formidable, superbe!" I was thinking, God, this is the sort of audience I deserve. So I go to Paris to see it, and it's fine, and Act Two starts and he was right. She did every word and you could have heard a pin drop. But she was stark naked! He'd altered the equation.

It made me laugh too but you see what I'm saying, don't you, that the thing which is going on up here is not literature walking about. That's not what it is. When I go back over my own experience I just remember things all the time where the idea was not a good idea, certainly with Shakespeare. And I don't mean either let's all do it as though it's happening in 1930 or something, let's all do it in jackboots to show what *The Tempest* is really about or whatever. I don't mean that; in fact I on the whole disapprove of that on purely practical grounds, sort of artistic practical grounds. I don't think theatre works as parable; it works as metaphor. This is an important difference. Let's say that you see *Coriolanus* and you think to yourself, "Mussolini." Now many people I would think have done so, or something like that, thought of some twentieth-century dictator or nineteenth-century dictator; it depends on where the play is done. If it's done in Latin America it might be somebody I can't call on now, but there would be a sense of a reference and application. This is to me how the thing is supposed to work; but as soon as you make everybody Italian and give them a shining brown belt and big boots and walking around in 1930s Italian Fascist style then it's not metaphor, then it becomes a sort of parable. I think that seldom works because in a way you're denying the sub-text's right to be sub, which is where its power is.

Do you know a play called *The Fire Raiser;* it's called *The Fire Bugs* in America, by the German-Swiss writer called Max Frisch. It's set in a bourgeois household, in Germany, in a town where a couple of arsonists are at work. Every now and again a building goes up in flames and nobody knows who is doing it. Into this little bourgeois household one day a very sinister man comes and insinuates himself into this house as the lodger. He moves in upstairs then brings a friend and insinuates the friend and now there's two lodgers, both upstairs. And all the time in the newspaper you hear another house has been burnt to the ground, a factory here and there, fire everywhere, and these two lodgers come and go; they don't say much, but they start bringing in cans of gasoline and storing it. So pretty soon the attic is full of cans of petrol. Downstairs is this quavering family saying to each other, "Well, I'm sure it's not them." Finally the first of these men comes downstairs and says to the householder, "Excuse me, would you happen to have a box of matches?" Then there's this awful kind of pause: he doesn't want to antagonize the guy, so he gets a box of matches and gives it to him. The guy goes out and goes upstairs. The man turns around to his wife and he says, "Now listen, if they were the arsonists they'd have their own matches." Then the house blows up.

It was perfectly clear to me what this play was about: how the Nazis came to power in Germany in the thirties. It was a perfect metaphor for it. I went around telling people this as though I'd written it, you know. It turned out that Max Frisch thought it was about the way the Communists came to power in Eastern Europe after the Second World War. My point is, I'm not sure he was any more right than I was, and if you had a third idea I'm not sure you would be any less right than he was or than I might be. In other words the power of metaphor is that it impacts, and just goes where you happen to see it from. Most of the time metaphors are not that powerful and they tend to suggest one correlative, and very often the writer has had that particular correlative in mind, and he's, as it were, manipulated it. But the work, which in some curious way, seems to be immortal insofar as we might be there to read it is a work where the author didn't think anything like that. If Melville had somebody saying, "You know, it seems to me that this great white whale here, it reminds me, it sort of seems to stand for the imperial experience," he'd say, "That's interesting, Ahab, yeah, I think you have a point . . ." Then the air would have gone out of the bag, right?

The empirical nature of the theatre as it happens is matched by a kind of brazen pragmatism on the part of writers like myself. I don't say that all writers are like myself, but I feel in a sense disappointingly pragmatic about these things. And very often a play takes its final form for reasons which are rather embarrassing to admit, and never more so than in this context and this milieu—where they are "studied." I'll give you a frivolous example from a play which I adapted and translated from one by Nestroy, the nineteenth-century Viennese comedian-actor who wrote innumerable plays and a handful of them are still in the Viennese repertoire. One of these we did at the National Theatre, we called it *On the Razzle*. There's a certain point in the play where they're in a restaurant, it was a curtain, it was a moment when an act finished and one wanted something, you know, which wasn't quite there.

I decided to have a waiter come on with what I called a flaming pudding, like a Christmas pudding, with lots of flaming spirit on it. It looked as though it would do the job. So we rehearsed and rehearsed, and of course you rehearse without props, the pudding or anything, you just do it, and finally we were there at the technical rehearsal: "OK where is the flaming pudding?" It turned out that because of the fire regulations at the National Theatre we couldn't have a flaming pudding. So then there was a pause for consultation, and everyone turned to me as if it was my fault. Finally I said, "Well, OK we better make it a cake with electric candles," so the fire people wouldn't mind. They said, "That's fine, we'll do that. Go and get me a cake and electric candles." I said, "Wait a minute, whose birthday is it?" Nobody in this play was having a birthday. So I then made it the birthday of one of the women in the hat shop. So I said, "OK it's her birthday."

When you do that—this isn't playwriting class, but I'll tell you anyway—you can't just suddenly say, "Oops, it's my birthday, here comes my cake," because the audience will not believe you. You have to get the birthday up front in Act One, and then have someone mention the birthday, and finally by the time it gets to the cake the birthday must have been in the play really and properly several times and then the cake will work. Now then, this play was translated from Nestroy, and without question somewhere there is an academic doing something about Nestroy or maybe even me and they say "ah." And then they write a paper or maybe set a question for some of you: "In *Einen Jux will er sich machen* (in the original) Mrs. Thing does not have a birthday. But in *On the Razzle* the plot has accommodated a whole new thread in which her birthday is really rather important. Why do you think that . . . ?" If this ever comes up you just write down because the National Theatre fire officers said, "Get that fucking pudding out of here!"

I want to say one more thing about this equation. Algebra doesn't actually offer the clearest image of this, perhaps a kind of three-dimensional geometry is involved because in fact the audience is implicated in this changing event. A lot of it is actually out of one's control, because what happens is the changes are entirely mysterious to the writer, the actors and everybody there. You can see the effect: you take these words on a Tuesday night and you get these people to say them and you get these light cues and you get these sound cues and you do everything, and on Tuesday night the whole thing takes off and it flies and everybody is happy and whatever and they understand it and they clap at the end and they go out and they say, "My God that was good, I'll tell all my friends to come and see it." Wednesday night, you get the same piece of paper, the same people, the same actors, the same lights, and it just lies there absolutely, you sit at the back and think something terrible has happened to this play. But you don't know what it is. In fact it's you.

In some strange way there's some collective force which acts like a chemical agent on this, and we act on that. This fourth wall, here, which you can't see, is there, which is like those toffee windows they have for movies so you don't kill an actor when you throw him through it. It's there all the time and when something just goes like a needle through that wall the event is just destroyed. Sometimes you exploit this; there are often plays where one character converses with the audience or at least addresses the audience and then turns back into the play. So in that sense the equation is extended deliberately. This is a very frail object, whoever the writer is, and maybe especially if it's Shakespeare—we always get back to Shakespeare but I think with good reason, because he's sort of there like a decanter, with that silver label around its neck saying "World Champ." Even with Shakespeare the extraordinary fragility of this event is something which I can hardly overstate for you. The paradisal dream of the playwright is to write a novel, because whatever you write—that's the way it stays. Everybody gets the same thing and it's the same tomorrow as well. It's a temptation all the time to get out of this appalling danger and write something which just stays the way you left it. The reason you don't is that it stays the way you left it.

I had a play called *Night and Day,* in which this fourth wall thing was responsible once for a sort of state of collective terror in the audience. It was as though some seventh veil of the seventh muse had just been shredded for a moment and the kind of horror and fright of that moment was so intense, and it was extraordinarily simple; and you also sort of laugh, because it's all so funny too. One of the characters, Ruth, uniquely in this play, was able to express her inner thoughts to the audience. So she had a voice for the people in the play and she also was able to have a voice for us, so we could hear what she was thinking. She was a married woman; in one scene she was in the garden and a young journalist shows up. She rather fancies him, but she is a fairly moral person and she doesn't want to do anything immoral; but she talks to this young man and then she cautions herself to "get out." She has made the point earlier that women like her, if they come across somebody to whom they are instantly attracted, will run away; they just run away fast in the opposite direction, and she claims to be one of them. So she's in the garden, young man there, and she's talking to him, and then she talks to herself: she has this very simple single line which is: "Run. Run, you stupid bitch."

Now, can I have a volunteer? Thank you. You've got one line to say so we can all hear it: it's "What did she say?" You're talking to your neighbour; it's a matinee on Broadway and you've come on the bus and you've done the shopping and you've gone to see this play which somebody said you ought to go see. They're all talking in British and fast and it's got irritating now. So what you do is you turn to your friend who has come in with you and you say to your friend, you simply say: "What did she say?" That's your cue. (Listen, you haven't got a problem; I'm Maggie Smith!) So, Maggie Smith: "Run." "What did she say?" "Run, you stupid bitch."

It was like the worst moment of one's life in a way.

I don't have a beautifully curved ending—well, I have, but it's a long way off. I'll tell you a very short poem. I didn't write it but when I read it, it seemed to me to be just the sort of poem that a playwright would need, wrapping up an hour of trying to explain what he tried to do and what people in the theatre think they're trying to do. It's a poem for two voices, written by an English poet called Christopher Logue. It goes like this:

> Come to the edge.
> It's too high.
> Come to the edge.
> We'll fall.
> Come to the edge.
> So they came.
> And he pushed them.
> And they flew.

Full Stoppard

Stephen Schiff

After acknowledging that "a significant minority" of the London audience for *Hapgood* "were not understanding the play on a purely narrative level," Stoppard "was told to volunteer to find a solution" before taking the play to America. Interviewing Stoppard in late February 1989 as he was revising *Hapgood* prior to its Los Angeles opening (and debating how much to simplify it), Stephen Schiff engages Stoppard in an extended discussion of the play and the extent to which mystification "might be part of the play's essential personality."

It is a warm, almost balmy late-winter evening in England's Buckinghamshire—a strange thing in itself. Stranger still, here is Tom Stoppard, whom his friend the director Mike Nichols calls "the only writer I know who is completely happy," and he's plainly not feeling happy at all. What he's really feeling is useless. Thuggees from hell are hunting Salman Rushdie, and the Czech government has, only hours earlier, sentenced Stoppard's good friend Václav Havel, the dissident playwright, to yet another term in prison—this time for nine months. All around him, writers are suffering for their words and deeds, and Stoppard, the crown prince of verbal razzle-dazzle, can do little more than pace about the conspicuously comfortable living room of his conspicuously comfortable Georgian mansionette, refusing to be soothed by the luxury a life in the theater has purchased. "I'm very depressed about Havel and the nine months," he says rather heatedly. "That's really upset me today, but in a sort of selfish way. I'm upset with myself, really, for my good fortune and powerlessness and things like that."

From *Vanity Fair,* 52, no. 5 (May 1989).

His fingers sift his shaggy curls. And then, almost hissing: "I mean, look at this fucking house and everything."

I do. The living room is peach-toned, high-ceilinged, and warm, with watercolors on the walls and books everywhere, including leather-bound editions of the plays—*Rosencrantz and Guildenstern Are Dead* (1967), *Jumpers* (1972), *Travesties* (1974), *The Real Thing* (1982), and the radio plays and television plays and one-acters and translations—that have made Stoppard, with Harold Pinter, the most celebrated of contemporary English playwrights. Soon his new drama, a complicated, oddly touching spy yarn called *Hapgood,* will join them—but not until after its run in America, which begins in Los Angeles in April. In the kitchen next door, his wife, Miriam, is guiding their fourteen-year-old son, Edmund, through the thickets of a Robert Graves poem, while two fat, docile dogs coax their caresses. Could any writer's life be plummier?

Yet Stoppard seems uneasy. He stalks, smoking Silk Cuts, and the way he smokes them is at once distracted and voracious. Also a bit odd. Stoppard likes to tilt the lighted tip upward and then sip, as if he were drawing nectar through a thick straw from some ethereal vessel above his head. It's a very showy way to attack a cigarette, and indeed Stoppard retains the air of the sixties dandy—he is still given to wearing purple jackets and swathing himself in scarves. His slightly effeminate beauty has aged more gracefully than that of his friend Mick Jagger, whose puckery looks have traditionally been the point of comparison for Stoppard's own. Now fifty-one, Stoppard more closely resembles the actors Tim Curry and Roger Rees—the massive head, the broad sweep of jaw, the plump upper lip that pours asymmetrically over the big teeth like soup over the side of a caldron. It's a rich, incongruous face, at once forthright and sybaritic—a face out of Caravaggio.

Suddenly he strides over to the stereo in the corner; a moment later, John Lennon is singing "Mother," the song in which he indulges in a lot of primal screaming at the end. "I just wanted to tell you this," Stoppard says, rather sweetly. "I tend to write each play to one record." And then, noticing my face, "Oh! I *knew* you'd be interested."

"Yes, we journalists like that sort of thing," I say. "How does it work?"

"Yes, well, I just kept playing this while I was writing *Jumpers.* It has nothing to do with the play, of course, but I always find it an extraordinarily moving track. For *Hapgood,* I listened to two or three tracks of *Graceland*—you know, Paul Simon—interminably, for three or four months. And with *Rosencrantz* there were two Bob Dylan tracks, 'Like a Rolling Stone,' and 'Subterranean Homesick Blues,' which is a lyric I've admired ever since. I *adore* it. It's one of those moments that gets to me better than even reading."

"You play this stuff while you work?" I ask.

"Well, in a way it stops me working. I stop and I go through the dialogue with this music on, and then I realize that it's just self-indulgence and turn it off. Work is really what one should do, isn't it?" And he clicks off the stereo and stands silently by the fireplace for a moment, as if pondering that daunting truth.

There has always been a shimmer of awe around Stoppard. I had been prepared for the verbal swashbuckler of legend, the punster whose leapfrogging wit had terrified the powerful and the glorious from London to Hollywood, the imp who filled interviewers' ears with reams of Wildean wordplay, all delivered in what the critic Clive James once called "eerily quotable sentences whose English has the faintly extraterritorial perfection of a Conrad or a Nabokov." But the real Stoppard turns out to be a lot easier to take than all that. He is thoughtful and disarmingly modest, and, as his friend the Broadway producer Emanuel Azenberg puts it, "there's a whole part of him that's just a plain old person. He's fun on a we-don't-sit-around-discussing-Proust basis." In conversation he can pursue a heady abstraction with the tenacity he brings to his plays—he's intent on pinning it down, getting it right—but he's not the sort of daredevil egghead that populates his comedies. An autodidact who never attended university, Stoppard has come by what knowledge he has the hard way, piece by piece. All of which he is the first to admit, though his interlocutors over the years have stubbornly refused to believe him. "My self-tutoring has always lagged behind what I was writing," he once said. "All my time is spent concealing what I don't know." And though there is something rather grand in his pampered lisp and the stentorian way he rolls his *r*'s, he is also remarkably reflective, down-to-earth, sincere—all the more so on this, the day of Václav Havel's sentencing.

He's pacing now, preparing the next utterance, and I can hear a faint clicking sound in his mouth, as though unformed words were bumping up against the hidden gate of his literacy. How to be useful, how to find one's place—these are the questions that besiege him, just as they besiege his Rosencrantz and Guildenstern, who cannot comprehend how they fit into the loftier universe of *Hamlet*'s Elsinore, and just as they besiege the various artists in *Travesties, Artist Descending a*

Staircase, and *The Real Thing.* Stoppard's characters are often poets and painters, intent only on making beauty in a world that castigates them, as it has sometimes castigated their creator, for being elitist, ineffectual, politically noncommittal. And Stoppard has frequently found himself defending Art for Art's Sake against those who would prefer art to preach and counsel and rage. He's fond of quoting Auden, who lamented that his poetry never saved one Jew from the gas chambers. "I get deeply embarrassed by the statements and postures of 'committed theater,'" Stoppard told an interviewer in 1973. "I've never felt that art is important. That's been my secret guilt." Yet Stoppard is always testing his own conscience; he has made forays into a more "committed" theater over the last several years (in such plays about Eastern-bloc repression as *Every Good Boy Deserves Favour, Night and Day, Professional Foul,* and *Dogg's Hamlet, Cahoot's Macbeth*), and Havel's predicament in particular gives him pause. "What one recognizes," he says, "is that one's own life is caught up in a tremendous apparatus of unnecessary strands and tangles. One becomes very conscious of one's own lack of asceticism about being a writer in England in 1989."

But is it really Havel he's thinking of now? Isn't he really facing his own frustration—and feeling ignoble about it? "Oh, yes—writer's block, you mean," he says rather exuberantly. "*That* frustration! Actually, I'm very depressed about it. I was grumpy with my family tonight because I've been so depressed all day. It's the sense that I've got absolutely no electric circuits left up there." Not that Stoppard isn't busy. *Hapgood* rehearsals are beginning in Los Angeles (with a superb cast: Judy Davis as Elizabeth Hapgood, the tough-but-romantic secret-service chief, and Simon Jones and Roger Rees as her agents); a Washington run will follow, and then maybe an opening in New York. And in July, Stoppard will direct his first film, a refurbished *Rosencrantz and Guildenstern Are Dead,* starring Richard Dreyfuss as the Player, and Roger Rees and Robert Lindsay as the eponymous nebbishes. What's more, Stoppard has just agreed to write a screenplay of John le Carré's next novel, *The Russia House,* to be directed by Fred Schepisi (*Roxanne, A Cry in the Dark*). All that, and yet there's still something missing—something central. The next big idea.

Ideas are what Stoppard's plays have always been about—or, rather, they're about the idea of Ideas, for the ideas themselves are not so much explored as they are dressed up in exquisite jabber and sent out on parade. "With any luck, I get sparked by something, switched on by something," he says. "But the notion that, for example, *Jumpers* is a contribution to philosophy is nonsense. It's a view of my work which embarrasses me, because the specialists in the field know something which I know myself: that I'm operating on a very naïve level. If I were writing an essay on any of these topics instead of a play, it would not be a profound essay." What Stoppard seeks in an idea is not a stand to take—he rarely knows which side of an argument he supports—or even an area of knowledge to navigate. He's looking for a structure, a little bomb of a notion explosive enough to generate funny characters and beguiling situations and the kind of paradox-happy logorrhea that makes his plays jingle and sing. In fact, Stoppard's formula might be summed up along the lines of "Great ideas make for great jokes." Certainly that would square with the accusations of shallowness and empty wizardry that are regularly flung his way. But jokes, paradoxes, tautologies—these, it turns out, are no small thing to Stoppard. As he will later demonstrate to me, they have their own unaccountable beauty—indeed, the fact that they are unaccountable enhances their beauty all the more. Which goes a long way toward explaining why I have always found Stoppard's airily spinning "shallowness" more profound than the weighty finger wagging of so many of his contemporaries. What he does with an idea is often a bigger thing—or at least a more spectacularly theatrical thing—than the idea itself.

"In *Hapgood*," he says, "the idea was to use the dualities in quantum physics as a metaphor for the duality in people—the duality about the people they love or the propositions they hold, even which side they're on in the Cold War. That was an idea I was excited about. But I finished *Hapgood* just over two years ago, and that's what I think of as the last thing I wrote. I mean, I've been working, but I haven't done what I'm supposed to be doing. So this is the Dark Ages as far as I'm concerned. And it affects everything. There's something unhealthy about it, because it means that, conversely, when I get something and I realize that there is a play I can now write, the joy of that is so intense that things which ought to matter stop mattering." What things? "Well, obviously if one of my children were ill, it would override. But he'd have to be pretty ill! It's disproportionate, you see." He stops and crumples onto the couch next to me, and then suddenly sits forward, bolt upright, sipping his cigarette and ruminating. When he talks, Stoppard often traces a kind of filigree in the air with his arms and hands, and now one of those arms snakes forward as though it had come alive by itself, gesturing to indicate the whole room, the family— everything. "I think what I'm trying to say is that if I'm not working, if I haven't got something for the next play, then all this is completely irrelevant. It doesn't help. It doesn't make life nicer."

As if on cue, his ménage trots in—not the three older boys, who are off at school, but Edmund and Miriam and those two tubby dogs. All of which, contrary to Stoppard's protestations, instantly makes life nicer. Stoppard's fog lifts. Edmund flops down on a corner chair, wraps headphones round his skull, and begins listening to John Lennon. And Miriam, looking svelte and tiny in a green knit pantsuit, sidles romantically up to Tom and, gazing deeply into his eyes, says, in her breathiest voice: "All right, I've got an eight o'clock meeting, and then my day's been rearranged; I'm seeing a rough cut of my video at 1:30, and I'm dubbing for the rest of the afternoon. And then the board meeting at eight, so I'll be back about nine."

TOM: Right. Nine. Now, I'm going in about noon. And I'll be back about six. And Thursday morning I've got this guy taking my photograph and then I'm taking Eddie.

MIRIAM: Oh. Well, I'm here tomorrow night, and I'll be here Thursday morning. But are you going to Bristol, because then I have to cancel my train back, you see?

TOM: That's no problem. Now, I heard from Peter Wood, and he said he didn't get something called his H-1, and it's almost certain that we won't be rehearsing in America on Tuesday.

MIRIAM: But that's just silly. You *just* have to get somebody powerful onto it. All it requires is the right phone call.

TOM: Well, I'll be in New York on Saturday.

MIRIAM: I'll be here. I have a text that needs looking after.

And so on. If this were a section of a Stoppard play, one might well be lost by now, as indeed audiences often complain they are at various points in Stoppard plays. But it wouldn't matter; the undercurrents would sweep one along into the next scene, and the scene after that. If one had been following the drama from the beginning—say, from about 1970, when Stoppard left his first wife and moved in with Miriam (who divorced her first husband, a veterinary surgeon)—one might realize how much she has changed. Once a rosy English pudgebunny, all moonfaced and bright-eyed like Julie Walters or Lulu, she has grown lithe and gravely beautiful, with a murmuring voice and a brunet sheen that remind one of Elizabeth Taylor. Miriam operates at a distinctly higher speed than Tom, and in Britain, according to their friend the actress Diana Rigg, "if you ask a taxi driver, he will have heard of Dr. Miriam Stoppard, but not necessarily of her husband." A dermatologist by training, she has become the compleat health-and-beauty pundit, a constant presence on TV and in the news-papers, and the author of groaning shelves full of books: *Miriam Stoppard's Book of Health Care, Everywoman's Lifeguide, Miriam Stoppard's Health and Beauty Book,* and on and on. "She's a very high-powered lady," says Tom's agent, Kenneth Ewing, "but when you see her in her gardening hat pruning the fruit bushes, she manages to seem very relaxed and have all the time in the world for you until she jumps into the next helicopter."

And now she gazes at Tom for a moment, and he at her, and at the same helter-skelter speed with which she has just recounted her schedule, she tells Tom how dear and wonderful Edmund looked the other day in Tom's old cardigan, and how all the women at the airport had gone mad for him, and then she and Tom surreptitiously turn their gaze toward Edmund bopping in his headphones, and then back toward each other—it's Love on Mount Olympus. For a long time, Stoppard was upbraided for the women characters in his plays: they were stick figures and foils, said his critics, and Stoppard didn't argue. But beginning in 1978 with *Night and Day,* and reaching a kind of apotheosis in *Hapgood,* Stoppard has been constructing dramas around strikingly attractive, intelligent, powerful women—women who, like Hapgood herself, can run the British secret service with spit-and-polish efficacy one minute and rhapsodize over a son's Rugby performance the next. Watching the Stoppards now, in their living room, one realizes how much the works of his new, "serious" period have been, among other things, valentines to Miriam.

Certainly she has given him a much calmer life than the one to which he had grown accustomed. Born Tomáš Straussler in Zlín (now called Gottwaldov), Czechoslovakia, Stoppard was almost immediately whisked away to Singapore; it seems he had a Jewish great-grandparent, and the shoe firm for which his father worked (as a doctor) thought that, in 1939, his family might well be safer there. But three years later, Singapore was on the verge of being invaded by the Japanese, and Tom and his mother and brother were transplanted once again, this time to India; his father, meanwhile, died in enemy hands. Much has been made of Stoppard's Czech roots. Like Clive James, many have associated his command of English with that of Conrad and Nabokov, who putatively achieved their dexterity by falling in love with a language not their own. Leaving aside for a moment the fact that Nabokov was raised speaking English and Russian with equal fluency, Stoppard himself pooh-poohs that sort of speculation. "I spoke only toddler's Czech," he says. "I went to an English-speaking school in India, and I was educated in English. English has been my first language ever since I could talk."

And England became his home after the war. His mother had married a British army officer, Kenneth Stoppard, and Tom went to school in Nottinghamshire and Yorkshire until 1954, when, at the age of seventeen, he quit to go live with his family in Bristol and become a famous journalist. For a while, he prospered, writing features, reviewing plays and films, even turning out humor columns. But in Britain in the late fifties, playwrights were the thing—John Osborne, Arnold Wesker, John Arden, and the rest of the "Angry Young Men." Stoppard tried his hand with a play he called *A Walk on the Water*, which was performed on British television in 1963. The play brought him to the attention of Kenneth Ewing, who was astounded by Stoppard's devil-may-care confidence. "I got him a job writing a BBC radio series about an Arab student—it was ridiculous, really, because everything he wrote was then translated into Arabic for broadcast overseas. At any rate, Tom was going home one day, and he was broke. So I lent him £40. Well, he turned right around and hailed a taxi. I went home on a bus."

It was around that time that Ewing, musing aloud, suggested to Stoppard that in *Hamlet,* when Claudius sends Rosencrantz and Guildenstern to visit the English king, that king might well have been Lear. Not long after that, Stoppard wrote a one-act play, in verse yet, called *Rosencrantz and Guildenstern Meet King Lear*. He expanded and restructured it over the next few years—and, happily, converted it into prose—and in 1966, *Rosencrantz and Guildenstern Are Dead* was performed by an amateur company at the Edinburgh Festival. Most of the reviews were bad, but, fortunately, a critic for London's *Observer* saw it; he declared it "the most brilliant debut by a young playwright since John Arden's." Those words sparked the interest of Kenneth Tynan, then the literary manager (under Laurence Olivier) of London's prestigious National Theatre, and in 1967, the play opened at the Old Vic, to ecstatic notices. In New York, its success was even more tumultuous. An interviewer asked the exhilarated Stoppard what the play was about, and, in an immoderate moment, he replied, "It's about to make me very rich." He was right.

Stoppard's ascent, in fact, was out of all proportion to the quality of his play, as good as it was. He seemed to fill a kind of cultural gap; he became, at thirty, the intellectuals' answer to the British Invasion. And though he was then, as he is now, a traditionalist and a conservative, his rakish aura suited the *Zeitgeist.* "At every party," says Diana Rigg, "he was always elegantly slouched in a corner with a cigarette between his fingers. The voice was never raised. And he was very much a clotheshorse, with a lot of feel appeal. Do you know what I mean by that? Soft, the cashmere or the vicuña—not the sharp look: rumpled, but expensive." As Ewing puts it, "The press loved him because he was lucid and good-looking, and his look fit in very well with the sixties. It was not the well-dressed, well-turned-out look of the fifties; it was a sort of challenging look. And he did resemble Mick Jagger a bit. Young people loved him. It was astounding the way the Americans took to him."

The first casualty of Stoppard's rise was his marriage. Jose Ingle had been a researcher for a London consumer magazine when Stoppard married her in 1965. She took Stoppard's success hard. "In her cups, she would tell Tom's friends how she had really written *Rosencrantz and Guildenstern,*" remembers one longtime friend. "And all the time, Tom was behaving with a kind of chivalric constancy. His friends were throwing up their hands because he was spending all his time looking after the children and doing the washing up. Then came the time when he decided it was over, at which point he behaved with a kind of frightening clarity, taking the two kids with him and setting up a new home with Miriam." Stoppard himself has little to say about the breakup. "It's so classical, it's slightly boring," he murmurs. "In some sense I began to belong to more people. It was that simple."

Mostly, though, he belonged to his work. When he wasn't writing the big plays—*Jumpers, Travesties, Night and Day, The Real Thing,* and now *Hapgood*—he was writing radio plays, screenplays, TV plays. Practically everything he touched turned to acclaim—and big box office. "Tom's a work animal," says Steven Spielberg, who became a close friend when he directed Stoppard's screenplay of *Empire of the Sun.* "For somebody who really is an artist," says Spielberg, "his work habits are really nose-to-the-grindstone." Tom and Miriam have converted a stable next to their house into a suite of offices, with two secretaries, a snooker room, a swimming pool, and Stoppard's prized collection of literary autographs—Wilde, Hazlitt, Beckett, Shaw, Hemingway. "But, actually, I don't get up in the morning and write there," he confesses. "I like to write in the kitchen, after everyone's gone to bed." In preparing a play, he outlines extensively. Then, when he knows the shape of what he calls "the vessel," he fills in, writing the dialogue with pen and ink, "And then I dictate it into a tape recorder so that somebody can type it—my secretary can't read my handwriting." All of which makes me suddenly imagine a series of wonderful cassettes on which Stoppard himself can be heard acting out each role. "Oh, heavens no!" he cries. "The tape sounds like this: 'Daphne says, What then, query. Costa says, We'll see. Daphne says, He says she says yes, brackets, query. Bracket, pause, close bracket.' It's a purely technical exercise."

The task currently at hand is *Hapgood,* which needs revising before it braves America. The play is like a John le Carré novel gone berserk, with a plot that twists its way through a labyrinth of double agents, twin-brother agents, twin briefcases, and hints of love affairs gone awry. On paper, it's an invigorating mix of textures and moods, and what spanks it along is the language—a tangy stew of quantum physics, spook-speak, and quicksilver repartee—and its heroine, the beguiling Mrs. Hapgood, who can almost be seen as an idealized Margaret Thatcher figure (Stoppard is a somewhat defensive Thatcherite): an iron lady with a steel-trap mind, but one who is also romantic and generous and movingly vulnerable. Unfortunately, *Hapgood* doesn't have the structural perfection that can make even Stoppard's least substantial plays feel satisfying, and, worse, audiences during its British run last year often found it impossible to follow. "*Hapgood* has been Tom's first halfway failure," says his old pal the actor John Wood. "He has not experienced the absence of complete international success before."

And now Stoppard faces a question: how accessible must he make *Hapgood?* In his other plays, it didn't matter so much when the audience missed a trope here or a reference there. But Stoppard has never before written a play that was so dependent on plot; in *Hapgood,* what's whizzing over spectators' heads is the very story he's trying to tell. For Stoppard, this is a thorny dilemma. After all, it's not the first time he's been accused of being high-falutin or mystifying. "But I resist the idea that one's work contains some kind of cryptogram," he says. "I'm not trying to make the plays difficult, God help me. Nobody could think that one would just, you know, be mischievous or perverse and try to make life hard for the audience." Still, doesn't he recognize that he, more than many playwrights, has a way of leaving his more literal-minded viewers scratching their heads? "Ah, well, I write very literary stuff—it's just the way I do it," he explains. "I don't have any philosophy, for example, that accounts for the fact that most of my characters appear to have been brought up in the same house, have gone to the same school, and have lived together for years before they were released into my plays, so they all have each other's speech rhythms and vocabularies. The whole thing is an artifice." He stops for a moment and with one hand gives his face a sudden brisk scrub. "Actually, it doesn't interest me to try and simulate life in some more plausible way. There are some writers, for instance, who are far more fascinated by the differentiation of character, and I obviously have no interest in that. I'm only interested in the felicitous expression of ideas, and very often when I'm rewriting, it doesn't matter who says something—if I need those lines elsewhere I'll give them to a different character. But the experience with *Hapgood* was that a lot of people just found it hard to follow. And so I was going to change it a bit for the American production. It's just that one is revolted by having to lay something out and explicate it so baldly that it offends one's aesthetic sense."

He's trying anyway, of course, altering small things here and big ones there. And as Steven Spielberg says, "Tom is a real problem solver. He works until he reaches a solution." But what to Tom Stoppard constitutes a problem? After all, for him, as for the quantum physicists he's been studying, the bottom line isn't certainty, it's uncertainty; for him, irresolution has the satisfying clink of truth. A typical Stoppard play will pit two characters against each other, each representing an opposing side of an argument, and no one will win; the dénouement will always emerge from some unexpected irrelevancy that ends the argument—usually with a deflating pop—without resolving it. (What gives the plays their whirligig spin is the way their perfectly balanced form always battles their messy content.) In short, Stoppard isn't so sure he wants to give up the mystification. He likes it—and he thinks audiences do too.

"What haunts me about this whole process of clarifying *Hapgood*," he says, "is that mystification might be part of the play's essential personality. Part of the play's appeal is the pressure you're under to work it out for yourself as it goes. I know I can smooth the narrative. The difficult question is, do you want the narrative smooth? This is the question that makes it an art form. And because it's an art form, there is no answer." Would he care to explain? "If *Hapgood* was a new engine for a Fiat, you would just take the car out and find out what is best. If you were designing the shape of the Fiat, the wind tunnel would tell you what is best. But if you were merely staging a competition for beautiful cars which didn't have to move, then it would all be much less certain."

Well, that may sum up the difference between science and art, but where does mystification come in? "Mystification is my word, and I withdraw it," he says. "I mean something much less toxic than that.

What I mean is that if you were able to take such an abstract thing as audience enjoyment and put it on a lab bench and work out what it is, you'd find that part of it is the audience having to do the work. That is true of certain kinds of jokes. In certain cases, and I don't mean this in any kind of condescending way, laughter is the sound of people congratulating themselves. And if the joke had been made that much easier, you wouldn't get the laugh—they'd have nothing to say 'Well done!' about."

And now we are back to great jokes, and I begin to see that the open-ended, unsettled nature of a superb joke—or its relatives, a superb paradox or a superb tautology—is for Stoppard a kind of paradigm of beauty; it's the atom of his art, irreducible, alive, complete in itself and yet forever sending out ripples. He's always adored those Samuel Beckett jokes that take the form of "Firstly, A; secondly, minus A" (the most succinct example might be the famous line in *The Unnamable:* "I can't go on, I'll go on"). He loves the old *Goon Show* tautology that runs something like "And then the monsoons came, and they couldn't have come at a worse time, bang in the middle of the rainy season." As Stoppard has pointed out, that joke is like a "snake in a funny hat eating its own tail"—at once infinite and completely contained. And now he tells me, "My favorite joke when I was a child of, you know, thirty-nine, was:

"'My great-grandfather was killed at Waterloo.'
"'Oh, really? Which platform?'
"'Oh, don't be ridiculous. What does it matter which platform?'
"I just adore the shape of that. [It probably helps to know that Waterloo is a London railroad station.] To me, that is an archetypal joke, because you think you've had it, and then you haven't had it. Paradox appeals to me. Paradoxes have a shape, like a piece of architecture. It's that which is appealing. They're like a thought process in concrete form—you can see the actual shape and structure of it." He's hit on something there, something resonant, and he knows it. And suddenly his body wilts into the couch, as if, having got to the bottom of what makes his art tick, he were finally spent. "Paradox and tautology," he murmurs. "They don't have to mean anything, lead anywhere, be part of anything else. I just like them. I've got an unhealthy love affair for them."

Looking at him now, with the fog rolling back into his face, I remember something John Wood told me. "Tom has changed over the years," he said. "There was an inevitable darkening, like seasoning wood. When I first met him in the sixties, there was a kind of anarchic joy in him, and it's still there, but it contains its own impossibility now. I can't say that life has disappointed Tom, but I think he once thought there must be some system behind the absurdity, and he found out that there isn't."

Or is there? Stoppard has been reading James Gleick's book, *Chaos,* about the new science that attempts to make sense of nature's senselessness, that attempts to systematize what appears to function outside of any system. There's a play in that somewhere, Stoppard knows—but what would it be? He will probably never go to jail for what he writes, or even for what he believes in, and the comfort his home and family provide may always give him pause. But if Tom Stoppard can continue to design gorgeous spinning jokes, jokes good enough to reveal the architecture of our thoughts—well, how many artists can claim to be more useful than that?

Welcome to the World of Tom Stoppard

Thomas O'Connor

In Los Angeles for rehearsals prior to the American opening of *Hapgood,* Stoppard was able to indulge the same vaguely disreputable taste in popular music he had attributed to Henry, the playwright-protagonist of *The Real Thing.* After having Henry agonize over his musical selections for "Desert Island Discs," Stoppard himself was a guest on the BBC radio program in 1985 and included the Beatles' "Love Me Do" and "Jump for Joy" by the Avon City's Jazz Band among his desert island discs. Most of his time in Los Angeles was spent not just rehearsing but rewriting *Hapgood* for an American production that was expected to go on to Washington, D.C., and New York. In the Los Angeles production, right after the intentionally baffling opening scene with its switching of briefcases, an actor turned, faced the audience and announced: "Okay, I'm Wates and you want to know what the hell is going on here." In rehearsals Wates's explanatory monologue—ostensibly delivered to CIA colleagues off-stage—lasted about eighteen minutes and was, Stoppard says, "not only interminable but unendurable." By opening night the monologue had been cut to seven minutes but was still a device Stoppard termed "A Child's Guide to *Hapgood.*" The Los Angeles production played to some appreciative audiences during previews but after opening night it faced completely packed houses of sullenly silent southern Californians who by subscribing to the entire Ahmanson Theatre season

From the *Orange County Register,* 2 April 1989.

225

were promised tickets to *The Phantom of the Opera.* Plans for *Hapgood* to have a Broadway run were abandoned.

I'm supposed to be one of your intellectual playwrights. I'm going to look a total . . . , aren't I, going on the radio to announce that when I was telling Jean-Paul Sartre that he was essentially superficial, I was spending the whole time listening to the Crystals singing 'Da Doo Ron Ron.'
—Henry the playwright, in *The Real Thing*

Tom Stoppard threw back his head suddenly and emitted a most un-English roar.

"I love Oldies 93! I am *mad* for . . . What is it? KODJ?" the playwright declared, the frostily polite British reserve dissolving into a grin of wicked charm.

"You see, I've become quite addicted on this visit to driving around Los Angeles, and made the happy discovery on the car radio that there's a station that does only '60s pop. We don't have that in England. It's wonderful. Every time I turn the radio on, there's a record I want to hear."

Coming from one of the wittiest, most erudite writers in the English-speaking world, Stoppard's unsolicited endorsement—of a Los Angeles radio station dedicated to bubble-gum music, to girl groups and Neil Sedaka—seems a dumbfounding turnabout.

Imagine Mike Tyson looking up from his latest knockout victim, beaming at the camera and shouting, "Where am I going? I'm going to the Kierkegaard Institute."

"Of course I am perfectly well aware of how fatuous and inane nearly all the lyrics are," added Stoppard, whose award-winning play, *The Real Thing,* featured a playwright character with the same musical passion.

"They're beneath contempt. I just like the noise."

Tom Stoppard loves to throw his audience off the scent, be it a full house of theatergoers or—on this occasion last week—one visitor, with whom he huddled over takeout lunch in a rehearsal room at the Los Angeles Music Center.

This is, after all, the playwright who turned a comic murder mystery into a debate on moral philosophy (*Jumpers*). Who assembled Lenin, James Joyce and a Dadaist artist for a circus-style parody of 20th-century theories of art (*Travesties*). Who startled the theater nearly a quarter-century ago by writing an entire play around two obscure characters from *Hamlet* (*Rosencrantz and Guildenstern Are Dead*). Who turned the tables on vicious theater critics *(The Real Inspector Hound)*. Who cast a full symphony orchestra as a character *(Every Good Boy Deserves Favour)*.

Stoppard doesn't write plays, he builds glittering theatrical erector sets—wit-strewn, mirrored theatrical mazes that alternately baffle and delight audiences with high-wire linguistic pirouettes and bizarre twists.

Consider the mystifying, split-second choreography of spies and spy-catchers that launches Stoppard's newest work, *Hapgood,* a brain-teasing mix of John le Carré-like espionage, particle physics and romance.

Hapgood has its US premiere this month at Hollywood's Doolittle Theatre, starring Judy Davis *(A Passage to India, My Brilliant Career)* as an enigmatic British spy master, and Roger Rees *(Nicholas Nickleby)* as a brilliant Soviet physicist.

The occasion is the first production of LA's Ahmanson Theatre operation in its temporary new headquarters at the 1,005-seat Doolittle. The Ahmanson itself, at the Los Angeles Music Center, is being readied for what is expected to be a two-year run of the musical *The Phantom of the Opera*. Landing the Stoppard drama's US premiere was a considerable coup for the Ahmanson producers.

Both Rees and director Peter Wood are holdovers from last year's critically acclaimed London production, and *Hapgood* is expected to go on this summer to Washington, DC, and New York.

"As in other plays I've written, the first scene is supposed to be virtually incomprehensible," Stoppard explained. "I spent *weeks* with two pieces of paper, doing diagrams of where everybody could go. It wasn't that I had to work it out in order to make it intelligible to the audience, but to make it intelligible to me.

"It's like the beginning of *Travesties* or *Jumpers*. For ten minutes, it's just sort of 'Hellzapoppin.' That's a sort of mannerism of mine. Then you clear it up and begin to explain it."

Stoppard is a tall, handsome man, still trim at age 51, with a great shock of brown curls and heavy, languid eyelids a rock star would envy. His smile reveals a slight overbite that explains the faint lisp in his soft voice.

In the manner of his adopted country (the Czech-born Stoppard moved to England at age eight), he is at once polite and aloof, deliberating over his words with great care but evincing more interest in learning the geography of Los Angeles than in discussing his work.

Kenneth Tynan once wrote that for Stoppard, "Art is a game within a game—the larger game being life itself, an absurd mosaic of incidents and accidents."

That the Cold War spies buzzing through *Hapgood* are merely a means to an end, a sort of dramatic Maguffin, is a standard part of the Stoppard game plan. His plays, he said, are always born of a fascination with some abstract idea in life.

This time it was notions about duality and uncertainty that have rocked the once-staid field of physics.

"All I knew was that in the last 50 years, the rock-solid basis to physics had disappeared," he said. "The deeper they looked, the less things were certain.

"I was looking for some kind of narrative which would serve partially as a metaphor for physics, and decided, rightly or wrongly, to turn to a kind of le Carré spy-thriller world.

"Believe me, it took an awful long time to get anywhere near knowing what to write about. My refrain is that the long, uphill struggle in playwriting is getting to the top of page one. Once I know roughly what I'm supposed to be doing, I find dialogue much easier to write."

Stoppard has no apology for the intellectual demands he makes on audiences, and it is worth noting that, however rigorous his plays, they have made him world-famous and wealthy (he and his wife, Miriam Stoppard, a physician and British TV star, split their time between an 18th-century country home and a posh London flat).

"One thing I can't stand is the sense that food has been cut up on the plate for the person who eats it," he said. "You've got to let the audience have their own knife and fork. Otherwise, they're not doing anything."

Stoppard puzzled over the suggestion that his plays show a special reverence for language.

"I have an enjoyment of language. Is that the same thing? Reverence? Well, I probably do, because I go into a kind of pain when it's used loosely and inaccurately. It's like a mental twitch."

He is incapable, he said, of writing inarticulate or foul-mouthed characters such as those created by David Mamet.

"I love Mamet's plays, but I have no idea how to do those characters. Something happens to those plays between the page and the performance; the text goes through some interesting transformation between type and human personality. That's not really true of the kind of plays I write; you can sort of see the play and hear it just by reading it.

"I don't write character parts on a conscious level. Because (my characters) are only brought into existence because of my desire to express certain ideas, (actors) have to deduce their characters from what they say."

This creates problems when actors demand background about a character from Stoppard. "I'm really baffled by the question, because then I have to invent something which doesn't contradict what I've written. That's the best I can do."

The problem is complicated by the inevitable, learned efforts to match Stoppard's own tracks with those of his characters.

"Do you like Evelyn Waugh? I rather like his attitude to his novels, that he considered them to be artifacts, with no more personal history than a pot. I invented this person aged 32; I didn't need the first 31 years. It's just this book with these people in it. Of course, Waugh was, in a sense, deceiving himself; as the creator, he had his own personal history and psychology.

"But he wasn't interested in any kind of self-analysis, and I must say I have absolutely the same temperament about my work.

"Because *The Real Thing* had an English playwright editorializing about writing and love and marriage and all that, it was perfectly obvious that when he was waving his prejudices around, he was pretty much speaking for me. But then so are the people (in the play) who contradict him. That's what playmaking is; you have to take everybody's side."

Even while he tinkers with *Hapgood* during rehearsals in Los Angeles ("Plays are never quite finished, really; you just abandon them when you run out of time, until you do them again"), Stoppard is wrestling with the idea of a play about his early youth, when his family fled Nazi-occupied Czechoslovakia for Singapore and India.

"I was eight when I left India for England. I felt I should be able to use my own experience of India to write something about the ethos of the British Empire. But right now (the idea) isn't really going. I've never really abandoned a play. In the end I've always found something I wanted to do, and I hope that happens with this one, too."

Stoppard will direct his first film this year, an adaptation of his *Rosencrantz and Guildenstern Are Dead*, starring Rees, Robert Lindsay and Richard Dreyfuss.

"I've only just now got interested in movies on their own terms.

I'd like to write a film of my own, as opposed to somebody else's book (Stoppard's screenplay adaptations include *Empire of the Sun;* he also collaborated on Terry Gilliam's controversial *Brazil*).

It was *Rosencrantz and Guildenstern,* the two comically hapless Shakespeareans trapped in an inexorable tragedy over which they have no control, that catapulted Stoppard to fame 23 years ago.

"Yes, I saw a stage production of it just a couple of years ago," he said. "It was still funny, which was the main thing. If it's not funny, it isn't anything."

Stoppard Ascending

Diana Maychick

Diana Maychick spoke to Stoppard one week prior to the opening on Broadway of Stoppard's "radio" play, *Artist Descending a Staircase.* One of Stoppard's intentions for *Artist*—as for his earlier radio plays *Albert's Bridge* and *If You're Glad I'll be Frank*—had been to create a radio play that could *only* be performed on the radio. The goal of fully exploiting the resources of a given medium gained further refinement in his desire, also harbored for decades, to write a radio play consisting entirely of sounds. The roasting he had received from both London and Los Angeles critics over the excessive intricacies of *Hapgood* may lie behind Stoppard's eagerness to claim that the "geometrical" intricacies of *Artist* are just a means to "allow me to get at ... emotions better" in a play that is "a love story." In any event, a recognition of the way "sequential hijinks" can not only force a greater "sense of reverberation" but also establish greater emotional resonance was clearly in the playwright's mind as he plotted the temporal geometry of *In the Native State* and *Arcadia.*

What you hear first—on a tape recorder—is a man dozing into an irregular snore.

Then you hear footsteps, a stealthy creak.

The sleeping man stirs, then he awakens.

You hear a thump, followed by wood cracking and the sound of a man falling down a series of steps. The sounds signify an *Artist Descending a Staircase,* and they come from the imagination of Tom

From the *New York Post,* 26 November 1989.

Stoppard, an artist himself, but one known for his sharp portraits with words.

"If I could, I'd like to write a complete play without words," Stoppard says, sounding ominously like Samuel Beckett gone wild.

A sinking feeling begins at that very moment, at the anticipation of a theatrical world without the bite and parry of Stoppard dialogue, evident in his stellar debut in 1967 with the Tony-winning *Rosencrantz and Guildenstern Are Dead* through his most recent Broadway play, the 1984 Tony-winning *The Real Thing*.

But the playwright later clarifies his revolutionary statement. He only wishes to ban words from radio dramas, that anachronistic art form that Stoppard almost single-handedly has kept alive.

Artist Descending a Staircase, in previews at the Helen Hayes Theater, where it will open on Thursday, began as a radio drama 15 years ago, around the time the playwright brilliantly concocted a drama about a fictional meeting among James Joyce, Lenin and Dada co-founder Tristan Tzara in *Travesties.*

"I guess I had been thinking a lot about art at the time, about the reasons for art, if there are such things," he said.

Indeed, the title *Artist Descending a Staircase,* seems a direct descendant of "Nude Descending a Staircase," the futurist painting by the other founder of the Dada movement, Marcel Duchamp.

"Other than the title, I didn't go into Duchamp too much," Stoppard said. "But after exploring the reasons for art, I did want to focus on the different perceptions of it." There is a pause. "But it's also a love story, isn't it?"

Artist Descending a Staircase is probably a love story first, focusing on the lifelong friendship of three artists and the woman they all loved. That she can't see their paintings seems a typically Stoppard touch, as do the lines about a sculptor who turns to molding sugar as giving "Cubism a new lease on life."

"I look at the construction of this play as a puzzle. That's why the time sequence seems so geometrical," he said about the 90-minute drama that goes backward and forward in time from the present to 1914, trying to determine how the artist in the first scene died. The mystery involves determining whether it was a suicide, an accident or a murder.

Set temporally in six parts, the play begins in the here-and-now. The next five scenes are each a flashback from the previous scene; the last five scenes are continuations of the fifth, fourth, third, second and first, respectively.

For non-math majors, it sounds more complicated than it plays. "What it allows me to do is reveal certain plot points in ways and in a time frame that forces the sense of reverberation," Stoppard says. "I also know that despite a career's worth of criticism to the contrary, I do try to deal with emotions. The sequential hijinks allow me to get at these emotions better. Because I am not just playing with words—not just trying to make them fit a scheme."

Since he wrote the drama, the playwright has resisted most attempts by producers to stage it.

"I didn't write it for the stage, I wrote it for the radio," he said, "and I didn't think I should test the fates. I always thought of it as an apple, not an orange."

Last year, King's Head Company, a fringe theater group housed in a north London pub, approached him again. "I knew the place as a customer," he said, "and I felt comfortable about them trying it."

A big hit, it moved to the Duke of York Theatre in the West End, where it ended a successful run last summer.

In New York, it's being produced and acted by some of Broadway's finest: Emanuel Azenberg, Robert Whitehead, Roger Berlind, among the former; and among the latter, Paxton Whitehead, John McMartin and Harold Gould.

"Given that I wrote it so long ago, there has been none of that last-minute frenzy of revision. I had the great liberty of really listening to the actors and the others, and I know everyone is doing a great job," he said. "There are fewer of those gnawing doubts with this one. I've realized I've been less involved than with any other project, but that I've gotten the best notices in my career."

Born in 1937 in Zlin, Czechoslovakia, Stoppard fled the Nazis with his family and moved to Singapore during World War II, an experience he called upon to write the movie *Empire of the Sun* for Steven Spielberg. After his father died, Stoppard moved to India with his brother and mother, who remarried an Englishman.

"As soon as we all landed up in England, I knew I had found a home," he said. "I embraced the language and the landscape, and the two came together for me in journalism."

At 17, he was writing about the arts for a local Bristol paper. "And that was all I wanted to do for quite a long time. But during one interview, I don't remember who I was talking to, I realized I had asked the same questions of the same person before, and that he had given me the same answers. The repetition scared me more than anything else."

And so a playwright was born.

"I don't have any schemes for writing," he says, "I just worry my way through ideas, hopefully all the way to dramas. I'm terribly slow at it, though."

There are some lines in *Artist Descending* that probably summarize why Stoppard's art takes time.

"Skill without imagination is craftsmanship and gives us many useful objects such as wickerwork picnic baskets. Imagination without skill gives us modern art."

Listening to them, he says, "Ah, yes, I did write that. And you know, I realize now, probably more than when I wrote the play, that you really need both."

It is clear that he has both. That theorem, geometric or not, needs no proof.

Script Jockey: The Flickering
Images of Theatre

Sid Smith

The film version of *Rosencrantz and Guildenstern are Dead* written and directed by Stoppard, was originally going to star
Sean Connery as The Player with Roger Rees and Robert
Lindsay as the hapless courtiers. After Connery backed out,
prompting legal wranglings and verbal recriminations within
the pages of *The Times,* Richard Dreyfuss was signed as The
Player. But it was only some time later that two actors of a
distinctly younger generation, Tim Roth and Gary Oldman,
were brought in to play Rosencrantz and Guildenstern. Interviewed by Sid Smith for the first issue of *The Theatre Magazine,*
Stoppard explained the changes he made in adapting his
stage play for the cinema and the difference the cast changes
had made in the film.

SMITH: What's the big difference between the stage and film versions
of *Rosencrantz and Guildenstern?*

STOPPARD: That I left out half the lines. It's a play about two people
waiting for other people to come in and go out, and the energy of the
piece has to be carried mainly by the language. In the movie they
aren't trapped like that: they can do the rushing about—which is what
happens. In the play it's like two people on a railway platform, and in
the film they're roaring around like this train. So there's a lot of
energy that gets used up in the physical momentum of this. And I
suspect that the energy is a constant: the more you use in the one the
less you need in the other.

From *The Theatre Magazine,* no. 1 (April 1991).

I sound as if I have a theory of adapting plays into films—which is of course nonsense. The work is more intuitive than that: I simply started again, thinking of it as a film. My big advantage was that I had no interest in protecting the play.

I wrote a film script of *Rosencrantz and Guildenstern* in about 1968. MGM bought the film rights and I wrote a script for John Boorman. It was a terrible script. I haven't got it but I vaguely remember it as being very word-heavy. And in those days I was thinking, 'Oh I must save my play.'

Now my attitude is completely different, and the reason we were doing a film script instead of just filming the play was that I said, 'Oh we must change everything because it could be really boring and far too long. Why don't we try and do a screenplay?' So I was liberated from the play really.

SMITH: Where did the impetus come from to change the play? Is it you that's changed? Or everybody? Or is it that film is expensive and there's financial pressure for you to make the thing more popular?

STOPPARD: It's everything. It's certainly true that when you're trying to raise money to make a film most of the time what you agree to do is not just to deliver a film, you agree to deliver a film which is x minutes long, maximum: two hours in our case. So, yes you're right about that.

But that wasn't even in my mind, actually. My real fear was that it would be too long for its own good. And it was written 25 years ago and not all of it is still to my taste: there are chunks of it—mainly in the character of The Player—which I don't actually *want* in the film. And some of the shorter lines, the duologues, they're probably more repetitive than they need to be.

It was really easy to cut. I know the phrase 'to murder one's children', but I never had any of that. Mainly I was interested in trying to add things which I was now able to think of because I could now change the *frame*—which frankly is the only important difference between theatre and film for me.

In the theatre you've got this medium shot, fairly wide angle, for two and a half hours. And that's it folks. You can't do jokes which depend on close-ups or different angles. That's what I was really thinking of. And I had a good time, actually.

SMITH: What about casting? You started off with Sean Connery as The Player—which did fit in with the usual image of the character as a grizzled and cynical old player-manager. But the eventual performer, Richard Dreyfuss, is notably younger. And in Tim Roth and Gary

Oldman you have two leads who are best known for playing psychopathic punks.

STOPPARD: When Sean Connery was doing The Player I cast it with people I'd grown up with. And when he pulled out and Richard Dreyfuss said he'd do The Player, I began to realise I'd forgotten how old I was.

It was written when I was 28 or something, and I suspect if you write a play when you're 28 the people in it are 28. And because I thought I was still 28, and because I was casting people I'd grown up with, the cast were all people in their 40s.

When we started again I decided this was wrong. And once I'd cottoned on to younger actors it became much more interesting and a much more modern-feeling film as a result.

SMITH: Which do you go to most often, the cinema or the theatre?

STOPPARD: Well, it's which I go to less least. The cinema and theatre always happen when I feel like working. My biological clock is such that I do at least three quarters of my work between 8 pm and 2 am.

But I go to the theatre more than the cinema because you can't get theatre on video. I don't have the time or inclination to see everything [at the theatre] and I'm usually behind with my work, so I go to things with which I've got a connection—I know someone in it, or who wrote it, or directed it.

SMITH: You've often spoken about your problems in coming up with plots. But when you've found a story—often from another source—you produce some very complicated and elaborate dialogue.

STOPPARD: I seem to have accepted uncritically (and unconsciously, actually) the principle that the playwright's job is to tell a story, that until you actually have a story you don't have anything—a story which works as well as an Arabian Nights story, which winds itself up and then goes and you want to get to the end. That seems to me the prerequisite.

But the problem is that I become stimulated by the *subject*—which is nothing to do with a story. The difficult part has always been that I don't have any stories ready to tell about anything, so there's a long period where I'm unable to write anything that I'm supposed to be writing because, whether it's going to be about the Empire or journalism or whatever, I can't work out who is in it and what they're doing. I know what they're saying and what they're arguing about but I don't know who they are.

But when I've constructed some story which isn't very, erm, *wieldy* (or whatever is the opposite of unwieldy) the hard part is over, because the dialogue grows organically: I just have to help it to grow.

SMITH: Have you tried to adopt strategies to get around this problem with story lines?

STOPPARD: Well, *Rosencrantz and Guildenstern* is built around *Hamlet*, of course. *The Real Inspector Hound* is basically an Agatha Christie story. And in *Travesties* the matrix is *The Importance of Being Earnest*. There are probably one or two others using the same method. In fact, eventually I got to the point where I thought, 'I've got to stop doing this: it's becoming a kind of mannerism.' But I can see now looking back it's that I didn't have to do the story.

And that's the great thing about film adaptations: le Carré or someone good at it has done all that part. It's what makes film adaptation so comfortable.

SMITH: We hear that you're looking at the screenplay of Sir Richard Attenborough's film about Charlie Chaplin.

STOPPARD: I've been talking to him. This film was supposed to be going ahead *now*—but it's in a pause. I've had some conversations and I'm reading the stuff to see if there's anything I can add. A very good writer has written a nice script and Attenborough is very keen on it. But the film is between one studio and another and—par for the course—they have one more writer than they need. So I don't know what I'll be doing with it, if anything.

Left to myself I wouldn't have mentioned it because the film writing world has its own rules and scripts keep floating around between writers. Without question it also happens to my scripts. I always feel that the union of writers is breaking ranks about looking at each other's scripts.

SMITH: So have you any more film plans?

STOPPARD: I'd like to direct another film I'd also written, something that's really my own but written for cinema instead of theatre. I'd like to write that this year.

SMITH: Any ideas for a plot?

STOPPARD: No. *(Laughs)*.

Third Ear

Paul Allen

Stoppard spent three years writing *In the Native State*, the radio play that, he says, may yet provide the groundwork for a film or stage play. Setting his play in one of the "native states" of India where he spent his boyhood, Stoppard intended to write a play "about the ethics of empire." Preparing, as he had before, with voracious reading—in moral philosophy for *Jumpers*, and in physics for *Hapgood*—Stoppard said he "must have read a million words about India when I needed a tiny fraction of that reading" for the radio play. Ultimately, however, his intention to write about the ethics of empire was pushed to one side when he "got interested in other things more." Paramount among those attractions may be the character of Flora Crewe herself; *In the Native State* is the most character-driven of all Stoppard's plays. Indeed, Stoppard elsewhere acknowledged, "I got more wrapped up in my characters than in previous plays, particularly Mrs Swan, and her feelings for her elder sister." If some of the strengths of *In the Native State* are a matter of serendipitous discovery, something of that same openness to unforeseen possibilities characterizes Stoppard's conversations of the time. Four days before *In the Native State* was transmitted on BBC Radio Three, Stoppard was interviewed on Radio Three's "Third Ear" program. Ostensibly he was there to discuss *In the Native State* and the recent film version of *Rosencrantz and Guildenstern Are Dead*. In fact, his conversation ranged widely from those topics to such questions as whether America is the most conformist country in the world. Whether Stoppard was talking about the

Broadcast on "Third Ear," BBC Radio Three, 16 April 1991.

intended subjects or topics that just came up, Miles Kington of *The Independent* found him "riveting either way because he was talking in the real sense of 'talk,' following a train of thought because it interested him. The opposite of 'chat,' in fact, which jumps on a train because the audience is going that way already. Down with television and chat, up with radio and talk." Stoppard's radio talk provided a foretaste of the richly nuanced, compelling talk that permeates his radio masterpiece, *In the Native State.*

ALLEN: Many things in Tom Stoppard's professional life seem to have come full circle recently. He went back to the play that made him famous 25 years ago, *Rosencrantz and Guildenstern Are Dead,* and he filmed it himself, winning the major award at the Venice Film Festival last year. If that surprised people, they were stunned when his next project turned out not to be another lucrative film but a return to BBC Radio, which had sustained him like so many other young playwrights in the 60s when he gave up journalism for a full-time career in drama. The play was *In the Native State,* which also took him back, in his imagination at least, to India, the subcontinent where he'd briefly lived in his itinerant childhood. The play takes place simultaneously in 1930 and 1990. In 1930 an adventurous but dying woman poet is having her portrait painted by an Indian artist. Sixty years on, the Indian's son shows the rather surprising result to the poet's sister back in London. It gives Stoppard a chance to reflect on the social and cultural themes of empire, race and the kind of love eventually found by some of his characters. When I met him in the Green Room during the recording I asked what the starting point for the play had been.

STOPPARD: Certainly the main one was a rather generalized idea to write about the Empire, and more particularly the ethics of empire. And I'm not saying that *In the Native State* is *that.* In a way, I still want to do that. But this play is some sort of introduction to the subject for me. One starting point, answering your question on a quite different level, was simply being asked to write a radio play and saying that I would. That tends to concentrate the mind, though not very quickly.

ALLEN: How, in quotes, "authentic" is the play? Your own experience, of India, your direct experience of India, is before you were eight years old, presumably?

STOPPARD: Yes, there's almost nothing of my experience in it, not even indirectly. On the other hand, India is the only Empire country

I would want to write about in any way. I was there between the age of four and eight and the country has always fascinated me. I never went back until this year and the visit back actually was in the nature of an experiment with memory as well, because I had quite a few images in my head which really were as nebulous as dreams, some of them. It was interesting to go back and put them back in their physical reality and see how the scale of things has changed. In a way it was chastening because I went back to a school which I attended; and I can remember being in this dormitory. (Education was different, you know; we were boarding when we were six and seven and all that.) I remember nights in this dormitory with the other boys. But in a sort of curious way it was never a real place. I didn't really think of it as being a real place. And it was very odd to go back to this school, which was closed for the winter when I was there but somebody got a key and they opened the door to the dormitory and there was this extremely ordinary room, rather smaller than I remembered, not really worthy of the intensity of the emotions I felt and associated with it. This was a couple of weeks ago; I'm still in a way reverberating.

ALLEN: So you went back after you'd written the play, not before you'd written it?

STOPPARD: That's right, yes. I'd written the play. Of course the play is set in 1930—that part of it which is set in India—so it wasn't a case of needing to go to India to research it or describe things, not at all. In fact, going back to India just after writing this play was more in the nature of a coincidence. It was much more to do actually with the Indian Film Festival inviting me and *Rosencrantz and Guildenstern are Dead* to come to Madras and I just thought "oh well, that's it," I'd wanted to go for years and now I'm going to go. The experience I had, as I say, after writing the play was one which was not particularly surprising to me. I was vaguely aware of its existence. That's the phenomenon of quite a lot of Indians of the older generation—having their own nostalgia for the British India days. I met several people who spoke in terms, you know, that it had all started to go wrong when the British left.

ALLEN: There's a sense in it for me of India being a kind of English Eden, a place to which you go to have an even more English time than you would actually here in England and of educated Indians feeling much the same way, and if they're not spending all their time reading and discussing Dickens, they're recreating English suburban life in the most improbable surroundings.

STOPPARD: Well, the British certainly did that, but not only the

British. One of the Indian actors in this play was telling me that he was brought up in a family to whom everything English was good and the loss and the passing of English influence was deeply regretted. I would say that's certainly a minority view among Indians, naturally enough. As for that recreation of the English Eden, I know exactly what you mean. In fact, it's more or less famous for being that. We built our houses in—I was going to say in the English style. In point of fact, Darjeeling where I spent most of my time is full of Scottish houses with Scottish names and it was quite fun walking around above the Bazaar Darjeeling and reading the names of these houses which are called Killarney Lodge and Gleneagles, still—though the roads are now renamed; Auckland Road is now Gandhi Road and so on.

The creation of this strange English time-warped society wasn't really entirely something one would love to be inside. It appeals to a certain side of me because I'm conservative by temperament and the English abroad tend to be a brake on the evolution of English society and manners and I always think that that evolution is far too fast so I'm quite pleased to be among people who've slowed it down. That doesn't mean that you really want to spend a lot of time with those people. One of the things that even as a child I was dimly aware of was that it enabled, in some cases, the worst side of people to come out, not always in deeply significant ways, sometimes in quite frivolous ways—for example, because an English family in India would as a matter of course have a number of servants, there was a tendency for people who were of no account in England at all to behave like duchesses as soon as they got east of Suez. We weren't actually English, as you know, so one was, I think, really neither in the British Raj world nor in the Indian world for most of the time I was there.

ALLEN: Is there any trepidation about writing Indian characters? I mean plainly in the past you've written . . . with all characters you are outside yourself and you've written about Lenin, about . . . there seems to me something slightly different about creating a character from another culture especially when you can be perceived as belonging to a culture which historically has exploited that one.

STOPPARD: I quite agree but the difficulty, particularly in this decade by the way, is not to write Indians who sound like Indians, which is hard enough, but to avoid writing characters who appear to have already appeared in *The Jewel in the Crown* and *Passage to India*. I mean the whole Anglo-Indian world has been so raked over and presented and re-presented by quite a small company of actors who appear in all of them (I'm very proud to say that Saeed is one of ours too), and so

I mean there is this slight embarrassment about actually not really knowing much about how to write an Indian character and really merely mimicking the Indian characters in other people's work. Because my own memory of living in India really hasn't been that much help because my conscious knowledge of how Indians speak and behave has actually been derived from other people's fictions.

ALLEN: In a number of your plays there is a sense of either characters or sometimes ideas in opposition, a kind of polarized feeling in which you very fairly give a shout to both sides. Now I suppose in a sense there's an Indian side and an English side to this play, but they don't seem to me to be quite so much in opposition and there seems to me more ... harmony? compassion? as a result in the play as a whole?

STOPPARD: Well, that's mixed up with the personalities of the two characters who have to carry nearly all of the dialectic in the 1930s scenes. I think that there *are* two oppositions at work in the play, but they're not cut and dried. Just to take the first and most obvious point, it's the Indian who loves things English—literature and his references are English and he obviously is in a kind of thrall to English culture. And it's the Englishwoman who finally says "It's all bosh, you know. It's your country and we've got it; everything else is bosh." The flavour I get off the play finally, I suppose because the last word is given to a real person called Emily Eden, who travelled around India in the mid-nineteenth century, because the last word is given to her and because it's caustic about the British and—what she actually says is she can't understand why the Indians don't cut all our heads off and think nothing more about it. Because that's the last word, I suppose the flavour of it is that *our* perspective on India actually distorts our own importance in the long run. So there are these currents in the play, but I was rather keen not to write a play which was a pair of conflicting polemics or editorials. That's really the problem with writing in any way about historical, political, social movements, oppositions ... I mean that's what's so hard, isn't it? I don't feel as if I've done it. I think it's a terribly hard balance. In a way, perhaps, the play now isn't actually *enough* about that subject, the subject which really provoked the play in the first place. Or one of the plays. You have to in a way find its serious subject matter, because there's quite a lot of chat in plays; it's their nature.

ALLEN: What's happened to divert the play? Is it simply that line by line characters take over?

STOPPARD: I suppose that is true. I mean it's certainly true of all plays in my experience that the process of writing the play determines the way it goes much more than one starts off thinking it will. I mean one of the reasons that I tend to deliver plays late, which I do, is that I can't shake off this idea each time that I can't possibly write anything until I've worked out exactly what's going to happen and why. I tend to start writing a play at the point where I just give up in despair and just *start* and hope that something works itself out. Clearly that's the way plays *ought* to be written because it allows them to be organic, and I think that if you work to plan too much from a set of principles as it were, just have a matrix and then knock the thing off in three weeks, I think probably you'd end up with something too schematic. But it's a frightening process (I mean, heavens, you know, we should all have such frights) but when one's living in this enclosed world where it assumes an unnatural importance to one's own life and well-being and future, it *does* become very frightening because you don't know how it's going to resolve itself, how it's going to manage to become a play really. And this is why perhaps . . . it's a play which I like and it's a play about *something* . . . but I don't think it's the play that I thought I'd write or the play which I still feel I ought to write.

ALLEN: You've been in the fairly unusual position within the last year of working, obviously, both on your latest piece of writing and one of your very earliest, *Rosencrantz and Guildenstern Are Dead,* which you've re-scripted and directed for the cinema. Now one of the reasons that you decided to direct it for the cinema, apart from being offered the chance to play with this wonderful machine and make a film was—I think I'm right in saying—that you thought that no other director would be ready to do sufficient violence to the original script in order to make it into a film as opposed to a filmed play. What violence did you do?

STOPPARD: Well, I left out half of it. And that's one thing. Mind you, that's not quite the situation because I'd written the script; and the director, you know, wouldn't do *that.* So *that* side of being disrespectful to the play I could do anyway; and then I could have given the result to a director. But in fact the situation would have become a bit embarrassing because by the time I'd finished the writing of the screenplay I had very firm ideas of how it was supposed to operate and how it would work and a sense that it wouldn't work at all unless it was done this way and this is what I meant and this is what you have to do. So it would have been embarrassing to have to go to somebody and say "listen, this is what you have to do," because directors want to make *their* films not *your* films. Even if I'd teamed up with somebody

244

who's very congenial in that way, it's actually impossible to tell a second person what you meant all the time.

It became very clear—I was going to say "retrospectively" but in fact during the process itself—that in film it seemed to me that writing and directing were the same job which for circumstantial reasons was often done by two people, which is not to say it always ought to be done by the same person. I don't consider myself to be a film director suddenly because I did my own film once. And it's equally true that one shouldn't assume that all film directors can write because, actually, they can't. So it's a tricky one, really. In an ideal world films should only be directed by writers but they should only be written by directors.

ALLEN: What is the actual difference, then, between film and theatre because in the theatre the whole time you're having to tell people what you really mean, presumably. You're there and that's the purpose of your being there in rehearsals of plays.

STOPPARD: Well, the main difference is that in the theatre the frame never changes. So a whole area of grammar isn't available to you and consequently it's much more an art form to do with utterance. I mean it's not *only* to do with that. In point of fact when you think of your own memories of particularly good theatrical moments over the years, I think most people would probably find if they examined it that a lot of things which they remember were never written down at all. They were simply not *in* the text. I mean you look it up and it says "Exit Lear" or something.

But that said, theatre obviously is about people talking to each other and one of the reasons that half—I say half because somebody told me I'd left half of the play out of the film, I've never actually counted the lines myself—but one of the reasons that an awful lot has gone missing is that it's in the way, it's unnecessary, it's not what you'd do if you were writing a film. And the great thing about . . . I mean the thing which saved the film really, I think, is that I didn't care. I didn't care to defend any of the play. I wasn't interested in protecting the play and politically speaking the main reason I directed the film is that I was the only person who had this attitude. Other people—one or two people—as it were recommended themselves for directing the film but they did so in terms which instantly disqualified them from the job because they were only too anxious to assure me how they revered text and would respect it at all times, which was actually not what I wished to hear.

ALLEN: You were also very interested, the last time we met, in writing about Americanness and the way that they have a conformity all their own so that the disappearance of collectivism in the world wasn't necessarily going to alter that. Since then we have got this new polarity in the world, if you like, developing; and we are, as we speak, at war. Do these things change very dramatically the mindset, if that's an acceptable phrase, of you as a writer?

STOPPARD: It probably should. It doesn't seem to. I mean, you're right, I would like to write about Americanness and Englishness, probably in the same play which would be one good way of doing it. Just looking at your question empirically, my feelings about that play are the same today while we are at war as they were a year ago. I don't know what conclusion to take from that but that's it.

Perhaps the things that interest me aren't affected by global events of that nature. I mean that's not really what interests me. I could speak a little about what *does* interest me, I mean I don't know whether it's quite relevant now, but it's . . . as you know I came here when I was eight and I don't know why, I don't particularly wish to understand why but I just seized England and it seized me. Within minutes it seems to me, I had no sense of being in an alien land and my feelings for, my empathy for English landscape, English architecture, English character, all that, has just somehow become stronger and stronger.

And now on the other side I'm very interested by the American character and how different it is from what it's supposed to be. I mean America has actually sold its own image in some rather successful way. So that in some very interesting way a nation which I think is *the* most conformist country anywhere—I mean to me it's a country of malleable susceptible conformists—has within it some true expression of maverick, pioneering glamour and audacity which is rattling about there and it leaks out. But it's the latter which has become the American image: a country of freebooters, adventurous adventurers.

And when you go there, one gets so sort of angry with the way they're all such . . . I'd better be careful here, what can I say, you stand on the corner of Madison and 57th or something and it says "DONT WALK" and the only people crossing the road—there's nothing coming for miles, you can see a quarter of a mile Sunday morning, you can see 800 yards that way and there's nothing coming and there's all these people standing on the corner waiting for the light to say "WALK" *except* the foreigners who are just ambling along because it's silly not to. I can't imagine the French or the Germans living with a government which says you can only drive at 55 miles an hour. They'd be out. They would be gone. Nobody would vote for them; there'd be a revolution. But the Americans in these huge cars just sort of trundle along like huge featherbeds at 55 miles per hour on these motorways built for going 110.

It's a very interesting country. I mean these are people who are only there, I mean their forebears, they're only there because they had the gumption to cross the Atlantic and get there and start again and they've all become sort of watered down into some other kind of people who are . . . I mean they have a sort of horror really of being out of line. I mean not 100 per cent of them of course but an interestingly large number of Americans don't really want to be out of line at all.

But as Kingsley Amis said many many years ago, and I've always remembered because it got me between the fourth and fifth rib, he's rather sick of people who go to America and are treated with overwhelming generosity and sweetness and never allowed to put their hand into their own pocket to buy a cup of coffee and they come back to England and start saying what's wrong with the Americans, and I don't really want to be of that number because I feel both things towards them.

ALLEN: Tom Stoppard, thank you very much.

STOPPARD: Thank you.

Tom's Sound Affects

Gillian Reynolds

The week that *In the Native State,* starring Felicity Kendal, was
to air on BBC Radio Three, the *Radio Times* devoted its cover
to a photograph of the actress along with the titillating headline "Felicity Kendal on Her Great Love Affair." Nine paragraphs into its cover story on Kendal as a "Thoroughly Modern Memsahib," the *Radio Times* dropped the bombshell quo-
tation in which Kendal confessed that her "love affair" was
"with India." That revelation probably came as a surprise to
readers who saw the *Radio Times* cover story on the same
news agents' racks as numerous tabloid stories linking Felicity
Kendal and Tom Stoppard romantically. Despite such attempts to emphasize the sensational, Kendal had been part
of the Stoppard production "team"—along with director
Peter Wood, designer Carl Toms, and actor Roger Rees—for
a full decade. After appearing as Christopher in *On the Razzle*
(Stoppard's 1981 Molnár adaptation), Kendal created the
role of Annie in *The Real Thing* (1982), starred as Dotty in
the 1985 revival of *Jumpers,* and created the title role in
Hapgood (1988). One of Stoppard's concerns during those
years—dating at least as far back as *Night and Day* (1978)—
was to counter the criticism that he did not write very good
parts for women. He more nearly fulfilled that ambition with
Annie in *The Real Thing* and in the title role of *Hapgood,* a
part written with Kendal in mind. But whereas *The Real Thing*
and *Hapgood* starred Felicity Kendal *and* Roger Rees, the focus of *In the Native State* is much more exclusively on women,
played by Felicity Kendal and Dame Peggy Ashcroft. Gillian

From the *Daily Telegraph,* 20 April 1991.

Reynolds's interview with Stoppard appeared the day before *In the Native State* was aired (while the *Radio Times* cover story was still on display at the news agents'). Several weeks after its BBC broadcast, *In the Native State* was published by Faber and Faber with a dedication "For Felicity Kendal."

A new play by Tom Stoppard is an event. That the world première of his latest, *In the Native State,* should be on Radio 3 tomorrow night is an event significant enough to merit the front cover of *Radio Times,* a place more usually reserved these days for television bimbos and bad boys.

It is a remarkable play, however. Funny and subtle, sharp, passionate and sensuous, it has Felicity Kendal as the heroine, Dame Peggy Ashcroft as her sister, and a story that moves about. John Tydeman, who commissioned it three years ago and has directed it, says it is the most mature thing Stoppard has written. "He's got real flesh and blood into those characters. I confess to having shed a tear or two."

The story is of Flora Crewe, poet, radical, lover of life and of many men, who goes to India in 1930 for her health. There she meets an Indian artist who paints her portrait. In 1990, years after her death, this portrait appears on the cover of an edition of her letters. The artist's son sees it, comes to London, meets Flora's sister, and shows her another portrait, a nude, painted at the same time but unseen for all these years.

Take it as a story, hear it as an allegory, understand it as a play about deciphering each other and decoding the past. It works brilliantly on any level, stealing into the air as conversation, lighting up the mind, leaving it changed.

Stoppard was late with it. He kept sending Tydeman postcards, despairing. "I've known him an awfully long time," he says of Tydeman. "He knows me awfully well and he knows I'm trying. I was trying to get him a play before the film of *Rosencrantz . . .* I just couldn't. Then they finished the film last July, I got going in September and delivered it in October.

"It began as odd pages, dialogue and stuff. I kept trying to find what play they belonged to. I thought I was going to write a play simply about the portrait of a woman writing a poem and her poem is about being painted. Then I found the idea of her poetry so perversely enjoyable I went on writing her poetry for far longer than you'd believe.

"I thought I wanted to write a stage play about the ethics of empire—there's still that to do. Here I got interested in other things more. I might do a play about empire. I might do one about Flora."

Flora is wonderful. She has shades about her of H. G. Wells's Ann Veronica. There is more than a passing resemblance to both Emily Dickinson and Sylvia Plath. She inspires. Mr Das, the painter, is under her spell, so are the Resident, the Rajah, the son of Mr Das, who knows only her picture, and Mr Pike, the American scholar who has edited her letters.

They are all in love with Flora and so, I suspect, is Tom Stoppard. For the audience, such romances often end in tears of boredom. Not here. Flora captures and conquers and dies far too young.

Stoppard's first plays, back in 1965, were for radio. *Albert's Bridge* won the Italia Prize in 1968, the money and prestige of which helped enormously to establish him. He goes on writing for radio when the stage, the cinema and television all jostle for whatever drops next from the end of his pen. "When people ask, why radio, they're really talking about money. That's what they mean. They want to know why do it when you could make more money somewhere else. And they're asking whether people hear it.

"That part of it doesn't worry me, but one is aware of it. Comparatively few people will hear it compared with television or the cinema. Instead of buying a ticket and sitting quietly in the dark for two hours you're answering the phone at the same time."

Does he listen to radio plays? "Yes, I do. Unfortunately I'm one of those people I was just describing. I listened to lots of *The Forsyte Chronicles* and to the Craig Raine *Andromache*. I heard a bit of the Christopher Logue one, *Kings*, but that was just another one of those evenings. My life doesn't accommodate radio drama much. I don't even see half the stage plays I want to.

"Sometimes I wish the BBC worked like a subscription library, with a catalogue of programmes you could buy or rent. [In fact, the BBC Radio Collection has over a dozen plays for sale on cassette, including Stoppard's own *Rosencrantz and Guildenstern Are Dead*.]

"To make 8–10.30 pm, say, undisturbed, can be done, but it's difficult. But one of the things about having something on the radio makes me pull myself together and *see* what's on the radio."

He appreciates sound. The season of his plays last summer on Radio 3 showed how well his texts repay a close ear; but he confesses an ambition to write something for radio with no dialogue at all. Perhaps he has already started. John Tydeman describes him in the studio the other week, playing with sound-effect horses' hooves, going click, click, click. "I suppose," he said, "a single coconut shell is an existential horse?"

Stoppard Basks in a Late Indian Summer

Russell Twisk

During rehearsals for *In the Native State,* Russell Twisk was able to observe the interaction between Stoppard and the play's director, John Tydeman. The BBC Radio's head of drama, Tydeman had also produced Stoppard's *If You're Glad I'll Be Frank* (1966) and *Artist Descending a Staircase* (1972) but declares of *In the Native State:* "I think it's the best thing he's ever written. It has flesh and blood. One is moved by it. So often in the past his cleverness has got in the way and he's hidden his feelings under the pyrotechnics. But he's really a soppy old thing." But if feelings are never far from the surface of *In the Native State,* the play is also carefully crafted. As Felicity Kendal, who played Flora Crewe, observes: "This play is to do with language rather than action and it lends itself particularly well to radio; it isn't the story that's the thing, it's the spider's web of ideas and circumstances, written very carefully with a lot of loops that loop into some-thing else." Besides discussing the genesis of the play with Stoppard, Twisk was able to capture Stoppard suggesting to Felicity Kendal line readings that underscored the emotional resonances of some of those loops. Twisk's interview ap-peared the same day *In the Native State* was first broadcast.

Tom Stoppard sits in the studio for the entire five days it takes to make his new radio play, *In the Native State.* He delights in the company of actors and finds rehearsals an agreeable team sport, a welcome contrast to the loneliness of writing.

From *The Observer,* 21 April 1991.

We meet high in Broadcasting House at the end of the day's recording. He watches with an ex-journalist's wary eye as I arrange my notes. He hunts for an empty ashtray, which is soon filled to the brim, and settles his lanky frame awkwardly into a chair.

In the studio he sits in a corner, wading through Peter Ackroyd's biography of Dickens, half listening to the actors experimenting with his words. First he likes to see what they make of his script; only then does he suggest changes, preferring counter-punching to punching. He explains: 'When you write a play it makes a particular noise in your head and at rehearsals I can see if the actors will reproduce that noise. Sometimes they have a better noise to offer. But typography is a curiously ambiguous medium for measuring the emotional temperature from moment to moment.' He confides his prejudices to the director 'to see whether he'll go along with any of them'.

The director, John Tydeman, who is also head of BBC drama, has worked with Stoppard for more than 25 years since he submitted his first 15-minute play to an experimental late-night series. Tydeman luxuriates in this mutual trust. He says: 'When Tom finishes his script, he feels that possession passes to the director and actors. He'll say "Do you mind if I change that word?" as though the script were mine.'

He cites as an example the highly-charged and erotic poem spoken by the heroine Flora Crewe, played by Felicity Kendal, towards the end. 'Sweat collects and holds as a pearl at my throat, lets go and slides like a tongue-tip down a Modigliani, spills into the delta, now in the salt-lick, lost in the mangrove and the airless moisture . . .' Stoppard says gently: 'Felicity, the word "mangrove" is not there entirely accidentally. It has a gender connotation too.' Tydeman says: 'I must confess that was one I missed . . .'

Stoppard is twitchy about the media because the tabloids are on the snoop at the gates. He's having a relationship with Felicity Kendal who plays the deliciously promiscuous Flora. In the play, her sister Mrs Swan, played by Peggy Ashcroft, says of the character: 'She used men like batteries. When things went flat, she'd put in another one.'

Off-air lives must add an extra Stoppardian dimension to the recording sessions. *Today* used a publicity shot of the production showing Stoppard and Kendal with Peggy Ashcroft in between. They billed it as the first picture of the couple together since denying rumours of a relationship. The production team thought it was in very bad taste. One said: 'There was dear Peggy sitting there being made to look like a female Pandarus.'

The play is about crossing boundaries between scandal and propriety; India and the Empire; left-wing Bloomsbury and the wealth of the Rajah; the Indian painter and the Englishwoman; the compliant ruled and the imperial power which knows its days are numbered; respectful Anglo-Indians versus the free spirit from England. Time melts too: between flashbacks to the nineteenth-century to Forties India and present-day London. There are many levels in a Stoppard script and they seem to change every time you examine them.

In the Native State was a year late in delivery: he got 'sidetracked' by the film he directed of *Rosencrantz and Guildenstern are Dead,* which is released on 24 May. 'I had to come crawling and apologise. They were very nice about it, BBC Radio must be the last bastion of courtesy.' But promising the play interfered with his peace of mind and made him feel guilty. 'It stood as an obstacle between me and any future I might have, but then retroactively I am in John's debt because I know the play wouldn't exist at all if he hadn't prevailed on me to do one.'

This turns out to be a familiar pattern in the birth of a Stoppard play. Enthusiastic commitment, followed by a growing sense of obligation, which eventually turns into a burden. He says: 'I think the cart has always been pulling the horse. I wrote my novel by owing it to someone. Moral obligations are somehow more enforceable. I hate not having anything going on as a writer. It depresses me.'

He needs more than one idea and began this wanting to write about a woman having her portrait painted while writing about the painter. He also wanted a play about the ethos of Empire in India, where he'd spent a few years as a young boy, leaving in 1946. His keenest memory is the smell of horse manure, replaced now by petrol fumes. He says: 'When ideas combine, then it begins to feel like the possibility of a play.'

At the end he feels drained, emptied out. 'I use everything I've got hanging around so that whenever I finish a play I have absolutely nothing left at all.' Is this emptying out an essential part of the creative process for him? 'I don't see why it should be, but it is. I wish I had a drawerful of ideas like other writers.'

The play swings through time with parallels, ambiguities, puns, paradoxes in hot pursuit of each other. Each reading or listening yields more. There's a commentary from an American editor, Pike, who adds pompous, over-explicit footnotes to Flora's text.

Stoppard says he dearly wants the play to make a film—'if only I could figure out what to do with Pike! I don't want to leave him out because he adds a dimension of spurious reality. Sometimes I think Pike should turn into captions which just stutter across the screen.'

He has tried for years to write a play that will work only on radio. He thought he had achieved it in *Artist Descending A Staircase,* but the King's Head kept asking and he thought it precious and priggish to keep refusing 'so I thought, let them find out—and I've never had such good notices for anything in years'.

The intimacy of a radio studio, relaxing with old friends, and redeeming hasty promises conspire to bring him back. 'It's quite un-like any other play-producing because you never do the whole play, you have a go at a scene, then you put it on tape and do the next scene and the thing accumulates. At the end of five days you feel "we could do it now," but you find you've done it.'

I've now listened to *In the Native State* three times, re-read the script and interviewed the author. My pleasure grows with finding more after each reading and hearing. It is a beautifully crafted play. When it becomes a film, at least a third of the dialogue will be lost. Don't miss it in its native state tonight. I certainly won't.

Is *The Real Inspector Hound* a Shaggy Dog Story?

Angeline Goreau

In New York for rehearsals of *The Real Inspector Hound,* Stoppard was as ready as ever to describe the play as "an entertainment...a mechanical toy." But if *The Real Inspector Hound* is a shaggy-dog story, it continues to snare numerous listeners. Despite Stoppard's steadfast denial that the play is anything more than a mere entertainment, it remains the only way his work is represented in the *Norton Anthology of English Literature,* the standard text at hundreds of American colleges and universities. At the same time that Stoppard shrugs off any sense of *Hound* having any greater significance, he quite happily comments on autobiographical and thematic elements in *The Real Thing* and *In the Native State. Arcadia,* the work in progress Stoppard discusses here, opened at the National Theatre in London on 13 April 1993 in a production directed by Trevor Nunn, who also directed the premiere production of *Every Good Boy Deserves Favour.* The cast of *Arcadia* included Emma Fielding, Allan Mitchell, Rufus Sewell, Samuel West, and Felicity Kendal.

Most playwrights who have suffered indignities at the hands of the critics—and who has not?—lie awake at one time or another inventing clever forms of revenge and then think the better of it in the morning. Tom Stoppard wrote *The Real Inspector Hound.*

In this broad—very broad—swipe at the enemy, two critics of dubious stripe, Birdboot and Moon, bumble their way through and

---

From the *New York Times,* 9 August 1992.

finally into the play they are supposed to be reviewing, to find in the end that an ignominious fate awaits. Together, they cover the spectrum of critical response: the highbrow Moon looking for "the nature of identity," while the lowbrow Birdboot throws himself on a box of Black Magic chocolates and tries to guess who the murderer is. In his romp through commonplace, Mr. Stoppard—who once worked as a critic himself—gives Moon lines like this: "There are moments, and I would not begrudge it this, when the play, if we can call it that, and I think on balance we can, aligns itself uncompromisingly on the side of life."

Oddly enough, *The Real Inspector Hound* was written on the heels of the playwright's first major critical success, *Rosencrantz and Guildenstern Are Dead* (1967). But Mr. Stoppard, as critics have so often observed, is a man of paradoxes. In a strange way, *Hound* is—among other things—a self-parody. And Mr. Stoppard has never been the sort of writer to resist the temptation of a naughty good time.

First staged in 1968, *Hound* is being revived on Broadway by the Roundabout Theater Company in a production directed by Gloria Muzio. In previews at the Criterion Center, it opens Thursday with David Healy and Simon Jones as the critics and Patricia Conolly, Anthony Fusco, Rod McLachlan, J. Smith-Cameron, Jane Summerhays and Jeff Weiss also in the cast. The playwright's farcical *15-Minute Hamlet* is on the bill as a curtain-raiser, with the same cast members delivering Shakespeare's lines in double, sometimes triple, time.

Mr. Stoppard, who lives in England, is in Manhattan for rehearsals, and on a hot soupy late July afternoon he briefly comes to rest at the University Club. Dropping into a chair with apparent exhaustion, he confesses to finding himself "at the lowest ebb of life—second day in New York at 4 o'clock in the afternoon. It's when jet lag catches up with you." And adds mischievously: "It has no ill effect on me other than decimating my vocabulary and the pace of cerebration."

The 55-year-old writer is known for the constant revision he subjects his plays to, reworking them while they are in rehearsal and frequently rewriting extensively for new productions of plays long ago "finished." He will not, however, be tinkering with what is arguably the shaggiest of all his plays. *The Real Inspector Hound* is also the only one of his plays that he has himself directed, in a National Theatre production in London five years ago.

"*Hound* is timeless in the truly pejorative sense . . . incapable of change," its author quips, when asked whether he finds it plays differently now from the way it did in the 60's.

"*Hound,*" he continues, "doesn't lend itself to deep scrutiny. It's an entertainment, just like a mechanical toy. It waves a flag, squeaks and turns a turtle and carries on. It's a logical structure with a vein of parody going through it. There's no *reason* to write a play like that. It's an enjoyment. And that is what it is. One hopes it will work out all right, because in the nature of theater there's this interesting transition between the text and the event. The ball can be dropped in many different ways. Or not dropped. *Hound* has been a lucky play. It sort of works out all right generally."

Like most writers who achieve immortality before death, Mr. Stoppard is regularly pursued by critics and academics looking for the key to his works. And, like most writers of good sense, he shies from exegesis.

"I don't trust writers who wax confidently about what they do and why they do it," he said. "In writing plays, I find that the problems—if that's what they are—are very mundane, and in a way surface. The wellspring of a play is often curiously uninteresting—it all derives from insubstantial stray images and ideas. What it doesn't arise from at all, I don't think, is anything like a complete sense of the whole. You know, What am I going to try to achieve here? What is it going to be about *underneath?*

"I seldom worry about underneath. Even when I'm aware that there *is* an underneath, I tend to try and suppress it further under, because theater is a wonderfully, refreshingly simple event. It's a story-telling event. The story holds or it doesn't. You don't get the point or its significance if it doesn't hold. The same would be true of a short story or a novel."

Until the late 80's, critics tended to view Mr. Stoppard's career as a progression from the early enfant terrible period, in which he dazzled audiences with erudition and verbal high jinks in such plays as *Jumpers* and *Travesties,* to the period in which he began to write plays with political subtext (*Night and Day,* for example, deals with freedom of the press), to a final coming to terms with life and feeling in *The Real Thing.*

The last new play of his to be produced in New York, *The Real Thing* was greeted by Frank Rich in *The Times* in 1984 as "the most bracing play that anyone has written about love and marriage in years." It went on to win five Tony Awards, including best play.

Because the hero was a dramatist, *The Real Thing* was thought to be much more autobiographical than it was, Mr. Stoppard said. In its earliest version, to avoid this difficulty, he tried to make the major character a novelist. But in the end, he said, he was forced to make him a playwright for structural reasons:

"The first idea I had was that I'd like to write a play in which the first scene turned out to have been written by a character in the second scene. That was all I started with. There is a strong—not autobiographical element—but strong editorial element because the man spouts opinions generally which I subscribe to. So in that sense there's a lot of me in it, more than in most plays, but only by virtue of the fact that the protagonist is a writer in London in 1980-odd."

In the last few years, New York has seen a revival of his Tony-winning *Rosencrantz and Guildenstern* and, in 1989, his radio play *Artist Descending a Staircase,* which received mixed reviews and closed after 36 performances. *Hapgood,* a new play, which was done in Los Angeles also in 1989, never came to New York. A complex comic spy thriller about physics, it had its admirers, but some critics thought that Mr. Stoppard had carried inscrutability beyond the pale.

"*Hapgood* has a physicist in it," he said, "who talks about physics a bit. But I don't think that actually is the problem. The intricacies of the spy plot are quite difficult. I think I'm not as good as John le Carré at doing that kind of story. But I find I'm talking about the play as though it failed in some way for me. In fact, I'm interested by it in so far as it *succeeded.*" He is thinking of reworking it in a "much simpler form," but clearly it's not a first priority.

A new play, *Arcadia,* has been "cooking" for the last three years, and is scheduled to open at the National Theatre in April. "I've got some of it written," he said, "but I've been working on films for a year, so I don't quite know what it needs." The play shuttles between the present day and 200 years ago. "I don't want to talk about it very much," he said tentatively. "It's about literary detection . . . about people speculating about what happens . . . and in theory the fun is seeing how wrong they can be, because we've been there and they haven't."

One film script he has been writing is for *Poodle Springs,* a novel that Raymond Chandler wrote four chapters of and that Robert Parker finished. Next year, he plans to rework a new radio play, *In the Native State,* for the stage. "The trick here," he said, "is to put the radio play aside and write a stage play about the same people."

In the Native State has more than a few references that, as in *The Real Thing,* look suspiciously autobiographical. Interestingly enough, it also returns to a much more straightforward narrative style. Though the action moves back and forth between the 1930's and the present, it tells two stories in a more or less traditional fashion. But the complexity remains in this play about the British Empire, which questions the received wisdom about colonization. "There are some internal contradictions," Mr. Stoppard asserted.

"I was interested in writing a play in which these arguments and counterarguments were properly weighed," he said. "I don't think a play's the best place to do it, frankly. One of the built-in ironies of being a playwright at all is that one is constantly trying to put into dramatic form questions and answers that require perhaps an essay, perhaps a book, but are too important and too subtle, really, to have to account for themselves within the limitations of what's really happening in the theater, which is that the story is being told in dialogue."

Mr. Stoppard said he uses "this ill-suited medium" to account for and dispose of his own preoccupations—"about matters like morality of empire, or the authenticity of romantic love"—with the reservation that "failure is almost built into a play if that is its true purpose, its true function. And so one avoids failure if one can, by denying that that is the function of the play. And one says that, no, that was merely an aspect or a sidelight of the play's function and the primary function is to tell an entertaining story."

What matters to him more than anything, he said, is the pleasure in writing itself. "My primary delight, which is a good enough word for the fuel that one needs to do any work at all, is in using the language rather than the purpose to which language is put...and more than language, I would say theater—the way theater works, through disclosure and surprise."

Surprise is what audiences have come to expect from Mr. Stoppard. But what seems to keep them coming back is that they never know exactly what form it will take.

In a Country Garden (If It Is a Garden)

David Nathan

Like *In the Native State, Arcadia* alternates between two radically different time periods and raises questions about how
the past impinges on the present and how the present can
understand (and misunderstand) the past. Although Stoppard says the "original impetus" for *Arcadia* was the desire to
write about the contrast between the classical temperament
and the romantic temperament "and how they might collide
and whether each one partook of the other," the play as
written touches upon "all kinds of things" he had not expected to include. Such serendipity in part reflects the rich-
ness of ideas in a play that deals with order and chaos, art
and nature, the arrow of time and the fate of the cosmos.
But unexpected dimensions of the play may also be found in
the characters' emotional depth in an intricately plotted work
that explores the unpredictable nature of love and sexual
desire. Speaking to David Nathan three weeks before the
play's opening, Stoppard was not going to be drawn regarding the plot. However, he was willing to reveal that the ambiguities of his bucolic *Arcadia* are rooted in the mathematical
intricacies of chaos theory. If its oscillation between time periods recalls *In the Native State, Arcadia*'s use of theoretical
mathematics extends the concerns of *Hapgood*, where quantum mechanics provides a metaphor for the uncertainties of
human personality. In fact, it is with a comparison to the
complexities of *Hapgood* that Nathan begins.

From the *Sunday Telegraph*, 28 March 1993.

It is five years since Tom Stoppard's last play, *Hapgood,* and people have lain awake ever since trying to figure out what its mix of quantum physics and double agents was all about. Perhaps it's not surprising then that questions about his new play, *Arcadia,* do not have Stoppard rushing to give a neat synopsis of the plot. He's not being unhelpful, far from it; it's just that he's loath to give explanations—not least, he says, because it spoils the fun.

Landscape gardening seems to be the starting point—the classical, formal garden or the romantic wilderness; though, as Stoppard hurriedly points out, even the wilderness can be contrived. This leads on to the difference between "those who have particular respect for logic, geometry and pattern, and those with a much more spontaneous, unstructured communion with nature."

After that things get a good deal murkier. "Um, anti-science," he says, "but not really *anti* so much as scepticism of science as the ultimate truth about the world." Then he gives up. "I know," he says pleadingly, "that talking about *Arcadia* in these terms is really not describing it very clearly, but if I were to get very clear I'd be telling you the story, which I would rather not do."

All the same, the new play would seem to pursue themes that go right back to his earliest work—questions about whether there is an underlying order in the world or simply chaos, and an awareness that either one only raises more questions. In his 1966 novel, *Lord Malquist and Mr Moon,* the latter asks: "If it is all random, what's the point?" To which Laura Malquist replies: "What's the point if it's all inevitable?"

No doubt a long conversation with the author prefaced the National Theatre's press release about *Arcadia.* It says: "In the garden room of a large country house in April 1809 sits Lady Thomasina Coverly, aged 13, and her tutor. Through the window '500 acres inclusive of lake' is about to succumb to the fashionable Gothic style; 'everything but vampires', as garden historian Hannah Jarvis remarks to academic Bernard Nightingale, in the same room, 180 years later. Bernard has arrived to uncover a scandal, which took place (if it ever did take place) when Lord Byron stayed there (if he ever did)."

Stoppard, munching on a prawn sandwich (if it is a prawn sandwich) during a break in rehearsal, says, "There was romantic and classical mathematics as well. Classical mathematics is certainly a phrase; romantic mathematics isn't, except I'm prepared to use the term for the purpose of an interview."

I begin to feel a little like Stoppard's Guildenstern—"what a fine persecution—to be kept intrigued without ever being quite enlightened."

"You see, I got tremendously interested in a book called *Chaos* by James Gleick which is about this new kind of mathematics. That sounds fairly daunting if one's talking about a play. I thought, here is a marvellous metaphor. But, as ever, there wasn't really a play until it had connected with stray thoughts about other things."

There seems little point persisting in trying to pluck out a play's mystery before seeing it, so we move on. Stoppard has never made a secret of the fact that he finds it very difficult to come up with a plot. When this one—whatever it is—came along, was he thrilled? "Oh yes, but then I still had the difficult part to work out. This time things fell into place fairly quickly and I was reasonably happy. It certainly works quite well on the level of what will happen next, which is the *sine qua non* of playwriting, telling a story.

"I think I did it in two or three months which is fast for me. I don't rough things out and then re-write. I can't do the 37th line until I'm happy with the 36th—even if I turn out to be wrong about it and change it later."

I mention that Christopher Fry once told me that he had laboured for two weeks on one line. Stoppard thought about this. "Two weeks is quite a long time for one line," he said at last, "but not too much, considering Oscar Wilde would put in a comma in the morning and take it out in the afternoon. Which line was it?"

Something about the unlaborious laburnum, I thought.

Had he been worried then that the play had been so long in coming? "Less worried than irritated," he said. "I was perfectly well aware that I was creating the interval myself by doing other things. I was constantly busy. I never spent a month trying to write a play and failing. But I got a bit disgusted with myself because I interpreted it all essentially as laziness. There's a kind of self-delusion that it will happen if you take a walk and have a think, or if you lie down for a while and work it out. Of course, that's all nonsense. It happens when you sit there with a pen in your hand, and it doesn't happen otherwise."

Stoppard once said, "I write plays because writing dialogue is the only respectable way of contradicting yourself." Nor has he changed much over the years.

"None of us is tidy; none of us is classifiable. Even the facility to perceive and define two ideas such as the classical and romantic in opposition to each other indicates that one shares a little bit of each."

So which does he lean to? "That's a really difficult question. They take turns to dominate, but I would say I lean to the classical in the sense that I associate it more with caution and introversion, rather than recklessness and extroversion. Extroversion is a performance art."

At 55 Stoppard says, gloomily, that he's started to feel the passing years, although there is little or no grey in the thick mop of hair and he could still pass for a good 10 years younger. This autumn the RSC will revive *Travesties* with Antony Sher, and it can't be too long before *Jumpers,* in which logic collides memorably with acrobatics, is considered ripe for disinterment. As for any more new plays, they will have to wait.

"The fact that I've got a new play coming out is an absolute guarantee that I'm not working on anything else," he says, as if it's a thoroughly shameful admission. He confirms this by adding, "It's terrible! When I reached 50 or thereabouts I thought I hadn't got enough time left to fiddle about so I tried to force myself to get going on something. It didn't work. I am thinking of rewriting my last radio play, *In the Native State,* for the stage, but that's not new work.

"It doesn't really matter," he says, all shrugs and gestures signalling quite the opposite. "There's no law that says you've got to write a play every three years until you're dead. On the other hand if I don't do that, what the hell am I doing? Playwriting is what I do, it's my identity."

Trevor Nunn, director of *Arcadia,* walks in as I'm leaving: "I expect you know what it's all about now," he says.

"Of course," I say. "Of course."

Plotting the Course of
a Playwright

Nigel Hawkes

Appearing on the day *Arcadia* opened, Nigel Hawkes's interview was accompanied by "Tom Stoppard's Science: A Playgoer's Guide," offering an explanation of such matters as chaos, thermodynamics, the arrow of time, Fermat's Last Theorem, and Newcomen's Steam Pump. Although favorable in tone, the article may have contributed to a sense that the play was more idea-driven than, say, *In the Native State*. First night reviews of *Arcadia*, which opened at the National Theatre on 13 April 1993, ranged from denunciations of "the play's central vacuum: its fatal lack of living contact between ideas and people" to celebrations of an "unusually moving" play in which "Stoppard's ideas and emotions seamlessly coincide." In any event, Stoppard's first full-length original play to be performed at the National since *Jumpers* was a triumph with audiences. *Arcadia* played to sold-out houses and the NT bookstalls broke all records for sales of a playscript. In part audiences may have responded intellectually by "wanting to know" just what an iterated algorithm may be or, indeed, how the play itself may be an iterated algorithm. But from the play's opening question to its surprisingly evocative and mysterious final dance, "wanting to know" embraces longings that are carnal as well as intellectual, romantic as well as spiritual. Whereas *Hapgood* begins with an intentionally baffling opening scene (and may leave much of the audience dumbfounded by the entire evening's proceedings), *Arcadia*

From *The Times*, 13 April 1993.

entices, intrigues, and only gradually mystifies its audience with the sense that there is more to be known. What, for example, are we to make of the silence of Gus, of his uncanny knowledge, of his comings and goings? What mysteries pervade the final dance, which spans generations, centuries, and—perhaps—much more? Speaking to Hawkes, Stoppard dismisses as an "illusion" the belief "that science was rapidly finding out all the answers, and would solve all the mysteries." However intricately it embodies scientific theory, *Arcadia* may itself be imbued with a sense of mystery that does not yield all its answers even as it invites us to join in the dance.

In a country house in Derbyshire, around 1810, a bright young girl stumbles on a discovery capable of revolutionising the way we look at the world. Chaos theory is born, makes a brief and unacknowledged bow, and is then forgotten again for 160 years.

Tom Stoppard's new play *Arcadia,* which opens at the National Theatre tonight, celebrates scientific ideas in a way which is unusual, if not unique, in British theatre. Stoppard has always pursued ideas like a boar after truffles, but seldom has he discovered such a rewarding hoard as he does in this play.

Chaos theory, entropy, the arrow of time, the second law of thermodynamics, population biology and Newcomen's Improved Steam Pump all have their moments as Stoppard explores the differences between the Classical and the Romantic imagination. The play shifts to and fro between 1810 and the modern day, creating a counterpoint against which he set a story of literary detection and scientific discovery.

Stoppard's mind began to work when he read James Gleick's book *Chaos* and saw that it might serve as a metaphor for a play about the antithesis between the Romantic and the Classical. Chaos theory in this respect represents the overthrow of determinism, the idea that nature behaves like a giant piece of clockwork whose functioning, once understood, can be perfectly predicted in advance. Chaos tells us that the world is not like that: even the motions of the planets, the most metronomic of natural phenomena, may ultimately be unpredictable.

The equations that represent chaos are simple in form, but complex to work out, and had to wait for the arrival of the calculator and the computer. In *Arcadia* they are discovered by Thomasina Coverly, a precocious and spirited girl who gets as far as she can with pen and paper. In the background as she works, the estate is being transformed to the sound of Newcomen's steam pump from the Classical calm of Capability Brown into a picturesque landscape of grottoes, gloomy woods and a tumbledown hermitage.

Tom Stoppard thus interweaves chaos theory with the rise of the Romantic movement. Is the play, then, an attempt to rewrite cultural history by suggesting that chaos theory ought to have been born at the same time as the Gothic novel? Stoppard disavows the idea.

"It isn't as tidy as that," he says. "In painting, literature, landscape gardening, these changes all happened sequentially. Over a hundred years, 1730 to 1830, they all seemed to go through that change, though not necessarily in concert with each other. I'm not really saying there was ever such a thing as Classical mathematics, and one doesn't talk about there being a Romantic phase in mathematics either. I think what one is really doing is taking advantage of one's enthusiasms."

Those enthusiasms include a pretty extensive reading of scientific books. "I have done a fair amount, but never in a spirit of dogged duty. I start thinking about a play because of the reading I've been doing, and then I do a lot more of it because of the play I've been thinking about. So it's circular, really. I do it entirely for stimulation and pleasure and ultimately I suppose I get a bit deeper into it, so that I know what's behind what I'm writing about."

A play, he says, cannot go into these subjects in any depth when compared with a book. Actually, *Arcadia* does succeed in conveying not only a lot of scientific ideas, but more unusually, something of the spirit behind them. For the average playgoer, I suggested, perhaps it goes about as far as one could get away with? "Well, even further..." admits Stoppard with a laugh.

"But I don't think any audience is homogeneous, in any theatre, for any play. So you're always really skirting the possibility of leaving some of your audience out of it. On the whole one tries not to. I mean, there are certain things that are deliberately there as a private language, and not just in this play. Talking to you as a journalist I can say that in a play I wrote about journalism there were phrases that only a journalist would have understood. But it gives a sense of authenticity and is understood by the few people in the audience who'd be familiar with that kind of thing. You hope that the overall narrative is strong enough to take people through to the main stations."

Arcadia doesn't give science all the best tunes. The character Bernard Nightingale, a literary don on the make, rounds splenetically on it. "Don't confuse progress with perfectibility," he says. "A great poet is always timely. A great philosopher is an urgent need. There's no rush for Isaac Newton. We were quite happy with Aristotle's cosmos. Personally, I preferred it. Fifty-five crystal spheres, all geared to God's crankshaft, is my idea of a satisfying universe."

This is not, however, Stoppard's own idea of science. "Bernard's polemic does not speak for me, no. It is a kind of performance art, anyway, the kind of speech that that man would make to a scientist, out of a sort of overflow of energy and mischief. I suppose that in theory I'd be capable of abolishing Bernard, I mean inventing a rival polemic."

In the play, that task falls to the earnest young scientist Valentine Coverly, studying the population dynamics of grouse with the aid of the estate's game books. "We're better at predicting events on the edge of the galaxy or inside the nucleus of an atom than whether it'll rain on auntie's garden party three weeks from now," he says. "The future is disorder. A door like this has cracked open five or six times since we got up on our hind legs. It's the best possible time to be alive, when almost everything you thought you knew is wrong."

It is this speech, not Bernard's, that strikes a chord with Stoppard. But he's anxious to insist that this isn't a play about science, or a play for scientists. "It's a play that just comes off that slice of the culture, and science is a large slice of our culture. There's nothing odd about the arts feeding off it, even though science plays about as small a part in the theatre as it does in the lives of most non-scientists."

Nor is the play's purpose didactic. "It all sounds rather as if I've got a policy on these things, which of course I haven't," Stoppard says. "I was jolly grateful to have an idea for a play, whatever it's about."

He sees anti-scientific sentiments as nothing new. "In any age, including the period around the year 1800, we had a kind of reaction against scientism by the poets of the time, so you find that Blake and Wordsworth and Coleridge as young men are resisting the thinking of that time that science was rapidly finding out all the answers, and would solve all the mysteries. The sense, or illusion, that science is doing exactly that seems to accompany every age, and creates an opposing force."

Last week Stoppard was trimming and tuning. Constructed as intricately as Aristotle's universe, *Arcadia* is not the easiest play to modify, but the first performances ran ten minutes over three hours. "You try to write it in a way that makes it impossible to leave anything out, or you haven't written it properly," he says. "Then you find you have to leave something out."

The final verdict on *Arcadia* belongs to the critics and the audiences, who must be satisfied if it is to succeed as a drama. But it's impossible not to applaud a playwright who sees culture as a seamless web, is interested enough to understand the part science plays in that culture, and brave enough to write a play around it. And, by the way, there are plenty of good jokes in it.

Bibliography

The following bibliography of Tom Stoppard's works and words about his works is arranged chronologically within each category. Plays and articles by Stoppard are listed in the order of their initial publication. Lectures, print interviews, and broadcast interviews are listed in the order—insofar as it can be determined—in which they were given. Where information about the date of an interview is not available, it is listed according to the date it was published or broadcast. Within these categories, the bibliography attempts to be comprehensive and is, therefore, necessarily incomplete. The editor will gratefully receive notification of articles, lectures, and interviews omitted from the following list. Intentionally omitted are news articles containing incidental quotations from Stoppard, audio and video recordings of plays, and acting editions of Stoppard plays (except for plays—or versions of plays—not otherwise published).

Works by Stoppard

Lord Malquist and Mr Moon. London: Anthony Blond, 1966; New York: Knopf, 1968; London: Panther, 1968; New York: Ballantine, 1969; London: Faber and Faber, 1974, 1980; New York: Grove Press, 1975.

Rosencrantz and Guildenstern Are Dead. London: Faber and Faber, 1967, revised 1967, 1978; New York: Grove Press, 1967, revised 1968; London and New York: Samuel French, 1967.

Albert's Bridge, in *Plays and Players*, 15 (October 1967), pp. 21–30; London: Faber and Faber, 1970.

Tango. By Slawomir Mrozek, translated by Nicholas Bethell, adapted by Tom Stoppard. London: Cape, 1968.

The Real Inspector Hound. London: Faber and Faber, 1968, revised 1970; New York: Grove Press, 1969.

Enter a Free Man. London: Faber and Faber, 1968; New York: Grove Press, 1972.

"Albert's Bridge" and "If You're Glad I'll Be Frank." London: Faber and Faber, 1969.

After Magritte. London: Faber and Faber, 1971.

Jumpers. London: Faber and Faber, 1972, revised 1973, 1986; New York: Grove Press, 1972, revised 1973, 1989 (paper), revised 1981 (cloth).

"Artist Descending a Staircase" and "Where Are They Now?": Two Plays for Radio. London: Faber and Faber, 1973.

"The Real Inspector Hound" and "After Magritte." New York: Grove Press, 1975.

Travesties. London: Faber and Faber, 1975; New York: Grove Press, 1975.

"Dirty Linen" and "New-Found-Land." London: Inter-Action Inprint, 1976; London: Faber and Faber, 1976; New York: Grove Press, 1976.

If You're Glad I'll Be Frank. London: Faber and Faber, 1976. [First published in 1969 with *Albert's Bridge*.]

The Fifteen Minute Hamlet. London: Samuel French, 1976.

"*Albert's Bridge*" and *Other Plays*. New York: Grove Press, 1977. [Contains *If You're Glad I'll Be Frank, Artist Descending a Staircase, Where Are They Now?*, and *A Separate Peace.*]

"*Every Good Boy Deserves Favour: A Play for Actors and Orchestra*" and "*Professional Foul: A Play for Television.*" London: Faber and Faber, 1978.

"*Every Good Boy Deserves Favor*" and "*Professional Foul*": *Two Plays*. New York: Grove Press, 1978.

Night and Day. London: Faber and Faber: 1978, revised 1979; New York: Grove Press, 1979; New York: Samuel French, 1980.

Dogg's Our Pet. In *Ten of the Best British Short Plays*, ed. Ed Berman, pp. 79–94. London: Inter-Action Inprint, 1979.

The (15 Minute) Dogg's Troupe Hamlet. In *Ten of the Best British Short Plays*, ed. Ed Berman, pp. 137–52. London: Inter-Action Inprint, 1979.

Dogg's Hamlet, Cahoot's Macbeth. London: Inter-Action Inprint, 1979; London: Faber and Faber, 1980.

Undiscovered Country. Adapted from *Das weite Land* by Arthur Schnitzler. London: Faber and Faber, 1980.

On the Razzle. Adapted from *Einen Jux will er sich machen* by Johann Nestroy. London: Faber and Faber, 1981, revised 1982.

The Real Thing. London: Faber and Faber, 1982, revised 1983, 1984, 1986, 1988; Broadway edition, Boston and London: Faber and Faber, 1984.

"*The Dog It Was That Died*" and *Other Plays*. London and Boston: Faber and Faber, 1983. [Contains *The Dissolution of Dominic Boot, 'M' is for Moon Among Other Things, Teeth, Another Moon Called Earth, Neutral Ground*, and *A Separate Peace.*]

Squaring the Circle. London and Boston: Faber and Faber, 1984. [Includes *Every Good Boy Deserves Favour* and *Professional Foul.*]

Four Plays for Radio. London and Boston: Faber and Faber, 1984. [Contains *Artist Descending a Staircase, Where Are They Now?, If You're Glad I'll Be Frank*, and *Albert's Bridge.*]

Rough Crossing. Freely adapted from *Play at the Castle* by Ferenc Molnár. London: Faber and Faber, 1985.

"*Dalliance*" and "*Undiscovered Country.*" Adapted from *Liebelei* and *Das weite Land* by Arthur Schnitzler. London and Boston: Faber and Faber, 1986.

Largo Desolato. By Václav Havel, translated by Tom Stoppard. London: Faber and Faber, 1987.

Artist Descending a Staircase. London and Boston: Faber and Faber, 1988. [First published in 1973 with *Where Are They Now?*]

Hapgood. London and Boston: Faber and Faber, 1988.

Stoppard: The Plays for Radio 1964–1983. London and Boston: Faber and Faber, 1990. [Contains *The Dissolution of Dominic Boot, 'M' is for Moon Among Other Things, If You're Glad I'll Be Frank, Albert's Bridge, Where Are They Now?, Artist Descending a Staircase*, and *The Dog It Was That Died.*]

The Boundary. Cowritten with Clive Exton. London: Samuel French, 1991; in *Antaeus*, no. 66 (Spring 1991), pp. 435–47.

Rosencrantz and Guildenstern are Dead: The Film. London and Boston: Faber and Faber, 1991.

In the Native State. London and Boston: Faber and Faber, 1991.

"*Rough Crossing*" and "*On the Razzle.*" London and Boston: Faber and Faber, 1991.

"*The Real Inspector Hound*" and *Other Entertainments*. London and Boston: Faber and Faber, 1993. [Contains *After Magritte, Dirty Linen, New-Found-Land*, and *Dogg's Hamlet, Cahoot's Macbeth.*]

Arcadia. London and Boston: Faber and Faber, 1993, reprinted with corrections 1993 (paper).

Articles by Stoppard

"A Very Satirical Thing Happened to Me on the Way to the Theatre Tonight." *Encore*, 10 (March–April 1963), pp. 33–36.

"Just Impossible." Review of "The Impossible Years." *Plays and Players*, 14 (January 1967), pp. 28–29.

"A Case of Vice Triumphant." Review of "The Soldier's Fortune." *Plays and Players*, 14 (March 1967), pp. 16–19.

"The Definite Maybe." *Author*, 78 (Spring 1967), pp. 18–20.

"Something to Declare." *Sunday Times*, 25 February 1968, p. 47.

"Confessions of a Screenwriter." *Today's Cinema*, 3 February 1969, p. 5.

"I'm Not Keen on Experiments." *New York Times*, 8 March 1970, sec. 2, p. 17.

"Joker as Artist." Review of *Magritte* by Suzi Gablik. *Sunday Times*, 11 October 1970, p. 40.

"Childbirth." [British] *Vogue*, 128 (May 1971), p. 54.

"In Praise of Pedantry." *Punch*, 14 July 1971, pp. 62–63.

"Orghast." Review of "Orghast" by Ted Hughes. *Times Literary Supplement*, 1 October 1971, p. 1174.

"Yes, We Have No Banana." *The Guardian*, 10 December 1971, p. 10.

"Playwrights and Professors." *Times Literary Supplement*, 13 October 1972, p. 1219.

Review of *A Supplement to the Oxford English Dictionary, Volume 1, A–G. Punch*, 13 December 1972, pp. 893–94.

"Acting out the Oil Game." *The Observer*, 8 September 1974, p. 24; "The Miss UK Sales Promotion," 15 September 1974, p. 27; "Disaster in Bangladesh," 22 September 1974, p. 27; "Festival of Soap Opera," 29 September 1974, p. 28. [Television reviews.]

"Welcome to the World: Presenting a New Arrival at Westminster Hospital." *Evening News*, 20 September 1974, sec. E, p. 1. [Full-page article on the birth of Stoppard's fourth son, Edmund.]

Introduction to *Glyn Boyd Harte: A Spring Collection*. London: Thumb Gallery, 1976.

"The Case for Peter Hall and the National: Three Big Guns of the Theatre—Tom Stoppard, Lord Goodman, Peter Stevens—Reply to Max Hastings." *Evening Standard*, 30 September 1976, pp. 24–25.

"Czech Human Rights." Letter to the editor. *The Times*, 7 February 1977, p. 15.

"Dirty Linen in Prague." *New York Times*, 11 February 1977, sec. 1, p. 27.

"The Face at the Window." *Sunday Times*, 27 February 1977, p. 33.

"Foreword." In *Forwards!: A Phantom Captain Book*, ed. Neil Hornick, p. 30. London: Unexpected Developments Ltd. in association with Aloes Books (distributed by Square Books), 1977. [Stoppard's contribution is one of forty-seven forewords written in response to an invitation to "write a foreword for a book without prior knowledge of its content or authorship"; the book, in fact, consists entirely of forewords.]

"But for the Middle Classes." Review of *Enemies of Society* by Paul Johnson. *Times Literary Supplement*, 3 June 1977, p. 677.

"Prague: The Story of the Chartists." *New York Review of Books*, 24, no. 13 (4 August 1977), pp. 11–15.

"Journalists' Closed Shop." Letter to the editor. *The Times*, 11 August 1977, p. 13.

"Human Rights in Prague." Letter to the editor. *The Times*, 17 October 1977, p. 13.

"My Friends Fighting for Freedom." *Daily Mail*, 20 October 1977, p. 6.

"Looking-Glass World." *New Statesman*, 28 October 1977, pp. 571–72.

"Nothing in Mind." *London Magazine*, 17 (February 1978), pp. 65–68.

"A 15-Year Wait for Nureyev's Mother." Letter to the editor cosigned by Alan Ayckbourn, Sir John Gielgud, et al. *Daily Telegraph*, 17 March 1979, p. 20. [Available on microfilm, *The Times*, 17 March 1979.]

Letter to the Headmaster of Downs School, 20 June 1978. In *The Downs School Record* (Bristol), no. 134 (1978), p. 62.

Introduction to *The Memorandum* by Václav Havel. New York: Grove Press, 1980; London: Eyre Methuen, 1981.

"Leftover from *Travesties.*" *Adam International Review,* 42, nos. 431–33 (1980), pp. 11–12.

"Tom Stoppard on the KGB's Olympic Trials." *Sunday Times,* 6 April 1980, p. 16.

"Borisov's Brief Freedom." Letter to the editor. *Sunday Times,* 15 June 1980, p. 12.

"Previous Non-convictions." Letter to the editor. *The Times,* 3 November 1980, p. 13.

"Stoppard Stops Off: The Playwright at Play in the Land of Free Time." *Washington Post,* 21 June 1981, sec. F, pp. 1, 10.

"Prague's Wall of Silence." Open letter to the president of Czechoslovakia. *The Times,* 18 November 1981, p. 10. Repr. as "Open Letter to President Husák," in *They Shoot Writers, Don't They?,* ed. George Theiner, pp. 57–59. London: Faber and Faber, 1984.

"Wildlife Observed: The Galapagos: Paradise and Purgatory." *The Observer Magazine,* 29 November 1981, pp. 38–42, 45–46, 48, 50.

Is It True What They Say about Shakespeare? International Shakespeare Association Occasional Paper No. 2. Oxford: Oxford University Press, 1982.

"Reflections on Ernest Hemingway." In *Ernest Hemingway: The Writer in Context,* ed. James Nagel, pp. 19–27. Madison: University of Wisconsin Press, 1984. [Transcription of a talk at the John F. Kennedy Library, Boston, 21 May 1982, as part of a conference on "Ernest Hemingway: The Writer in Context."]

"Lech's Troubles with Chuck, Bruce and Bob." *The Times,* 31 May 1984, p. 14. [On *Squaring the Circle.*]

"Freedom, But Thousands Are Still Captive." *Daily Mail,* 12 February 1986, p. 6. [On the release of Anatoly Shcharansky.]

"Arrests in Prague." Letter to the editor cosigned by Charles Alexander, et al. *The Times,* 4 October 1986, p. 9.

"Human Rights." Letter to the editor. *The Times,* 13 February 1987, p. 17.

"Going to Bat for Britain." *House & Garden,* 159 (November 1987), pp. 22, 26, 28, 30.

Foreword to *Publish and Be Damned!: Cartoons for International PEN.* Ed. Mark Bryant. London: Heinemann Kingswood, 1988.

"Some Quotes and Correspondence." Letter (about *Hapgood*) to nuclear physicist J. D. Polkinghorne with Polkinghorne's reply. In the Aldwych Theatre *Hapgood* production program, 8 March 1988. London, n.p.

"Harold Pinter: The Poet of No-Man's-Land." By John Peter with two-hundred-word comments from Tom Stoppard, Simon Gray, Christopher Hampton, John McGrath, and Howard Brenton. *Sunday Times,* 7 October 1990, sec. 7, p. 13.

"Going Back." *The Independent Magazine,* 23 March 1991, pp. 24–30. [On the experience of returning to Darjeeling, where Stoppard spent his boyhood.]

"Connery Dispute." Letter to the editor. *The Times,* 13 October 1990, p. 15. [Stoppard's response to being "maligned" by Sean Connery in an interview with George Perry, "The Man Who Is King," *The Times,* 6 October 1990, "Saturday Review" section, pp. 16–17.]

"Coda: To Film or Not to Film." *Premiere* (New York), 4, no. 3 (November 1990), p. 134.

"In Search of Childhood." *Daily Mail,* 4 May 1991, pp. 17, 19. [On his recent visit to India.]

"Let Iran Make Amends on Rushdie." *The Observer,* 16 February 1992, p. 22. [An edited version of a speech given at a gathering of Salman Rushdie's supporters in London on 14 February 1992.]

"Stop the Onslaught." Letter to the editor cosigned by Phyllis Auty, Tony Benn MP, Sir William Deakin, Michael Foot, et al. *The Guardian,* 22 May 1992, p. 24. [Regarding Bosnia-Herzegovina.]

"Drama Reduction on Radio 3." Letter to the editor cosigned by Douglas Adams, Harold Pinter, et al. *The Times,* 30 June 1992, p. 15.

"*Jumpers* and Olivier." Letter to the editor. *The Times*, 11 July 1991, p. 19. [Stoppard's response to a comment about *Jumpers* by Arnold Wesker, "Raise the Living abovc thc Dead," *The Times*, 3 July 1991, p. 13.]

"Tom Stoppard." In *The Pleasure of Reading*, ed. Antonia Fraser, pp. 147–52. London: Bloomsbury, 1992. Repr. as "Late to Read, Early to Rise," *The Times*, 12 September 1992, "Saturday Review," p. 17. [An essay on his early reading.]

"BBC's Quality Cut for Radio Drama." Letter to the editor cosigned by John Mortimer, et al. *The Independent*, 12 November 1992, p. 28.

"The Uncut *Jumpers*." Letter to the editor. *Financial Times*, 22 April 1993, p. 22. [Correction of a reviewer's comment that Kenneth Tynan made extensive cuts in *Jumpers* prior to its premiere.]

Lectures

Elsa Chapin Memorial Lecture, Lobero Theater, Santa Barbara, Calif., 8 December 1974. Partial transcript included in Sylvie Drake, "Tom Stoppard—The Entertainer," *Los Angeles Times*, 12 December 1974, sec. 4, p. 26.

"The Language of Theatre," a public lecture at the University of California at Santa Barbara, 14 January 1977. Partial transcript included in Kenneth Tynan, *Show People: Profiles in Entertainment*, pp. 44–123. New York: Simon and Schuster, 1979. Partial transcript also available in Jonathan Silver, "Stoppard Takes the 'Modest Course,'" *Daily Nexus* [UCSB student newspaper], 17 January 1977, pp. 1, 8.

"Gleanings from London: Tom Stoppard," transcript of a lecture and question-and-answer session, *Readers Theatre News* (San Diego State University), 4, no. 2 (Spring 1977), pp. 3–4.

"An Evening with Tom Stoppard," a public question-and-answer session at the American Conservatory Theater, San Francisco, 27 March 1977. Recording and partial transcript: ACT.

Lecture regarding the use of psychiatry as a political weapon in the USSR. Town Hall, St. Albans (England), winter 1978–79. Partial account in D. J. Daniell, "Forward with Stoppard," *Theatre News*, 11, no. 8 (May 1979), pp. 20–22.

"The Text and the Event: From Writer to Actor" and "The Text and the Event: From Writer to Critic," the Clark Lectures, Trinity College, Cambridge University, 8 and 15 February 1980. Partial transcripts contained in Philip Gaskell, "*Night and Day:* The Development of a Play Text," in *Textual Criticism and Literary Interpretation*, ed. Jerome J. McGann, pp. 162–79. Chicago and London: University of Chicago Press, 1985. [Professor Gaskell quotes from his private recordings, which are now held by the Department of English, Keio University, Mita Minatoku, Tokyo, Japan.]

"The Event and the Text," a public lecture at San Diego State University, San Diego, California, 4 November 1981. Videotape: Media Library, SDSU.

"The Event and the Text," a lecture in conjunction with the Third International Conference on the Fantastic, Boca Raton, Florida, 13 March 1982.

"Reflections on Ernest Hemingway," a talk at the John F. Kennedy Library, Boston, 21 May 1982, as part of a conference on "Ernest Hemingway: The Writer in Context," sponsored by Northeastern University in cooperation with the Hemingway Society. Transcription in *Ernest Hemingway: The Writer in Context*, ed. James Nagel, pp. 19–27. Madison: University of Wisconsin Press, 1984.

"What Makes a Play Play," a public lecture at Rice University, Houston, Texas, 22 October 1982. Partial account included in Eric Gerber, "Life Imitates Art with Playwright Tom Stoppard Center Stage," *Houston Post*, 23 October 1982; repr. in *Performing Arts* microfiche, vol. 9 (November 1982), card 39:A13.

"The Event and the Text," a public lecture sponsored by the Literary Society, Fairleigh

Dickinson University, Teaneck-Hackensack campus, Teaneck, New Jersey, 15 November 1983.

"Platform Performance," a public lecture and question-and-answer session sponsored by the National Theatre, London, 15 November 1984.

"Direct Experience," the Dawson-Scott Memorial Lecture at the London P.E.N. Writers' Day, South Bank Centre, London, 23 March 1985. Introduction by Harold Pinter. Panel discussion chaired by Francis King, with questions from the floor; panel participants: Arthur Miller, Fay Weldon, Harold Pinter, Tom Stoppard, and Malcolm Bradbury. Recording: National Sound Archive.

"The Less Than Sacred Text," the Darwin Lecture, Darwin College, Cambridge, 26 November 1985. Recording: Office of the Master, Darwin College. Partial account by Valerie Grosvenor Myer, "Stoppard on the Bard," *Plays and Players*, no. 386 (February 1986), p. 6.

"The Event and the Text," the Whidden Lectures, McMaster University, Hamilton, Ontario, 24–26 October 1988. Stoppard presided at a question-and-answer session on 25 October and gave an informal talk on 26 October. See Tom Stoppard, "The Event and the Text: The Whidden Lectures 1988," transcribed and edited by Doreen DelVecchio, *Ta Panta* [McMaster University Faculty Association], 6, no. 1 (1988), pp. 15–20.

Question-and-answer session with Tom Stoppard, Peter Wood, and Roger Rees following a preview performance of *Hapgood*, James A. Doolittle Theatre, Los Angeles, 9 April 1989. Arranged through the auspices of ACTER [A Center for Theatre, Education, and Research], the University of California at Santa Barbara.

Lecture in support of Salman Rushdie, the Stationer's Hall, London, 14 February 1992. Transmitted live by BBC-2 on "Arena" as "What Is There to Be Done?: Three Years of the *Fatwa*." Also speaking: Günter Grass, Martin Amis, and Salman Rushdie. Edited version of lecture published as "Let Iran Make Amends on Rushdie," *The Observer*, 16 February 1992, p. 22.

"Platform Performance," a public question-and-answer session sponsored by the National Theatre, London, 14 April 1993. Partial account by Sandra Barwick, "If Anyone Asked You Who You Are . . . ," *The Independent*, 17 April 1993, p. 13.

Lecture and question-and-answer session, Texas Center for Writers, University of Texas at Austin, 13 October 1993. Subsequently broadcast by KUT, Austin. On theater as event, with reference to changes made in the Swiss-German production of *Arcadia*.

Address to the Friends of the University Library, Harry Ransom Humanities Research Center, University of Texas at Austin, 14 October 1993. In Austin to present his archives to the Harry Ransom Humanities Research Center, Stoppard spoke on his life with books and earliest memories of collecting books.

Plenary Address, South Central Modern Language Association meeting, Austin, Texas, 15 October 1993.

Print Interviews

1966

Knight, John. "Saturday Night Sunday Morning." *Sunday Mirror*, 18 December 1966, p. 13.

1967

Anonymous. "Londoner's Diary: Worried Author." *Evening Standard*, 8 April 1967, p. 6.

Day-Lewis, Sean. "Plays and Players: Shakespeare Plus." *Daily Telegraph*, 8 April 1967, p. 13.

Dunn, Cyril. "Briefing: Footnote to the Bard." *The Observer*, 9 April 1967, p. 23.

Harper, Keith. "The Devious Route to Waterloo Road." *The Guardian*, 12 April 1967, p. 7.

Dodd, John. "Success Is the Only Unusual Thing about Mr. Stoppard." *The Sun*, 13 April 1967, p. 3.

Davies, Hunter. "Stoppard Goes." *Sunday Times*, 23 April 1967, p. 13.

Lewis, Peter. "How Tom Went to Work on an Absent Mind and Picked up £20,000." *Daily Mail*, 24 May 1967, p. 6.

McLoughlin, Shaun. "Another Moon Called Earth." *Radio Times*, 22 June 1967, p. 33.

Anonymous. "'What's All This About?'" *Newsweek*, 7 August 1967, p. 72.

Adams, Bernard. "Tom Stoppard on 'Teeth.'" *Radio Times*, 24 August 1967, p. 19.

Sullivan, Dan. "Young British Playwright Here for Rehearsal of 'Rosencrantz.'" *New York Times*, 29 August 1967, p. 27.

Halton, Kathleen. "Tom Stoppard: The Startling Young Author of the Play *Rosencrantz and Guildenstern Are Dead*." [American] *Vogue*, 150 (15 October 1967), p. 112.

Glover, William. "Theater Week: Enter Playwright, Successfully." AP Wire Service, 19 November 1967. Lincoln Center Drama Collection, New York Public Library.

Tallmer, Jerry. "Closeup: Rosencrantz' Friend." *New York Post*, 8 December 1967, p. 55.

Gale, John. "Writing's My 43rd Priority, Says Tom Stoppard." *The Observer*, 17 December 1967, p. 4.

Hedgepeth, William. "Playwright Tom Stoppard: 'Go Home British Boy Genius!'" *Look*, 26 December 1967, pp. 92–96.

1968

Prideaux, Tom. "Uncertainty Makes the Bigtime." *Life*, 9 February 1968, pp. 75–76.

Hastings, Ronald. "Rosencrantz Was Not the First." *Daily Telegraph*, 17 February 1968, p. 13.

Gordon, Giles. "Tom Stoppard." *Transatlantic Review*, no. 29 (Summer 1968), pp. 17–25. Repr. in *Behind the Scenes: Theater and Film Interviews from the "Transatlantic Review,"* ed. Joseph F. McCrindle, pp. 77–87. New York: Holt, Rinehart and Winston, 1971. [Interview conducted in March 1968.]

Louis, Patricia. "See the Father. See the Baby. See the Father Playing with the Baby. Doesn't the Father Look Happy? Yes, He Does." *New York Times*, 24 March 1968, sec. D, p. 3.

Anonymous. "The Talk of the Town: Playwright-Novelist." *New Yorker*, 4 May 1968, pp. 40–41.

Funke, Lewis. "Tom Stoppard." In *Playwrights Talk about Writing: 12 Interviews with Lewis Funke*, pp. 217–31. Chicago: Dramatic Publishing Co., 1975. [Interview conducted in 1968.]

1969

Leonard, William. "'R&G Are Dead' Brings Life to 'Hamlet' Legend." *Chicago Tribune*, 27 April 1969, sec. 5, pp. 7–8.

1970

"The Times Diary: Non Stop." *The Times*, 11 April 1970, p. 8.

1972

"Interview with Tom Stoppard." In the National Theatre *Jumpers* production program, 2 February 1972. London, n.p.

Gussow, Mel. "Stoppard Refutes Himself, Endlessly." *New York Times*, 26 April 1972, p. 54.

Natale, Richard. "I'm Always Chasing Peacocks." *Women's Wear Daily*, 27 April 1972, p. 12.

Tallmer, Jerry. "Tom Stoppard Pops in on the Cast." *New York Post*, 26 August 1972, p. 15.

Wahls, Robert. "Footlights: The Stage as a Chessboard." *New York Sunday News*, 24 September 1972, p. 8.

Rosenwald, Peter J. "The Theater." *Wall Street Journal*, 25 September 1972, p. 12.

Rosenwald, Peter J. "Stoppard's Sweet and Sour." *Time Out*, 3 November 1972, p. 31.

Norman, Barry. "Tom Stoppard and the Contentment of Insecurity." *The Times*, 11 November 1972, p. 11.

1973

"Londoner's Diary: Jumping About." *Evening Standard*, 29 January 1973, p. 16.

Hill, Frances. "Quarter-Laughing Assurance: A Profile of Tom Stoppard." *Times Educational Supplement*, 9 February 1973, p. 23.

McCulloch, Joseph. "Dialogue with Tom Stoppard." In *Under Bow Bells: Dialogues with Joseph McCulloch*, pp. 162–70. London: Sheldon Press, 1974. [Interview conducted 20 March 1973.]

Watts, Janet. "Tom Stoppard." *The Guardian*, 21 March 1973, p. 12.

Leech, Michael. "The Translators: Tom Stoppard: *The House of Bernarda Alba.*" *Plays and Players*, 20 (April 1973), pp. 37–38.

Edwards, Sydney. "Bricklayer Named Stoppard." *Evening Standard*, 13 April 1973, p. 8. [On Stoppard directing *Born Yesterday* and completing a play entitled *Galileo* for performance in the London Planetarium.]

1974

Hudson, Roger, Catherine Itzin, and Simon Trussler. "Ambushes for the Audience: Towards a High Comedy of Ideas." *Theatre Quarterly*, 4, no. 14 (May 1974), pp. 3–17. Partially reprinted in *New Theatre Voices of the Seventies: Sixteen Interviews from "Theatre Quarterly" 1970–1980*, ed. Simon Trussler, pp. 58–69. London: Eyre Methuen, 1981. [Interview conducted January 1974.]

Donnelly, Tom. "Donnelly's Revue: Jumping for Joy." *Washington Post*, 17 February 1974, sec. P, pp. 1, 5.

Leech, Michael T. "Wave of Success for *Jumpers* Author Tom Stoppard." *Christian Science Monitor*, 6 March 1974, sec. F, p. 6.

Topor, Tom. "Lunch with a Playwright." *New York Post*, 10 April 1974, p. 64.

Gussow, Mel. "*Jumpers* Author Is Verbal Gymnast." *New York Times*, 23 April 1974, p. 36.

Kalem, T. E. "Ping Pong Philosopher." *Time*, 6 May 1974, p. 85.

Owen, Michael. "Stoppard's New Electric Notion." *Evening Standard*, 24 May 1974, p. 26.

Mahon, Derek. "Tom Stoppard: A Noticeable Absence of Tortoises." [British] *Vogue*, 164 (June 1974), p. 21.

Hebert, Hugh. "Domes of Zurich." *The Guardian*, 7 June 1974, p. 10.

Amory, Mark. "The Joke's the Thing." *Sunday Times Magazine*, 9 June 1974, pp. 65, 67–68, 71–72, 74.

Smith, A. C. H. "Tom Stoppard." *Flourish* [RSC Club news-sheet], no. 1 (10 June 1974).

Hayman, Ronald. "First Interview with Tom Stoppard: 12 June 1974." In *Tom Stoppard*, by Ronald Hayman, 4th ed., pp. 1–13. Contemporary Playwrights Series. London: Heinemann; Totowa, N.J.: Rowman & Littlefield, 1982.

Hayman, Ronald. "Profile 9: Tom Stoppard." *New Review*, 1 (December 1974), pp. 15–22.

Eichelbaum, Stanley. "'Call Me the Thinking Man's Farceur.'" *San Francisco Examiner*, 11 December 1974, p. 69.

Taylor, Robert. "It's Really About . . . ." *Oakland Tribune*, 11 December 1974, p. 31.

Drake, Sylvie. "Stage Notes: Tom Stoppard—The Entertainer." *Los Angeles Times*, 12 December 1974, sec. 4, p. 26.

Hogan, William. "Stoppard's Non-Absurdity." *San Francisco Chronicle*, 13 December 1974, p. 66.

Tischler, Gary. "It Was No Day for an Interview." *Fremont* (Calif.) *Argus*, 20 December 1974, p. 23.

1975

Ferguson, T. S. "What's Happening: Stoppard up West." *Sunday Telegraph*, 3 August 1975, p. 13.

Wetzsteon, Ross. "Theatre Journal: The Heir to Shaw Comes to Broadway." *Village Voice*, 6 October 1975, pp. 105–6.

Marowitz, Charles. "Tom Stoppard—The Theater's Intellectual P. T. Barnum." *New York Times*, 19 October 1975, sec. 2, pp. 1, 5.

Gussow, Mel. "Playwright, Star Provide a Little Curtain Raiser." *New York Times*, 31 October 1975, p. 21.

Seligsohn, Leo. "Tom Stoppard: Intellect's the Thing for Playwright." (Long Island, N.Y.) *Newsday*, 4 November 1975, sec. A, pp. 4–5, 17.

Wetzsteon, Ross. "Tom Stoppard Eats Steak Tartare with Chocolate Sauce." *Village Voice*, 10 November 1975, p. 121.

Stasio, Marilyn. "Cue Theatre: Tom Stoppard's Mad Mushrooms." *Cue*, 29 November 1975, p. 15.

1976

Glover, William. "Stoppard Leaving 'Circus' for Man and Dog." *Cincinnati Enquirer*, 11 January 1976, sec. G, p. 5. [AP Wire Service story.]

Grant, Steve. "Serious Frivolity." *Time Out*, 18 June 1976, p. 7.

Anonymous. "Stoppard's Last Words." *The Guardian*, 19 June 1976. [Brief interview regarding *Every Good Boy Deserves Favour*.]

Semple, Robert B., Jr. "How Life Imitates a Stoppard Farce." *New York Times*, 21 June 1976, p. 45.

Hayman, Ronald. "Second Interview with Tom Stoppard: 20 August 1976." In *Tom Stoppard*, by Ronald Hayman, 4th ed., pp. 138–46. Contemporary Playwrights Series. London: Heinemann; Totowa, N. J.: Rowman & Littlefield, 1982.

Wood, Peter. "A Conversation." In the National Theatre *Jumpers* production program, 21 September 1976. London, n.p.

1977

Kerensky, Oleg. "Tom Stoppard." In *The New British Drama: Fourteen Playwrights since Osborne and Pinter*, pp. 168–71. London: Hamish Hamilton; New York: Taplinger, 1977.

Cook, Bruce. "Tom Stoppard: The Man behind the Plays." *Saturday Review*, 8 January 1977, pp. 52–53.

Christon, Lawrence. "*Travesties*—A Footnote Follies from Stoppard." *Los Angeles Times*, 9 January 1977, "Calendar" section, p. 48.

Leonard, John. "Tom Stoppard Tries on a 'Knickers Farce.'" *New York Times*, 9 January 1977, sec. 2, pp. 1, 5.

Bradshaw, Jon. "Tom Stoppard, Nonstop: Word Games with a Hit Playwright." *New York*, 10 January 1977, pp. 47–51. Repr. as "Tom Stoppard Non-stop," *Telegraph Sunday Magazine*, 26 June 1977, pp. 29–30, 32, 34.

Schwartz, Tony. "Tony Schwartz." *New York Post*, 12 January 1977, p. 31.

Silver, Jonathan. "Stoppard Takes the 'Modest Course': Portrays a Personal View of Theater." *Daily Nexus* [University of California at Santa Barbara student newspaper], 17 January 1977, pp. 1, 8.

Jackson, Beverley. "Patient Tom Stoppard." *Santa Barbara News-Press*, 18 January 1977, sec. B, pp. 6–7.

Drake, Sylvie. "The Importance of Being Stoppard." *Los Angeles Times*, 20 January 1977, sec. 4, p. 12.

Maves, C. E. "A Playwright on the Side of Rationality." *Palo Alto* (Calif.) *Times*, 25 March 1977, p. 16.

Eichelbaum, Stanley. "So Often Produced, He Ranks with Shaw." *San Francisco Examiner*, 28 March 1977, p. 24.

Bladen, Barbara. "Playwright Sees Plays as 'Rational.'" *San Mateo* (Calif.) *Times*, 29 March 1977, p. 29.

Weiner, Bernard. "A Puzzling, 'Traditional' Stoppard." *San Francisco Chronicle*, 29 March 1977.

Taylor, Robert. "Tom Stoppard's Plays Are More Than Just 'Clever Nonsense.'" *Oakland Tribune*, 17 April 1977, sec. E, p. 2.

May, Clifford D., with Edward Behr. "Master of the Stage." *Newsweek*, 15 August 1977, pp. 35–40.

Tynan, Kenneth. "Withdrawing with Style from the Chaos." *New Yorker*, 19 December 1977, pp. 41–111. Repr. in Tynan, *Show People: Profiles in Entertainment*, pp. 44–123. New York: Simon and Schuster, 1979.

1978

Glaap, Albert-Reiner. "From the Horse's Mouth: Questions from German Students to Living British Dramatists." *Anglistick & Englischunterricht*, 5 (1978), pp. 103–14. [Brief comment on *Dirty Linen* and *New-Found-Land*.]

Mortimer, Penelope. "Tom Stoppard: Funny, Fast Talking and Our First Playwright." [British] *Cosmopolitan*, January 1978, pp. 30–31, 39.

Shulman, Milton. "The Politicizing of Tom Stoppard." *New York Times*, 23 April 1978, sec 2, pp. 3, 27.

Edwards, Sydney, and Michael Owen. "Scoop Stoppard." *Evening Standard*, 9 June 1978, p. 26.

"Londoner's Diary: Rights and Writers." *Evening Standard*, 11 June 1978, p. 18.

Anonymous. "Tom Stoppard Puts Case for Soviet Jews." *The Times*, 12 July 1978, p. 7.

Brayfield, Celia. "Stoppard: I Think I'm a Don't-Know." *Evening Standard*, 15 August 1978, p. 3.

Huckerby, Martin. "Arts Diary: KGB to Blame in the End." *The Times*, 17 August 1978, p. 12.

Mills, Bart. "Tom Stoppard Moves into Political Writing." (Long Island, N.Y.) *Newsday*, 7 September 1978, p. 62.

Peterborough. "London Day by Day: African Prescience." *Daily Telegraph*, 26 September 1978, p. 18.

1979

Gaskell, Philip. Interview with Tom Stoppard, 9 January 1979. Partial transcript in Philip Gaskell, "*Night and Day:* The Development of a Play Text," in *Textual Criticism and Literary Interpretation*, ed. Jerome J. McGann, pp. 162–79. Chicago and London: University of Chicago Press, 1985. [The recording of Professor Gaskell's interview is now held by the Department of English, Keio University, Japan.]

Kuurman, Joost. "An Interview with Tom Stoppard." *Dutch Quarterly Review of Anglo-American Letters*, 10 (1980), 41–57. [Interview conducted in March 1979.]

Hardin, Nancy Shields. "An Interview with Tom Stoppard." *Contemporary Literature*, 22 (Spring 1981), 153–66. [Interview conducted in April 1979.]

Lawson, Carol. "Stoppard-Previn Drama to Play at the Met Opera." *New York Times*, 6 June 1979, sec. C, p. 22.

Hebert, Hugh. "A Playwright in Undiscovered Country." *The Guardian*, 7 July 1979, p. 10.

Say, Rosemary. "Show Talk." *Sunday Telegraph*, 8 July 1979, p. 14.

Green, James. "My Frightful First Nights . . . : They Turn Tom Stoppard over Inside—But He Is Always There." *Evening News*, 13 July 1979.

Gussow, Mel. "Stoppard's Intellectual Cartwheels Now with Music." *New York Times*, 29 July 1979, sec. 2, pp. 1, 22.

Berkvist, Robert. "This Time, Stoppard Plays It (Almost) Straight." *New York Times*, 25 November 1979, sec. 2, pp. 1, 5.

1980

Young, Pauline. "Interview with Tom Stoppard: Pauline Young Talks to Our Leading Dramatist: London, 16 January 1980." *Madog Arts Magazine* (Department of Arts and Languages, Polytechnic of Wales), Spring 1981, pp. 12–27.

Connolly, Ray. "Atticus: Stoppard in Greeneland." *Sunday Times*, 20 January 1980, p. 32.

Henninger, Daniel. "Theater: Tom Stoppard and the Politics of Morality." *Wall Street Journal*, 1 February 1980, p. 17.

Hayman, Ronald. "Double Acts: Tom Stoppard and Peter Wood." *Sunday Times Magazine*, 2 March 1980, pp. 29–31.

Hall, Anthea. "Men about the House." *Sunday Telegraph*, 22 June 1980, p. 10.

1981

Gollob, David, and David Roper. "Trad Tom Pops In." *Gambit*, 10, no. 37 (Summer 1981), pp. 5–17.

Pendennis. "Dialogue with a Driven Man." *The Observer*, 30 August 1981, p. 18.

Peterson, Karla. "Public Recognition Baffles Stoppard, English Playwright." *Daily Aztec* [San Diego State University student newspaper], 30 October 1981, pp. 5, 7.

Ruskin, Phyllis, and John H. Lutterbie. "Balancing the Equation." *Modern Drama*, 26 (December 1983), 543–54. [Interview conducted in October 1981.]

Jones, Welton. "Stoppard Coup Assures SDSU a Fortnight of Rare Drama." *San Diego Union*, 1 November 1981, sec. E, pp. 1–2.

Hagen, Bill. "Today's Truth, by Tom Stoppard." *San Diego Tribune*, 6 November 1981, sec. C, p. 1ff.

1982

DeVries, Hilary. "Playwright Tom Stoppard: Wit Ricochets off Every Surface." *Christian Science Monitor*, 8 July 1982, Western Edition, sec. B, pp. 1–4. [Regarding Stoppard's visit in May to Northeastern University, Boston, to deliver the keynote address for a conference on Hemingway.]

Coveney, Michael. "Step by Step with Stoppard." *Financial Times,* 27 November 1982, p. 16.

1983

Bennetts, Leslie. "Friendship Characterizes Stoppard Play Rehearsals." *New York Times,* 22 November 1983, sec. C, p. 13.

Levene, Ellen. "Stoppard Looks at Love and Freedom." (Long Island, N.Y.) *Newsday,* 25 December 1983. In *Performing Arts* microfiche, vol. 10 (January 1984), card 62:F1–F2.

1984

Gussow, Mel. "The Real Tom Stoppard." *New York Times Magazine,* 1 January 1984, pp. 18–23, 28.

Corliss, Richard. "Stoppard in the Name of Love." *Time,* 16 January 1984, pp. 68–69.

Kroll, Jack. "A Dazzling Gift of Play." *Newsweek,* 16 January 1984, pp. 82–83.

Freedman, Samuel G. "Stoppard Debates the Role of the Writer: Political Duty Is Questioned." *New York Times,* 20 February 1984, sec. C, p. 13.

Buck, Joan Juliet. "Tom Stoppard: Kind Heart and Prickly Mind." [American] *Vogue,* 174 (March 1984), pp. 454, 513–14.

Gore-Langton, Robert. "Sea-Sickness at the National." *Plays and Players,* no. 373 (October 1984), p. 17. [On *Rough Crossing.*]

Owen, Michael. "Tom Storms Back to the National." *The Standard,* 12 October 1984, p. 28. [On *Rough Crossing.*]

Asquith, Ros. "City Limits Interview: Tom Stoppard." *City Limits,* 19 October 1984, pp. 79–80.

O'Connor, Garry. "Two Men on an Ocean Wave." *Sunday Times,* 21 October 1984, p. 39.

1985

Sanders, Vicki. "He Makes You Want to Listen." *Miami* (Fla.) *Herald,* 29 January 1985. In *Performing Arts* microfiche, vol. 11 (February 1985), card 78:D10–D11.

Rousuck, J. Wynn. "In *The Real Thing,* Stoppard's Trying for Realism—For Once." (Baltimore, Md.) *Sun,* 28 April 1985. In *Performing Arts* microfiche, vol. 11 (May 1985), card 110:D7–D8.

Fallowell, Duncan. "Theatrical Incest and Acquisitive Lust." *The Times,* 23 August 1985, p. 8.

Davies, Russell. "Stoppard Directs." *The Observer,* 8 September 1985, p. 17. [On *The Real Inspector Hound.*]

1986

Shakespeare, Nicholas. "A New Wineskin from old Vienna." *The Times,* 17 May 1986, p. 18.

Sullivan, Dan. "Stoppard: Getting the Right Bounce." *Los Angeles Times,* 2 June 1986, sec. 6, pp. 1, 6.

Colvin, Clare. "The Real Tom Stoppard." *Drama,* 43, no. 161 (1986), pp. 9–10.

Mitchell, Sean. "Just Who, Really, Is Tom Stoppard?" *Los Angeles Herald Examiner,* 18 December 1986. In *Performing Arts* microfiche, vol. 13 (November 1986–February 1987), card 110:A5–A6.

1987

Killen, Tom. "Stoppard Giving Answers." *New Haven* (Connecticut) *Register,* 15 March 1987. In *Performing Arts* microfiche, vol. 13 (May 1987), card 146:F2.

Owen, Michael. "Mr Stoppard's Oblivion Boys Club Band." *London Evening Standard,* 5 June 1987, pp. 22–23.

Watts, Janet. "Stoppard's Half-Century." *The Observer,* 28 June 1987, pp. 17–18.

Darnton, Nina. "The Reel Thing." *New York Post,* 9 December 1987. In *Film and Television* microfiche, vol. 15 (January 1988), card 13:F12–F13.

Champlin, Charles. "New Day Dawns for 'Sun' Writer Tom Stoppard." *Los Angeles Times,* 10 December 1987, sec. 6, pp. 1, 9.

Thomas, Bob. "Spielberg Creates an 'Empire.' " *Santa Barbara News-Press,* 18 December 1987, "Scene" section, pp. 19–20. [AP Wire Service story.]

Lee, Luaine. "Stargazing: The U.S. According to Stoppard." *Pasadena* (Calif.) *Star-News,* 18 December 1987, "Extra" section, p. 2.

Lee, Luaine. "Writer Says He's Suited to His Craft." *Pasadena* (Calif.) *Star-News,* 27 December 1987, sec. B, pp. 1–4.

1988

Guppy, Shusha. "Tom Stoppard: The Art of Theater VII." *Paris Review,* 109 (Winter 1988), 26–51.

Freedman, Richard. "Writer Stoppard Felt Close to *Empire of the Sun.*" (Springfield, Mass.) *Sunday Republican,* 24 January 1988. In *Film and Television* microfiche, vol. 15 (February 1988), card 24:F8–F9. The same interview with two additional paragraphs appears as "Author Stoppard's Wartime Experiences Nearly Mirrored Those of *Empire's* Hero." (Newark, N. J.) *Star-Ledger,* 24 January 1988. In *Film and Television* microfiche, vol. 15 (February 1988), card 24:F10–F11.

Owen, Michael. "Spy Society." *Evening Standard,* 4 March 1988, p. 24. [On *Hapgood.*]

Lewis, Peter. "Quantum Stoppard." *Observer Magazine,* 6 March 1988, pp. [58–59].

Billington, Michael. "Stoppard's Secret Agent." *The Guardian,* 18 March 1988, p. 28.

Bennetts, Leslie. "Five Top Playwrights in a Dialogue, with Arthur Miller Adding Drama." *New York Times,* 18 June 1988, p. 9. [Account of symposium on "The Challenge of Writing for the Theater Today," sponsored by the First New York International Festival of the Arts.]

"Playwrights at the Cliff-Edge." *The Economist,* 9 July 1988, p. 85. [Quoting Stoppard's remarks on 17 June 1988 at the First New York International Festival of the Arts.]

Lewin, David. "Laugh? I Could Have Spied." *Mail on Sunday,* 13 November 1988, "You Magazine," pp. 66–68, 74.

1989

Schiff, Stephen. "Full Stoppard." *Vanity Fair,* 52, no. 5 (May 1989), pp. 152–57, 214–15. [Interview conducted 22 February 1989.]

O'Connor, Thomas. "Welcome to the World of Tom Stoppard." *Orange County* (Calif.) *Register,* 2 April 1989, "Show" section, pp. K3–K5. In *Performing Arts* microfiche, vol. 16 (1989), card 82:B9–B10.

Stayton, Richard. "The Mysterious Tom Stoppard." *Los Angeles Herald Examiner,* 14 April 1989, "Weekend" section, p. 6.

Maychick, Diana. "Stoppard Ascending." *New York Post,* 26 November 1989. In *Performing Arts* microfiche, vol. 17 (January 1990), card 13:C7–C8.

"Peterborough: Coined Phrase." *Daily Telegraph,* 3 June 1989, p. 13. [Regarding Stoppard's use—in *Hapgood* and in a screenplay—of a phrase from Anthony Minghella's *Made in Bangkok:* "And yet, here you are."]

Rothstein, Mervyn. "A One-Act Dialogue Starring Tom Stoppard." *New York Times,* 26 November 1989, sec. 2, pp. 5, 39.

1990

Johnstone, Iain. "The Man Who Turns Words into Gold." *Sunday Times,* 23 September 1990, sec. 5, pp. 1, 7. [On Stoppard winning the Golden Lion of Venice award for direction of *Rosencrantz and Guildenstern are Dead.*]

McGurk, Tom. "Playing God to Raise Ros and Guil from the Dead." *Mail on Sunday,* 23 September 1990, p. 29.

Ciment, Michel. "Écrivain Mercenaire, Écrivain Exigeant: Entretien avec Tom Stoppard." *Positif: Revue de Cinéma,* no. 361 (March 1991), pp. 25–32. [Interview conducted 24 September 1990 on Stoppard's work as film director and screenwriter; translated into French.]

Denison, D. C. "The Interview: Tom Stoppard." *Boston Globe,* 16 December 1990, p. 8.

"Tom Stoppard." *San Jose* (Calif.) *Mercury News,* 16 December 1990. In *Film and Television* microfiche, vol. 18 (January 1991), card 8:B7.

1991

Seidenberg, Robert. "*Rosencrantz and Guildenstern are Dead:* Tom Stoppard Adapts Tom Stoppard." *American Film,* 16 (February 1991), pp. 48–49.

Jackson, Kevin. "Tiffin and Sympathy." *The Independent,* 2 February 1991, p. 46. [On *In the Native State.*]

Dolen, Christine. "Tom Stoppard Directs Tom Stoppard." *Miami* (Fla.) *Herald,* 10 February 1991. In *Film and Television* microfiche, vol. 18 (March 1991), card 25:B5–B6.

Stevenson, William. "For Some, Screenplays Aren't Just Writes of Passage." *Variety,* 11 February 1991, p. 127.

Chesshyre, Robert. "Tom Stoppard: Putting on the Ritz." *Daily Telegraph,* 16 February 1991, "Weekend Magazine," pp. 16–20, 22.

Hartigan, Patti. "*Rosencrantz* the Movie Has the Stoppard Stamp." *Boston Globe,* 17 February 1991, sec. A, pp. 7, 10.

Brunette, Peter. "Stoppard Finds the Right Man to Direct His Film." *Los Angeles Times,* 20 February 1991, sec. F, pp. 1, 8–9.

Rosenberg, Scott. "Stoppard Lens a Hand." *San Francisco Chronicle,* 24 February 1991, sec. E, pp. 1, 4.

Stanley, John. "Move Over, Hamlet." *San Francisco Chronicle,* 24 February 1991, "Datebook" section, pp. 23–24.

Truss, Lynne. "Stoppard Making Sense." *Interview,* 21 (March 1991), p. 48.

Ryan, Desmond. "Writer Tom Stoppard Turns Movie Director." *Philadelphia Inquirer,* 3 March 1991. In *Film and Television* microfiche, vol. 18 (April 1991), card 35:C2–C3.

Roca, Octavio. "Tom Stoppard, Film Director." *Washington Times,* 12 March 1991, sec. E, p. 1. In *Film and Television* microfiche, vol. 18 (April 1991), card 35:C4–C5.

Christiansen, Richard. "Stoppard on the Go: The Playwright Makes His Debut as Director with *Rosencrantz.*" *Chicago Tribune,* 14 March 1991, "Tempo" section, p. 3.

Johnson, Reed. "The Play's the Real Thing for Stoppard." *Detroit News,* 14 March 1991. In *Film and Television* microfiche, vol. 18 (April 1991), card 35:B14–C1.

Hall, Carla. "Stoppard, Playwright in Waiting." *Washington Post,* 27 March 1991, sec. B, pp. 1, 11.

Smith, Sid. "Script Jockey: The Flickering Images of Theatre." *The Theatre Magazine* (London), no. 1 (April 1991), pp. 16–19.

Smith, Sid. "Alternative Scene: Radio: Stoppard & Burgess." *The Theatre Magazine* (London), no. 1 (April 1991), pp. 31–32. [Brief comment on *In the Native State*.]

Kunk, Deborah J. "Will Power." *St. Paul* (Minn.) *Pioneer Press-Dispatch*, 9 April 1991. In *Performing Arts* microfiche, vol. 18 (May 1991), card 66:D7.

Murray, Steve. "Stoppard Brings Talents from Stage to Screen." *Atlanta Constitution*, 18 April 1991, sec. F, p. 11.

Smith, Sid. "Sound Barrier." *Time Out*, 17–24 April 1991, p. 145. [On *In the Native State*.]

Sarler, Carol. "Thoroughly Modern Memsahib." *Radio Times*, 20–26 April 1991, pp. 18–19, 22. [Cover story on Felicity Kendal includes comments from Stoppard about *In the Native State*.]

Reynolds, Gillian. "Tom's Sound Affects." *Daily Telegraph*, 20 April 1991, "Weekend" section, p. 24. [On *In the Native State*.]

Donovan, Paul. "Return of the Native." *Sunday Times*, 21 April 1991, "Review" section, pp. 1–2. [On *In the Native State*.]

Twisk, Russell. "Stoppard Basks in a Late Indian Summer." *The Observer*, 21 April 1991, p. 75. [On *In the Native State*.]

Billington, Michael. "In Search of the Real Tom Stoppard." *The Guardian*, 11 May 1991, "Guardian Guide" section, pp. XVI–XVII.

Pendreigh, Brian. "A Playwright Coy about Private Lives." *The Scotsman*, 17 May 1991. [Prior to the opening of *Rosencrantz and Guildenstern are Dead* as a film, Stoppard returns to the Cranston Street venue where the play had its Edinburgh Fringe premiere.]

Owen, Michael. "Stoppard and the Nearly Man." *Evening Standard*, 17 May 1991, pp. 24–25.

Rodger, Michelle. "Stoppard Stars in His Real-Life Mystery Drama." *Daily Express*, 1 June 1991, p. 36.

Franks, Alan. "Stoppard Stoppered." *The Times*, 29 June 1991, "Saturday Review" section, pp. 4–5.

Talty, Stephen. "Inside *Billy Bathgate*." *American Film*, 16 (July 1991), pp. 32–35, 44.

1992

Goreau, Angeline. "Is *The Real Inspector Hound* a Shaggy Dog Story?" *New York Times*, 9 August 1992, sec. 2, pp. 5, 8. [Interview conducted 27 July 1992.]

Raymond, Gerard. "Inspecting the Real Tom Stoppard." *TheaterWeek Magazine*, 31 August 1992, pp. 13–19. [Interview conducted 31 July 1992.]

Twisk, Russell. "Stoppard's State of Grace." *The Observer*, 11 October 1992, p. 63. [On *In the Native State*.]

Bamigboye, Baz. "Stoppard Seals Love for Felicity with a Starring Role." *Daily Mail*, 14 November 1992, p. 3. [Brief comments regarding *Arcadia*.]

1993

Smith, Alex Duval. "Face to Face with the Two Clives." *The Guardian*, 4 January 1993, sec. 2, p. 9. [Four paragraphs by Stoppard regarding Clive James.]

Edwardes, Jane. "Head Case." *Time Out*, 21 March 1993, pp. 14–15.

Fallon, James. "Just a Chat with Tom Stoppard." *W Europe* (Paris), April 1993, pp. 46, 49. [Conducted during rehearsals of *Arcadia*.]

Nathan, David. "In a Country Garden (If It Is a Garden)." *Sunday Telegraph*, 28 March 1993, sec. 2, p. XIII.

Billington, Michael. "Joker above the Abyss." *The Guardian*, 2 April 1993, sec. 2, pp. 2–3.

Lawson, Mark. "Tomcat's New Tale." *The Independent Magazine*, 10 April 1993, pp. 20–24.

Hawkes, Nigel. "Plotting the Course of a Playwright." *The Times*, 13 April 1993, p. 29.

Capitol Radio interview, London, 25 May 1974. Cited in Cheryl Faraone, "An Analysis of Tom Stoppard's Plays and Their Productions (1964–1975)," p. 105. Ph.D. diss., Florida State University, 1980.

"Today." BBC Radio Four, 11 June 1974. Interview by Michael Sheils regarding *Travesties*.

1975

"Critics' Forum." BBC Radio Three, 4, 16, 18 January 1975. Panel discussion led by J. W. Lambert (4, 16 January) or Oleg Kerensky (18 January) with Margaret Drabble, Tom Stoppard, and Basil Taylor. Transcript: BBC Script Library.

"The Book Programme." BBC-2, 13 May 1975. Tom Stoppard with book choice. Transcript not available.

"Omnibus." BBC-1, 21 September 1975. "Exton, Stoppard & Co. at the Eleventh Hour," a documentary filmed while Clive Exton and Tom Stoppard were at work cowriting *The Boundary* for "The Eleventh Hour," a series of television plays each conceived, written, cast, and produced in a single week. Transcript not available. Partial account in *Sunday Times*, 21 September 1975, "Television" column.

1976

"Profile." Interview by Alastair Lack for Topical Tapes, 7 April 1976. Recording: National Sound Archive, LP37321 b01.

"Kaleidoscope." BBC Radio Four, 16 April 1976. Interview by Edwin Mullins regarding *Dirty Linen*. Transcript: BBC Script Library.

"Kaleidoscope." BBC Radio Four, 20 April 1976. Brief comment regarding *Travesties*. Transcript: BBC Written Archives Centre.

"Start the Week." BBC Radio Four, 17 May 1976. Interview by Richard Baker regarding *Dirty Linen*. Transcript: BBC Script Library.

"Today." BBC Radio Four, 31 May 1976. Interview regarding the move of *Dirty Linen* to the West End. Transcript not available.

"Kaleidoscope." BBC Radio Four, 22 September 1976. Interview by Paul Vaughan with Tom Stoppard and Martin Esslin regarding *Dirty Linen* and the process of writing. Transcript: BBC Script Library.

"The Playwright: Tom Stoppard." Independent Television, 27 September 1976. Half-hour program with Benedict Nightingale includes discussion of and extracts from *Dirty Linen, Rosencrantz and Guildenstern Are Dead, Jumpers,* and *The Real Inspector Hound* with concluding discussion of *Travesties*. Transcript and videotape: Thames Television, London.

"Tom Stoppard in Conversation with Anthony Smith." London: British Council, 1977. Literature study aids series. Recorded 17 December 1976. Recording and pamphlet: British Council.

1977

"The World This Weekend." BBC Radio, 27 February 1977. Gordon Clough interview regarding treatment of dissidents Stoppard met on his trip to Moscow. Recording: National Sound Archive, LP37494 f02.

"The Secret Workshop." BBC Radio Three, 9 March 1977. Interviews by Ian Rodger with various writers about radio and the part it has played in their lives. Recording: National Sound Archive, T38317.

"André Previn Meets." BBC-1, 29 May 1977. Interview by André Previn. Transcript not available.

"Tonight." BBC-1, 29 June 1977. Interview by John Timpson.

"Kaleidoscope." BBC Radio Four, 1 July 1977. Interview by Sheridan Morley with Tom Stoppard, André Previn, and Ronald Hayman regarding *Every Good Boy Deserves Favour*. Transcript: BBC Script Library.

1978

"Tom Stoppard." Interview by Stephen Banker regarding *Jumpers*. Washington, D.C.: Tapes for Readers, 1978.

"Start the Week." BBC Radio Four, 12 June 1978. Interview by Richard Baker about Shakespeare; interview by Anthony Clare about *Every Good Boy Deserves Favour* opening at the Mermaid Theatre. Partial transcript: BBC Written Archives Centre.

"Kaleidoscope." BBC Radio Four, 15 June 1978. Interview by Paul Vaughan regarding *Every Good Boy Deserves Favour*. Transcript: BBC Script Library. Recording: National Sound Archive.

"Kaleidoscope." BBC Radio Four, 10 November 1978 (recorded 7 November 1978). Interview by Michael Billington regarding *Night and Day*. Transcript: BBC Script Library. Recording: National Sound Archive, LP38669 b03.

"The South Bank Show." London Weekend Television, 26 November 1978 (recorded 22 November 1978). Interview by Melvyn Bragg; includes scenes from the West End production of *Night and Day* and a scene, performed in the LWT studios by Edward Petherbridge and John Stride, from *Rosencrantz and Guildenstern Are Dead*. Videotape: LWT.

1979

"Round Midnight." BBC Radio Two, 23 January 1979. Interview by Nigel Havers about the German Federal Prize. Transcript not available.

"Kaleidoscope." BBC Radio Four, 30 January 1979. Interview by Michael Billington about the Evening Standard Drama Awards.

"Today." BBC Radio Four, 16 May 1979. Interview by Helen Palmer regarding the British American Acting Company.

"Kaleidoscope." BBC Radio Four, 22 May 1979 (recorded 17 May 1979). Interview by Michael Oliver with Tom Stoppard and Ed Berman regarding *Dogg's Hamlet, Cahoot's Macbeth*. Recording: National Sound Archive, LP38768 b01.

"Tonight." BBC-1, 29 June 1979. Interview by Michael Billington at the National Theatre about all the Stoppard plays in production, especially *Undiscovered Country*. Transcript not available.

"Panorama: Under Surveillance." BBC-1, 9 July 1979. Interview by Michael Cockerell about the plays of Václav Havel and the political situation in Czechoslovakia. Transcript: BBC Script Library.

"Profile: Ed Berman." BBC Radio Four, 13 July 1979. Interview by Janet Cohen regarding Ed Berman. Recording: BBC tape no. TLN28/214G467.

"Kaleidoscope." BBC Radio Four, 17 July 1979. Paul Vaughan interview regarding *Dogg's Hamlet, Cahoot's Macbeth*. Transcript: BBC Script Library.

"Kaleidoscope." BBC Radio Four, 2 August 1979. Interview by Russell Davies with Tom Stoppard, Otto Preminger, Nicol Williamson, Robert Morley, Sir Richard Attenborough regarding *The Human Factor*. Transcript: BBC Script Library. Recording: National Sound Archive, LP38962 b04.

"The Arts Worldwide." BBC Radio, October 1979. Interview by Nigel Lewis regarding imprisonment of five social reformers in Czechoslovakia. Recording: National Sound Archive, LP39136 f02.

"Friday Night . . . Saturday Morning." BBC-2, 2 November 1979. Interview by Tim Rice. Transcript not available.

1980

"Today." BBC Radio Four, 14 February 1980. Interview by Graham Leach regarding the reenactment in Munich of the 1979 Prague trial of Václav Havel and members of Charter 77. Recording: National Sound Archive, LP39476 f04.

1981

"Drama Up to Now." BBC Radio Four, 8 May 1981. Program by John Russell Brown includes extracts from Stoppard interviews "Our Changing Theatre" (BBC Radio Four, 23 November 1970) and "Arts Commentary" (BBC Radio Three, 10 November 1972). Transcript: BBC Script Library.

"Week's Good Cause." BBC Radio Four, 11 October 1981. Appeal on behalf of Writers and Scholars Educational Trust and its magazine *Index on Censorship*. Recording: National Sound Archive, C 68/26 7872 R.

"Various Stages: No. 1 *On the Razzle*." BBC Radio Three, 24 October 1981 (recorded 19 October 1981). Interview by Ronald Hayman with Tom Stoppard, Peter Wood, Felicity Kendal, Dinsdale Landen, Mary Chilton, Harold Innocent, Ray Brooks, and Carl Toms regarding *On the Razzle*. Transcript: BBC Script Library. Recording: National Sound Archive, T41918.

"Tom Stoppard." KPBS-TV, San Diego, 26 January 1982 (recorded November 1981; rebroadcast KCET-TV, Los Angeles, 1 February 1982). Interview by Helen Hawkins regarding *Rosencrantz and Guildenstern Are Dead* and *Mackoon's Hamlet, Cahoot's Macbeth* (Stoppard's adaptation of *Dogg's Hamlet, Cahoot's Macbeth* for San Diego State University). Videotape: Media Library, SDSU.

1982

"Reputations." BBC-2, 25 July 1982. A program on Kenneth Tynan, moderated by Anthony Howard. Transcript: BBC Written Archives Centre.

"Channel Four News." Channel 4, London, 15 November 1982. Interview by Stephen Phillips with Tom Stoppard, Peter Wood, Roger Rees and Felicity Kendal regarding *The Real Thing*. Videotape: Independent Television News, London, tape no. 15831.

"Kaleidoscope." BBC Radio Four, 17 November 1982. Interview by Michael Oliver regarding *The Real Thing*. Transcript: BBC Written Archives Centre. Recording: BBC tape no. YLN46/463L824.

1983

"The World Tonight." BBC Radio Four, 25 January 1983. Interview by Geoffrey Wareham regarding Stoppard opening an exhibition illustrating the plight of Soviet Jews. Transcript not available.

"Writers on Writing: A Series of Conversations with Richard Hoggart." Independent Television, 22 April 1983. Interview by Richard Hoggart about writers whose work Stoppard admires or regards as an influence. Transcript: Television South, Southampton.

"Kaleidoscope." BBC Radio Four, 8 June 1983. Interview by Natalie Wheen regarding *The Dog It Was That Died* and Stoppard's writing for radio. Transcript: BBC Written Archives Centre. Recording: BBC tape no. TLN23/505x706.

"Frank Delaney." BBC TV, 17 October 1983. Interview regarding translations and adaptations for film, television, stage, and radio; also deals with *The Real Thing*. Videotape: BBC Viewing Service, Centre House.

1984

"Morning Edition." National Public Radio, 5 January 1984. Interview by Jay Kernis regarding *The Real Thing*.

"Kaleidoscope." BBC Radio Four, 2 March 1984. Interview by Sheridan Morley regarding *Jumpers* and a new Manchester production of the play. Transcript: BBC Written Archives Centre. Recording: BBC tape no. YLN09/578D994.

"Gloria Hunniford." BBC Radio Two, 25 May 1984. Interview about Stoppard's career and about cast changes in *The Real Thing*. Transcript not available. Recording: BBC tape no. LZA548L865.

"Morning Edition." National Public Radio, 4 June 1984. Interview by Renée Montagne regarding Tony awards for *The Real Thing;* includes comments by Jeremy Irons, Glenn Close, and Alan Carr.

"Solidarity with Stoppard." Television South, 16 April 1984. Program on the making of the Television South production of *Squaring the Circle* (31 May 1984); includes interviews by Jill Cochrane with Tom Stoppard, Richard Crenna, and Mike Hodges as well as excerpts from the production. Part of the arts magazine series "Putting on the South." Videotape: Television South, Southampton.

1985

"Desert Island Discs." BBC Radio Four, 12 January 1985 (recorded 8 January 1985; rebroadcast 18 January 1985). Interview by Roy Plomley about Stoppard's life and work and which eight gramophone records he would take to a desert island. Transcript: BBC Written Archives Centre. Recording: National Sound Archive, T47599.

1986

"Sunday." BBC Radio Four, 16 February 1986. Interview by Trevor Barnes regarding Stoppard's demonstration on behalf of Soviet Jews. Recording: BBC tape no. 86RA3007NH0.

"Breakfast Time." BBC-1, 17 February 1986. Live interview by Glyn Worsnip from the National Theatre, where Stoppard organized a day-long vigil reading the names of ten thousand Soviet Jews refused exit visas. Videotape: BBC Viewing Service, Centre House.

"News at 10." Independent Television, 17 February 1986. Interview by Joan Thirkettle regarding Soviet Jews. Videotape: Independent Television News, London.

"All Things Considered." National Public Radio, 17 February 1986. Interview by Vera Frankl regarding Soviet Jews.

"First Night Impressions." BBC Radio Four, 14 May 1986. Interview by Robert Cushman regarding *Jumpers, Professional Foul,* and *Travesties*. Recording: National Sound Archive.

"Breakfast Time." BBC-1, 20 May 1986. Interview regarding *Dalliance,* Schnitzler, *Professional Foul,* and cricket. Videotape: BBC Viewing Service, Centre House.

"Round Midnight." BBC Radio Two, 26 May 1986. Interview regarding Stoppard's career and the National Theatre. Transcript not available. BBC tape no. 86ZA2885LLO.

"Today." BBC Radio Four, 15 July 1986. Interview by Jon Silverman regarding refuseniks in the USSR and the sentencing of Alexei Magarik. Recording: BBC tape no. CLN28/86VB2802.

"Saturday Review." BBC-2, 18 October 1986. Interview by Russell Davies regarding Václav Havel and *Largo Desolato* being staged at the Bristol New Vic. Videotape: BBC Viewing Service, Centre House.

1987

"PM." BBC Radio Four, 11 February 1987. Interview regarding a Valentine celebration for charity at the Prince of Wales Theatre. Transcript not available. Recording: BBC tape no. YLN706/87VC0623.

1988

"Talking Theatre." BBC Radio Four, 6 January 1988. Interview by Robert Cushman. Recording: BBC tape no. SLN704/86LF1016.
"Channel Four News." Channel 4, London, 9 March 1988. Interview by Stephen Phillips with Tom Stoppard, Peter Wood, and Nigel Hawthorne regarding *Hapgood*. Videotape: Independent Television News, London, tape no. 34099.
"John Dunn Show." BBC Radio Two, 29 February 1988.
"Review." BBC-2, 13 March 1988. Interview by Kate Kellaway regarding *Hapgood;* includes comments by Dr. Patricia Lewis, a nuclear physicist. Videotape: BBC Viewing Service, Centre House.
"The Late Show with Clive James." BBC-2, 11 November 1988. Weekly discussion program with guests Lord Annan, Dr. Norman Stone, and Tom Stoppard discussing spies.
"Prisoners of Conscience." BBC-2, 8 December 1988. Account by Stoppard of the story of a prisoner of conscience; part of a series about people jailed for their beliefs.

1989

"Because the Scenery is Better." BBC-2, 7 January 1989. Interview on how Stoppard started with radio plays, as part of a program regarding the production of BBC Radio Drama.
"London Plus." BBC-1, 6 February 1989. Interviews by Richard Bath with Tom Stoppard, Derek Jacobi, Harold Pinter, Sally Meades, and Richard Luce regarding their call for the government to save the British Theatre Association Library from closure.
"Morning Edition." National Public Radio, 12 April 1989. Interview by Sarah Spitz of KCRW, Santa Monica (Calif.) with Tom Stoppard, actor Simon Jones, and director Peter Wood regarding U.S. premiere of *Hapgood*. Recording: National Public Radio.
"Today." NBC TV, 26 April 1989. Interview by Heidi Schulman with Tom Stoppard and Peter Wood regarding U.S. premiere of *Hapgood*.
"Today." BBC Radio Four, 29 December 1989. Interview regarding Václav Havel on the day Havel became president of Czechoslovakia. Recording: BBC tape no. CLN952/89VB5206.

1990

"Kaleidoscope." BBC Radio Four, 4 July 1990 (revised and rebroadcast 5 July 1990). Interview by Paul Allen in advance of a BBC Radio season of eight Stoppard plays; includes discussion on the nature of radio plays and *Rosencrantz and Guildenstern are Dead.* Stoppard's comments on *Night and Day* and *Professional Foul* (both included in the BBC Radio season of Stoppard plays) are excerpts from a conversation which, reedited, was broadcast in a much fuller version on 14 September 1990. Transcript: BBC Written Archives Centre.

"Kaleidoscope." BBC Radio Four, 14 September 1990. "On the Cutting Room Floor," interview by Paul Allen at Pinewood Studios, where Stoppard was in the last stages of post-production on the film *Rosencrantz and Guildenstern are Dead*. Transcript: BBC Written Archives Centre. Recording: BBC tape no. SLN037/90FK3705.

1991

"Morning Edition." National Public Radio, 18 March 1991. Interview by David D'Arcy regarding film of *Rosencrantz and Guildenstern are Dead*.

"Third Ear." BBC Radio Three, 16 April 1991 (rebroadcast 4 June 1991). Interview by Paul Allen regarding *In the Native State*, the filming of *Rosencrantz and Guildenstern are Dead*, and a possible play on Americanness and Englishness. Recording: National Sound Archive, B8138.

"Channel Four News." Channel 4, London, 9 May 1991. Interview by Fiona Murch with Tom Stoppard and Peter Wood regarding *Rosencrantz and Guildenstern are Dead*. Videotape: Independent Television News, London, tape no. 35968.

"Metro." Independent Television, 18 May 1991. Interview by Ian Drury regarding *Rosencrantz and Guildenstern are Dead*. Videotape: London Weekend Television.

"PM." BBC Radio Four, 14 June 1991. Interview regarding the death of Dame Peggy Ashcroft. Recording: BBC tape no. CLN124/91VP2424.

1992

"The Charlie Rose Show." WNET-TV, New York, 30 July 1992. Live interview in advance of the Broadway opening of a revival of *The Real Inspector Hound*.

"New York and Company." WNYC Radio, New York, 31 July 1992. Live interview by Leonard Lopate.

Interview by Ralph Howard. WINS Radio, New York, ca. 7 August 1992 (recorded 31 July 1992).

"Show Biz Today." CNN Television, 19 August 1992 (recorded late July 1992). Interview by Cynthia Tornquist with Tom Stoppard and Simon Jones. Broadcast by CNN and by Fox television affiliates.

"Morning Edition." National Public Radio, 18 September 1992. Interview by Tom Vitale regarding *The Fifteen-Minute Hamlet*. Comments by Simon Jones (Hamlet) and Gloria Muzio, director. Transcript: National Public Radio.

1993

"Kaleidoscope." BBC Radio Four, 15 April 1993. Interview by Robert Dawson Scott regarding *Arcadia*.

"Meridian." BBC World Service, 7 September 1993. Interview with Tom Stoppard introducing a series of his plays beginning with a new radio version of *Rosencrantz and Guildenstern Are Dead* produced by Gordon House (World Service, 12 September 1993). Partial accounts of the interview by Sue Gaisford, "A Big Lick from an Old Bulldog," *Independent on Sunday,* 12 September 1993, "Arts" section; and Helen Meany, "Voices in the Night," *Irish Times,* 14 September 1993, p. 10.

Index

McMaster University, 199
Measure for Measure, 68
Melville, Herman, 208
Memorandum, The, 191
Merchant, The, 145
Mermaid Theatre, 113–14, 115
Metropolitan Opera House, 129
Miller, Arthur, 26–27, 85
Milligan, Spike, 96
Mitchell, Alan, 173
Molnár, Ferenc, 132, 173, 174, 189, 190
Morning Star, 111
Moscow, 110
Mussolini, Benito, 207
Muzio, Gloria, 257

Nabokov, Vladimir, 26, 87, 101, 214, 218
Nash, Paul, 128
National Theatre, 1, 6, 11, 12, 13, 15, 16, 20, 31, 38, 46, 47, 57, 126, 130, 145, 172, 174, 178, 184, 203, 208–9, 219, 256, 257, 259, 262, 265, 266
Naturalism, 151–53
Nestroy, Johann, 165, 174, 189, 190, 208, 209
New-Found-Land, 85, 89
Newman, Paul, 70
Newton, Isaac, 268
New York Daily News, 171
New York Post, The, 171
New York Review of Books, The, 107
New York theater, 73, 82, 181–82
New York Times, The, 30, 80, 107, 144, 168, 171, 182, 258
Next Time I'll Sing to You, 22, 188
Nichols, Mike, 186, 212
Night and Day, 7, 8, 115–16, 118–19, 122–24, 125, 127–28, 130, 131–32, 135–38, 139, 141–44, 146–49, 151–54, 158, 162–63, 169, 175, 184, 186, 189, 199, 210–11, 218, 248, 258
  1978 West End production of, 115–16, 118–19, 123–24, 127–

28, 130, 131, 136, 139, 146–49, 152
  1979 Broadway production of, 130, 135, 141–42, 210–11
  female characterization in, 123–24, 135–36, 148–49, 169, 186, 210, 218, 248
  journalism in, treatment of, 116, 122–23, 127, 131–32, 137–38, 162–63
  naturalistic form of, 115–16, 131, 135–36, 151–54, 158
  origins of, 116, 122–23, 131, 139, 152, 189
  political ideas in, 141–44, 258
  reception of, 115–16, 141–42
Normal Heart, The, 196
Norton Anthology of English Literature, 256
"Nude Descending a Staircase," 232
Nunn, Trevor, 48, 204, 264

Observer, The, 17, 47, 54, 94, 165, 219
Occupations, 63, 68
Oldman, Gary, 235, 237
Old Ones, The, 145
Old Possum's Book of Practical Cats, 29
Old Vic Theatre, 13, 16, 94, 174, 195, 219
Olivier, Sir Laurence, 16, 20, 174, 180, 219
On the Razzle, 174, 189–90, 208–9, 248
Orlov, Irina, 109
Orlov, Yuri, 109
Osborne, John, 29, 54, 94, 146, 165, 183, 188, 219
Oxford Theatre Group, 16, 46

Parker, Robert, 259
Party, The, 63, 68
Pennington, Michael, 177
Perfect Spy, A, 181
Petherbridge, Edward, 116
Philanthropist, The, 108
Philby, Kim, 181
Phoenix Theatre, 124, 127